CHANGING FORMS
OF EMPLOYMENT

Economic recessions, as well as periods of growth, are obvious and immediate manifestations of change, which have a direct effect on the experience of employees, households and work organisations. However, fluctuations in the economy, important though they are, have to be distinguished from underlying trends, which might generate pressures towards a more fundamental reshaping of social institutions.

These trends include the growth of the service economy, technological changes, and the erosion of the 'male breadwinner' model of the gender division of labour. They have resulted in strains and ruptures in the organisation and regulation of employment and related institutions including trade unions, employers and households. The task of the next decade is both to reconstruct relationships and to renew institutions.

Changing Forms of Employment examines the impact of these different trends under three headings: regulation, deregulation and corporations; the recomposition of skills and employment; and change in gender relations.

Rosemary Crompton is Professor of Sociology at the University of Leicester. **Duncan Gallie** is Official Fellow at Nuffield College, the University of Oxford. **Kate Purcell** is Principal Research Fellow at the Institute of Employment Research, the University of Warwick.

CHANGING FORMS OF EMPLOYMENT

Organisations, skills and gender

Edited by

Rosemary Crompton, Duncan Gallie and Kate Purcell

London and New York

First published in 1996
by Routledge 1996
11 New Fetter Lane, London EC4P 4EE

Simultaneously published in the USA and Canada
by Routledge
29 West 35th Street, New York, NY 10001

Routledge is an Independent Thomson Publishing company

Typeset in Baskerville by
Keystroke, Jacaranda Lodge, Wolverhampton

Printed in and bound in Great Britain by
T.J. Press (Padstow) Ltd, Padstow, Cornwall

British Library Cataloguing in Publication Data
A catalogue record for this book is available from the British Library

Library of Congress Cataloguing in Publication Data
Changing forms of employment : organisation, skills, and gender /
edited by Rosemary Crompton, Duncan Gallie, and Kate Purcell.
p.   cm.
Includes bibliographical references and index.
ISBN 0–415–13371–8 (alk. paper). — ISBN 0–415–14116–8
(pbk. : alk. paper)
1. Work. 2. Employment (Economic theory) 3. Occupations.
4. Industrial organisation. 5. Skilled labor. 6. Discrimination in
employment. I. Crompton, Rosemary. II. Gallie, Duncan.
III. Purcell, Kate.
HD4901.C425   1995
331—dc20   95-25433
CIP

ISBN 0-415-13371-8 (hbk)
ISBN 0-415-14116-8 (pbk)

CONTENTS

CONTENTS

FIGURES

TABLES

CONTRIBUTORS

John Allen Senior Lecturer in Economic Geography, Faculty of Social Sciences, The Open University.

Peter Armstrong Professor of Accounting, University of Sheffield.

Irene Bruegel Reader in Urban Policy Studies, School of Land Management and Urban Policy, South Bank University.

Rosemary Crompton Professor of Sociology, University of Leicester

Paul Edwards Professor of Industrial Relations, Warwick Business School, University of Warwick.

Duncan Gallie Official Fellow, Nuffield College, Oxford.

Abigail Gregory Lecturer in French, Department of Modern Languages, University of Salford.

Nick Henry Lecturer in Geography, School of Geography, University of Birmingham.

Bryn Jones Senior Lecturer in Sociology, School of Social Sciences, University of Bath.

Alice Lam Senior Lecturer in Human Resource Management and Industrial Relations, University of Kent.

Tony Lane Reader in Sociology, Department of Sociology, University of Liverpool.

Paul Marginson Professor of Human Research Management and Employee Relations, University of Leeds.

Jacqueline O'Reilly Senior Research Fellow, Science Centre, Wissenschaftzentrum Berlin (WZB).

John Purcell Professor of Human Resource Management, University of Bath.

Kate Purcell Principal Research Fellow, Institute of Employment Research, University of Warwick.

Jill Rubery Professor of Comparative Employment Systems, Manchester School of Management, UMIST.

Carole Thornley Lecturer in Industrial Relations, University of Keele.

Judy Wajcman Professor of Sociology, School of Social Science, Australian National University, formerly Principal Research Fellow, Industrial Relations Research Unit, University of Warwick.

1

WORK, ECONOMIC RESTRUCTURING AND SOCIAL REGULATION

*Rosemary Crompton, Duncan Gallie
and Kate Purcell*

During the 1980s, following the election of a Conservative government in 1979, de-industrialisation in Britain was accompanied by levels of un-employment unheard of in the postwar years and the virtual destruction of occupational communities centred on coal, steel and shipbuilding. Nationalised industries were sold off, whilst legislation systematically removed a series of rights and protections relating to employees and their representative bodies, most notably in respect of trade unions but also for other occupational groups such as professionals. There was a corresponding erosion of employment rights and the collective social insurances (such as, for example, employment protection legislation and unemployment benefit) together with other welfare provisions which had been key elements of the social 'citizenship' rights established as part of the postwar consensus (Marshall 1963), and an increasing emphasis upon the requirement for *individual* (self) provision.

There was, therefore, widespread evidence of change in specific aspects of employing organisations, employment, and employment-related institutions between the mid-1970s and the mid-1990s. However, how far could these be said to reflect more fundamental changes in the nature of employment, and employment-related institutions? These issues lay at the centre of the discussions at the second conference organised by the journal *Work, Employment and Society* (WES) in September 1994, at which the papers in this book were first presented.[1] In a similar vein, the first WES conference in 1989 had taken as its theme: 'The 1980s: A Decade of Change?'[2] However, despite the transformations of the 1980s, as Brown and Morris (1990) wrote in the WES special issue that followed: 'uncertainty as to how much and what changed in the 1980s [was] a dominant theme of the papers'.

By the middle of the 1990s, was it possible to be any more confident as to whether substantive changes had, it fact, taken place? We believe that the answer is a qualified 'yes'. In this introductory chapter, we identify

1

three key areas of change, following a brief discussion of two respects in which the concerns of economic sociology in 1994 are rather different from those of 1989.

First, there has been a shift of emphasis towards comparative work, suggesting an increasing awareness not only of the importance of national specificities, but also of the need to locate the British case within the international and European context in order to understand change and continuity in employment-related issues. This reflects a growing concern with the possible impact of internationalisation (or 'globalisation') given the deregulation of national markets, together with the increasing prominence of international institutions such as those associated with the European Union.

Second, a recurring theme in economic sociology during the 1980s, reflecting both rising levels of women's employment as well as the critiques of 'second-wave' feminism, concerned the need to move beyond the boundaries of 'work' as employment, and to recognise the interconnections between all kinds of 'work' including work in the household, caring work, other kinds of voluntary work – as well as paid work (Pahl 1984; Deem 1990). This need to recognise 'work' as extending beyond the boundaries of employment is now widely accepted.

However, a certain 'fuzziness' relating to the conceptualisation of 'work' was also reflected in another prominent theme of 1980s (and 1990s) sociology – that is, the demise of 'work' as a 'key sociological concept' (Offe 1985). 'Work', it was argued, is no longer a key source of social identity at the end of the twentieth century, and the organisation of 'work' – most notably, the occupational order – no longer provides a useful framework within which social institutions and behaviour may be analysed (Beck 1992; Bauman 1982). These arguments have been paralleled by a growing emphasis upon the causal significance of consumption, rather than production-related activities in contemporary societies.

Growing internationalisation, as well as changes in the division of labour between the sexes, are major topics under investigation in the following chapters. These do not directly address the debates relating to the decline of the 'work society', but we shall briefly return to this topic in the concluding paragraphs of this introduction.

MAJOR THEMES

'Change' is ongoing, and it would not be too difficult to characterise any particular ten-year period during the twentieth century as 'a decade of change'. With the exception of major disruptions such as war or revolution, it is problematic to tie social change to a specific point in time. Nevertheless, there are historic periods when it becomes ever more apparent that taken-for-granted understandings, and accepted conceptual frameworks, have declined in explanatory value. The period 1980–95 has been such a time, during which the effects of a concatenation of trends have been reflected in the extensive reappraisal of existing theories and frameworks.

Economic recessions – as well as periods of growth – are obvious and immediate manifestations of change, which have a direct effect on the experience of employees, households and work organisations, and would be drawn upon in any explanation of actual events. However, fluctuations in the economy, important though they are, have to be distinguished from underlying trends which might generate pressures towards a more fundamental reshaping of social institutions. We discuss these trends under three broad headings: changes in the organisation of production and productive activity (particularly those associated with the growth of service-dominated – in employment terms – economies); the impact of technological change and information technology; and the decline of the 'male breadwinner' (or single earner model of employment and house-hold). These trends, we would argue, have resulted in strains and ruptures in the organisation and regulation of employment, and related institutions including trade unions, employers, and households. The task of the next decade is both to reconstruct relationships, and to renew institutions.

Changes in the organisation of production and productive activity

Here we would identify a series of linked developments which have often been discussed under the general rubric of a supposed transition from 'Fordism' to 'post-Fordism'; that is, a shift from the predominance of economies driven by manufacturing industries characterised by a mass, relatively homogeneous, semi-skilled workforce, towards economies dominated by employment in services, associated with a more hetero-geneous, fragmented workforce. These 'ideal-typical' production systems have their organisational correlates. Large-scale productive activities were accompanied by bureaucratic systems of personnel administration and stable organisational careers. The development of flexible production systems, it is argued, has been accompanied by organisational 'delayering' and the decline of the long-term, single organisation, career.[3]

The shift to service employment can hardly be denied. For example, in Britain, employment in services has grown from 53 per cent of total employ-ment in 1971, to 73 per cent in 1993 (*Employment Gazette* 1994). As we shall argue, developments in technology have been of considerable importance in facilitating flexible systems of production and work organisation in services, which by their very nature often have to be available outside the 'standard hours' associated with the 'standard worker'. Furthermore

3

(although this is not true of all service workers), the product of service work – the service – requires the exercise of different qualities and skills, often of an interpersonal nature (Hochschild 1983) compared with those associated with manual and low-level work in manufacturing industry.

The emergence of new occupations, as well as the restructuring of old occupations and skills, has generated new problems of control, classification and regulation. During an industrial era (in the West) dominated by large-scale manufacturing industry, the regulatory systems which emerged (sometimes described as 'mature' systems of Industrial Relations and Collective Bargaining; see Ross and Hartmann 1960) tended to be dominated by those established in the leading industries, although there were, of course, significant cross-national variations in this regard.

'Fordism' and the dominance of manual trade unions have also been linked to Keynesian economic policies of demand management and other forms of macroeconomic intervention (Harvey 1990). In Britain, the Conservative government has since 1979 rejected such attempts to regulate the economy, and has been committed to a radical market philosophy, promoting increased labour market flexibility (Beatson 1995). Thus successive Conservative governments have sought to remove or privatise welfare protections and regulatory institutions, to stimulate the market for labour and skills by reducing rates of income tax at the upper levels, and to shift the balance between direct and indirect taxation. As a recent report (Rowntree Foundation 1995) has demonstrated, the political decision to go down the road of deregulation and marketisation has resulted in social polarisation to a much greater extent in Britain than in other countries which have not taken the same path.

Nevertheless, the fact that many of the changes that we have experienced in the UK might be held to be the outcome of explicit political intervention should not be allowed to obscure the fact that profound changes have been under way as far as the organisation of production in capitalist economies is concerned. The shift to services is characteristic of all advanced economies (Esping-Anderson 1993), and there is a growing internationalisation associated with factors such as attempts to remove institutional boundaries within the European Union (EU) and the opening up of new markets in Eastern Europe. Decentralisation and subcontracting are on the increase. All of these changes have generated the need for new structures of regulation, even as the old ones are being removed.

The impact of technological change and information technology

Discussions of technological change within economic sociology from the 1960s tended to focus primarily upon its impact upon the work task and the labour process, as well as upon levels of employment overall.

4

Technological developments, particularly those associated with computer-isation, were seen as leading to the 'deskilling' of white-collar work, as well as the possible upgrading of manual employment, and thus to the blurring of a boundary which had long been held to be of crucial importance in industrial societies – that between 'white' and 'blue' collar work (Blauner 1964; Crompton and Jones 1984). These discussions were taking place within a context in which women's employment – particularly in low-level, clerical jobs – was increasing rapidly, leading to an apparently anomalous situation in which low-level non-manual women were being ranked 'above' their manual male partners in employment status terms. Together with these debates relating to the impact of 'new technology' on the nature of work, there were more apocalyptic predictions concerning the possibility that opportunities in employment were themselves being wiped out by its introduction (Jenkins and Sherman 1979).

The impact of computer technology on the nature of employment has indeed been profound, particularly in industries such as finance and in other mass white-collar industries, and in sectors of production such as vehicles. However, in Britain, debates about the possible job losses associated with the introduction of new technology tended to fade into the background following the massive unemployment consequent upon deindustrialisation in the first half of the 1980s. Nevertheless, it may be suggested that they have re-emerged in another guise in the debates around the topic of 'lean production' – stripped of management jargon, 'lean' production means fewer workers. Here, however, technological improvements are seen as a part of a package of innovations which are argued to be essential in order to achieve economic competitiveness (Womack et al. 1990). For example, 'lean' supply chains ('just-in-time' or kanban systems), dependent upon the information supplied by new technology, are central to the development of lean production.

Innovations in information technology, therefore, have been central to the development of such systems, which have revolutionised not just the organisation of production, but also major service sector industries such as retail, and the hotel and catering industry. In these industries, they have both encouraged the expansion of new professional services associated with the design of new information systems, as well as facilitated the sophisticated deployment of non-skilled labour, often hired as 'non-standard' workers. Here, 'just-in-time' systems are also accompanied by a 'just-in-time' labour force.

Apart from its effect on the organisation of the workforce, there has been a widespread view that new technologies have been transforming the composition of skills. However, there has been little agreement about the precise way in which this has been occurring. Some have stressed their potential for enhancing the work roles of employees, through enabling more complex decisions to be taken at lower levels in the organisation, while others have underlined their potential for centralising information and deskilling lower-level employees. Past research has provided some support for both views. However, given the sheer diversity of the new forms of technology, much of the evidence produced by economic sociologists on the impact of automation and computerised systems has become outdated. Faced by the rapid restructuring of work organisations, it has become essential to examine afresh the nature of skill trends and the way in which they have affected (and have been influenced by) traditional skill classifications.

At another level, however, the impact of information technology has been even more profound. The speeding up of information flows, together with the enhanced capacity to transfer capital and resources between different regions and nation states, has enormously increased both the flexibility of larger organisations as well as the possibilities for growth of multinational and global companies. Such companies have capacities for action which transcend nation-state boundaries, and there are very real fears of their potential to move both jobs and capital, thus destabilising national economies and employment structures. This kind of power places implicit (and sometimes explicit) constraints on national regulatory agencies.

The decline of the 'male breadwinner'

Women have always made a significant contribution to material production. However, with the coming of industrialism there also developed the ideology of 'separate spheres', in which the 'natural' sphere of women was deemed to be that of the home and family, whereas that of men was employment and the market (Davidoff and Hall 1987). Thus there emerged the 'male breadwinner' model of the articulation between paid employment and the household, associated with a characteristic gender division of labour. This model has (to varying extents and at different times in different countries) been reinforced by the deliberate exclusion of women from paid work – in particular, from better-paid and higher-status employment. Trade unions in particular have fought for the principle of the 'family wage' – that is, a wage sufficient to support a working man and his family, and the demand for a family wage had as its corollary the assumption that women should not take 'men's' jobs.

Whether this historical trajectory was a consequence of patriarchal exclusion (Hartmann 1976) or working-class resistance (Humphries 1982) is not an issue that concerns us here. Rather, we wish to make the point that the 'standard employee' – in respect of systems of employment regulation, organisational structuring, trade union organisation, and so on – has historically been assumed to be a male, full-time worker, and that this was reflected in economic sociology until the 1970s. In fact, the ideological underpinnings of this model were already being eroded, and were made explicit in the critiques of 'second-wave' feminism. However, the efforts of women to achieve a real, rather than a formal, equality with men within the sphere of employment have taken place within an institutional framework constructed on 'male breadwinner' principles, leading to further strains and tensions.

Since the 1950s and 1960s, there has been a growth of married women's employment in all Western countries. This has often been associated with the expansion of 'non-standard' – particularly part-time – employment. It might be argued that the growth of non-standard employment for women has, in effect, perpetuated a modified form of the male breadwinner model, and that its import may therefore be discounted. We would not agree. Not only is there increasing evidence of the entry of women into full-time work (often associated with entry into higher level jobs as well: Harrop and Moss 1994), but it is also apparent that many kinds of non-standard work are expanding rapidly, and that the single-wage household is in decline (Watson 1994; Beatson 1995; Rodgers and Rodgers 1990).

Changes in the gender division of labour, together with the growth of non-standard employment, suggest the need to reassess, and possibly renew, the institutions which mediate between employment and the household over the domestic life cycle. Principles of social insurance based upon the notion of a 'family wage' cannot simply be carried forward, and the assumption that caring work can be left to the household (i.e. women) is becoming increasingly divorced from reality.

We have argued, therefore, that there have been major changes associated with work, production and employment, which may be briefly summarised as: the shift to the service economy and other changes associated with 'post-Fordism'; the implementation of information technology; and the decline of the male breadwinner. Governmental politics in Britain since 1979 may have stripped out social protections and enhanced economic and social polarisation, but it would be naive to assume that a change of political complexion on the part of government would mean a return to the *status quo ante*. Social scientists, however, would argue that any changes in the future can be usefully informed by considered social science commentary and empirical research, and this spirit informs the chapters that follow.

THE CONTRIBUTIONS

In the first two sections of this introductory chapter, we have tended to emphasise the necessity for the renewal and restructuring of institutions which regulate employment and the labour market in the light of the changes that we have identified. Many of the chapters in this book, however, also serve to make the equally important argument that, even in

7

circumstances in which market forces might apparently reign supreme, labour contracts are inherently social, and that, as Durkheim (1984) argued: 'All that is in the contract is not contractual'. That is, human beings do not enter into employment and other economic relationships as random, atomised, individuals, but bring with them a series of tacit under-standings and cultural assumptions, linkages to other social networks, etc. (Granovetter 1985). From a variety of perspectives and standpoints, therefore, the chapters in this volume are concerned with the *persistence* of the social structures shaping economic institutions, as well as the impact of market deregulation, and the need for re-regulation, new institutions, and modifications in the light of the trends noted above. They have been organised into three parts: I Regulation, deregulation and corporations; II The recomposition of skills and employment; III Change in gender relations.

Regulation, deregulation and corporations

Rubery (Chapter 2) emphasises that the labour market cannot be reduced to crude notions of supply and demand, but is institutionally regulated. However, these institutions are in a process of transformation. She is highly critical as to the effects of their deliberate removal and forced decline, and pessimistic as to the capacity for anything approaching informed or rational decision-making in an increasingly fragmented and opaque labour market. Thus Thurow's model of job matching between employers and employees, for example, no longer applies, as employers become increasingly unable or unwilling to deliver 'good' jobs, and employees become justifiably sceptical of the employers' capacities to do so. It is not true that these developments are a consequence of unstoppable trends – in the British case, for example, institutions (early retirement schemes, Family Income Supplement, and so on) have been created in order to *increase* the supply of low-wage labour.

Paradoxically, removing institutions in order to give firms increased freedom to operate in the labour market renders their labour market information less complete, and long-term training and investment plans are jeopardised. There is a danger that these kinds of changes, together with uncontrolled and discretionary employer operation in the labour market will simply lead to a proliferation of 'junk jobs', thus undermining the capacity for social reproduction (e.g. the reproduction of skills; the bringing up of children). Rubery argues, therefore, that rather than further deregulation, there is a need for the rebuilding and renewal of labour market institutions.

Both Edwards *et al.* (Chapter 3) and Allen and Henry (Chapter 4) focus upon species of the 'new' employers and organisations emerging as a consequence of both deregulation, as well as the expansion of boundaries facilitated by improvements in technology and communications. These are multinational corporations (Edwards *et al.*) and international contract services (Allen and Henry). Lane (Chapter 5) examines a truly global industry – shipping – in which the growth of flags of convenience, together with that of an international labour bazaar for seafarers, has resulted in the nearest approximation to a completely unregulated market amongst all of the empirical examples of industries and occupations discussed in this book.

Edwards *et al.* are critical of the existing typologies by which multi-national corporations (MNCs) have been classified. They suggest that a relatively straightforward distinction between 'nationally' and 'globally' oriented approaches is the key to understanding different kinds of multi-nationals, the former retaining a strong identity with their home base, the latter being more 'international' and directive. This dichotomous classification is used to organise their empirical data, which are drawn from the Second Company Level Industrial Relations Survey, together with separately collected case study evidence. They do identify a tendency towards globalism, although this was relatively weak – most corporations included in their study did not monitor their national operations very closely, and tended to accept prevailing national regulatory mechanisms.

The multinational corporations investigated by Allen and Henry – international companies in the contract services industry – were rather different from those which were the main focus of Edwards *et al.*'s research (although their sampling frame did not exclude services, both of their case study examples were from manufacturing). Allen and Henry found that these 'hollow' contract service corporations can find themselves over-stretched in their efforts to administer a highly flexible workforce spread across a range of sites – which are not actually owned by the service contractor. This leaves the way open for local service contractors more attuned to local conditions – who are able, moreover, to take advantage of local 'custom and practice' as far as matters such as recruitment are concerned (for example, an informal 'arrangement' with the police force concerning recruitment to security jobs).

A similar appreciation of the significance of a rather different 'local' context is noted by Lane, who describes how shipboard conventions allow some sense of order to prevail for most of the time in circumstances (e.g. no common linguistic understanding amongst crews) which by any orthodox standards would be a recipe for chaos. However, this tenuous remnant of social order is set against an industrial background in which there has been a sustained growth in flags of convenience (FOCs), and today half of the world's deep sea labour force are to be found on such vessels. A combination of political and economic factors has been responsible for this growth – and amongst the latter, paramount is the opportunity to purchase ever-cheaper seafarers from the worldwide 'labour bazaar'. This has been increasingly augmented by even less expensive recruits from countries, such as China, Russia and Croatia, which have undergone a 'market turn' in respect of their economies. Such multinational crews on FOC ships are amongst the least protected employees anywhere.

To varying degrees, therefore, these three empirical chapters all draw attention to the persisting significance of the social despite the effects of market deregulation (and in some cases, the absence of any regulation whatsoever). This should not, however, be allowed to obscure the fact that overall, the actions of the corporations and employers under investigation had been to enhance the precariousness and insecurity of employment, and there were few if any signs of any 'voluntary' attempts to reverse this process. Lane does suggest that the sheer scale of maritime disasters in environmental terms has generated some efforts at self-regulation within the industry, mainly directed at pollution and safety. Although it is true that the MNCs studied by Edwards *et al.* did respect national conventions, it nevertheless remains the case that in general, the more global MNCs expressed an antipathy towards trade unionism and tended to avoid countries which they perceived to be strongly unionised.

The recomposition of skills and employment

A central concern of economic sociology has been the relationship between the widespread process of restructuring in industry and the development of skill structures (in the sense of the level of task complexity and of the ways in which skills are graded and classified). The conventional view sees the skill structure as in some sense a deterministic product of the level of technical development or of the impersonal workings of the market. The chapters here show that this is an altogether inadequate way of conceptualising the process of skill development. Skill structures are to a very substantial degree socially constructed. The way they are defined is affected by employer beliefs about the effectiveness of different forms of work organisation, the capacity of the organisations representing employees to influence skill classifications and the characteristics of educational systems which are themselves influenced by the policies of national governments. The chapters in Part II, then, seek both to elaborate the processes involved in skill formation and to give concrete illustrations of the way in which the skill structure has been changing.

Jones (Chapter 6) provides the most general statement of the deficiencies of conventional assumptions about skill processes. In particular, he criticises the view that the skill structure is regulated in a spontaneous way by price-clearing competitive markets. The so-called 'market' for skill, he argues, approximates more closely to a sphere of micro-political regulation, in which institutional norms determine the criteria for entry into specific skill

10

markets, the way in which skills are rewarded, the way in which tasks are defined at a more detailed level, the rights of the different parties and the way in which the rules themselves are decided. He examines two occupational groups which might be thought to be particularly clear cases approximating to the neo-classical model – self-employed workers in the construction industry and higher-level engineers. In the British context, both are often seen as representing skill markets where institutional or normative regulation is relatively low. But Jones shows that, in practice, this is far from correct. In the case of self-employed construction workers, pay rates are derived from wider industry regulations, while recruitment is heavily reliant on relatively stable social networks. In the case of higher-level engineers, the non-commodity nature of skills is apparent in the central role of publicly funded educational institutions in defining the nature of qualifications, the responsibilities falling to employers for the final stages of training and entitlement and the importance of tacit rights of career opportunity in structuring the employment relationship.

Gallie (Chapter 7) sets out to depict, with data from a national survey of employees, the general direction of policies with respect to skill change since the mid-1980s and their implications for the wider nature of work roles. In contrast to the view that the general tendency has been for employers to deskill their workforces, the evidence indicates that the main tendency has been towards upskilling, in the sense of increased task complexity. This has been the case for employees in all social classes, other than non-skilled manual workers. Increased task complexity has meant the enrichment of jobs in terms of creating greater variety, allowing employees to make fuller use of their skills and providing opportunities for self-development. On the other hand, it has been associated with an increased intensification of work. Further, it is clear that the relationship between growth in the complexity of tasks and the way in which the wider work role is defined is a contingent one and, indeed, in practice has been gender specific. While both men and women have seen the skill requirements of their jobs increase, it is only in the case of men that there is evidence of a shift towards greater decentralisation of control over decision-making about the task. It is clear that employer decisions about work organisation are in no sense highly determined outcomes of technical change, but reflect prevailing managerial philosophies and deep-set cultural beliefs about the capacities of different categories of labour.

The problematic nature of the relationship between skill as task complexity and skill as formalised in occupational classifications is brought out by Thornley (Chapter 8). She highlights the bargained and inherently unstable nature of the translation of task skills into specific grading structures, through a detailed study of nursing. The definition of skill categories becomes an arena for conflicting strategies not only between

11

the employer and the representatives of employees, but also between different types of employee organisation. She traces the three-way historical struggle between the Royal College of Nursing (with its ambitions of securing professional closure of the nursing workforce), the government as employer (with its recurrent attempts to cut costs through grade dilution), and the Trades Union Congress (TUC) affiliated unions (which sought to get increased recognition for the real skill content of lower-graded staff). This provides the context for her analysis of the highly contentious current debate on the structure of the nursing workforce, with the emergence of new proposals for a more flexible grading structure, relating rewards more directly to tasks and complementing the role of traditional entry qualifications with a new emphasis on continuous training.

Lam (Chapter 9) shows how the real skills of those in specific occupational positions are not simply given by the educational system or by the nature of the production technology, but are moulded by the everyday work process that results from the way organisations are designed. These organisational models may differ considerably between societies. Lam shows this by focusing on the skills and work roles of engineers, drawing on original comparative research in Britain and Japan. She finds that British organisations are characterised by a 'mechanistic' structure, with a high degree of segmentation between managerial and technical functions. In contrast, organisations in Japan approximate more closely to an 'organic' structure, allowing a greater degree of horizontal communication between management and engineers. These differences have major consequences for the extent to which there is a shared technical culture, for the diffusion of knowledge within the organisation, and for the breadth of skill development. The pattern of work organisation in Japan encourages engineers to develop a far wider range of non-technical or organisational skills than their British equivalents, and this enables them to handle more efficiently new product developments and a rapidly changing technical environment.

In short, while the economic restructuring since the mid-1980s has seen in general a rise in the skill content of jobs, this has been the product of specific organisational policies, reflecting the interplay of managerial philosophies, internal power relations and external constraints, rather than the result of some form of technological determinism. It has affected different groups in the workforce to very different degrees and its implications for wider work roles has differed between the sexes. Moreover, the relationship between increased task complexity and organisational skill classifications is inherently problematic. It has provided and will continue to provide one of the central sources of conflict and negotiation within employment organisations.

Change in gender relations

The three chapters in Part III explore the reflexive impact of household gender divisions of labour and gendered employment relations in labour markets and work organisations. Female economic activity rates vary among European countries but, in the period under review, there has been a progressive increase in women's employment, coupled with a decrease in single-earner households throughout Europe. If, as we argue, this is indicative of a decline in the male-breadwinner household, are such trends also facilitating a decrease in gendered employment segregation and/or the operation of increasingly 'gender-neutral' labour markets?

All of the contributors are concerned to explore the factors which facilitate and obstruct change in the gendering of employment and opportunities. Gregory and O'Reilly (Chapter 10) concentrate on two industries – banking and retail grocery – to investigate the relationships between national, institutional, cultural and sectoral factors on the different patterns of part-time employment in two European countries. Bruegel (Chapter 11) looks at household migration between UK regional labour markets to investigate whether there is any evidence of a reduction in female 'tied migration' as a result of women's increased economic activity. Wajcman (Chapter 12) focuses on one occupational group – managers in large multinational companies – who are unequivocally full-time continuous members of the labour force, comparing the characteristics, attitudes and experience of women and men who had achieved senior management status in organisations with an explicit commitment to provide equal opportunities in employment.

Gregory and O'Reilly's study provides an example of how national employment legislation and fiscal policy reinforce employment practices and mitigate tendencies towards labour process and structural convergence in sectors which do not operate in a global context. They examine the different patterns of part-time employment to assess the evidence for convergence between the two industries' use of labour and organisation of working time, teasing out the relative impacts of labour market regulation, industry-specific structural and technological factors, and socio-cultural factors relating to the demand for and supply of labour. In terms of labour market regulation, they conclude that legislation provides fewer constraints on employers and less protection for employees in the UK than in France, making part-time employment a relatively easy and cheap option for British employers. Conversely, there is little incentive for French employers to create part-time jobs, where flexible working patterns tend to be employee-controlled rather than part of employer strategies to maximise productivity and minimise labour costs. Staffing decisions are taken in the light of established and emerging organisational practice. For example, French banks have used part-time hours to reduce overstaffing, whereas British banks were preoccupied by concern to retain trained staff on part-time contracts to counteract the predicted 1990s smaller cohorts of new entrants to the labour market: the traditional source of labour to counterbalance gender-linked 'natural wastage'.

In France, full-time employment continues to be regarded as the norm by both employers and employees, and where employees work part-time they tend to work longer hours than their UK equivalents, have more advantageous employment contracts and be involuntarily part-time: that is, younger women entering the labour market for the first time rather than 'women returners' with dependent children. Thus, the increase in part-time employment in France does not reinforce established gender relations to the same extent as in the UK. French part-time employees are less likely than their UK equivalents to be disadvantaged in terms of employment rights and it is more often a *rite de passage* between education and full-time employment than relegation to permanent secondary labour market status. On the other hand, in sectors where part-time employment is largely female and confined to relatively routine work tasks (which is commonly the case in France as in the UK), it provides fewer promotion or training opportunities, less flexibility for employees and is essentially demand- rather than supply-led (Horrell and Rubery 1991). Such 'atypical' employment reinforces women's dependency in the household and subordinate status at work, although their 'component' wages (Siltanen 1994) may be an increasingly *essential* component of the household income. It is perhaps not surprising that part-time employed women are more likely than those in full-time employment to take primary responsibility for domestic work and childcare and to have more sexist attitudes to domestic divisions of labour, but it cannot be assumed that their earnings or power within the household are negligible.

This is tentatively borne out by Bruegel in her study of household employment-led inter-regional migration in Britain, using data from the Office of Population Censuses and Surveys (OPCS) Longitudinal Sample and the 1989 Labour Force Survey. Starting from the assumption that women's increasing labour market participation leads to a greater incidence of conflicts of interest in households faced with the option of job-moves which involve geographical relocation, she compared rates of migration between 1971 and 1989. She found, not unexpectedly, that women in sampled partnerships remain considerably more likely than men to have relocated because of their partners' employment-led migration, and that households with non-employed wives have relatively greater migration rates: but full-time employed women are more likely than those in part-time employment to be involved in relocation related to their husbands' employment. This could suggest a polarisation of 'career-rich' households whose capacity to relocate is enhanced by their joint marketable skills, professional competences or ability to negotiate and manage 'commuting' work patterns

– a trend which has also been noted in other research (Harrop and Moss 1994). It could also be indicative of household negotiations where one-and-a-half jobs have been found to be economically and socially compatible with parenting: wives with managerial and professional part-time employment are found to have been considerably less likely to have moved because of their partners' employment than either their full-time or non-employed equivalents. Female managers married to male managers had the greatest propensity to relocate between 1988 and 1989, but they were twice as likely as other managerial wives to be self-employed, suggesting that they may be atypical of managers in general and perhaps have greater flexibility than most self-employed people. Longitudinal analysis of women's and men's relative earnings indicates clearly that women who move jobs tend to be disadvantaged by discontinuities of employment, whereas men appear to gain from changes of employer or occupation (Elias and Gregory 1994: 43). Bruegel's analysis highlights the complexity of the variables involved and the need for further qualitative research to explore this increasingly volatile and relatively uncharted aspect of labour market operation.

Finally, Wajcman's survey of senior managers in five multinational companies with established credentials as 'equal opportunity' employers addresses the issue of gendered careers within organisations. In all the companies, women were under-represented at senior management level – defined, for ease of sampling, as managers earning a minimum annual salary of £40,000. Wajcman surveyed matched samples of women and men from this population and was able to identify similarities and differences between them. She found that, although these women were quintessentially adhering to the 'normal' (male) work/career model of continuous employment, and worked comparably long hours to their male colleagues, there were very clear differences between men and women with respect to functional responsibilities, family responsibilities, and attitudes to and perceptions of career development.

Her findings suggest that social and organisational custom and practice reproduce the status quo, particularly in a recessionary context where opportunities are decreasing rather than expanding. Male definitions of occupational excellence and appropriate promotion attributes discriminate against and discourage women. The most radical difference is the extent to which the female managers had clearly made choices to accommodate their career progression, to an extent which the men had not. Although similar proportions of men and women with children reported 'family commitments' as one of the barriers to their career development, more than two-thirds of the female managers did not have children, while more than two-thirds of the males had dependent children living with them: well over a quarter of the males had non-employed wives and nearly all were living with a partner, compared to under three-quarters of the women, who were more likely to be single, separated or divorced. The male managers sampled tended to be more likely than the women to subscribe to 'traditional' views about gender differences and their implications for women's suitability as managers and, indeed, previous research has indicated that men who have non-employed or essentially dependent wives and a traditional domestic division of labour at home are likely to have ideological views about gender which lead them to reinforce rather than challenge workplace gender norms (Ungerson 1983: 38). Wacjman suggests how cultural structures and processes within the organisations reinforced ideological boundaries within organisational and occupational labour markets, defining them in ways intrinsically resistant to change.

DISCUSSION

Fifty years ago Polanyi delivered a memorable critique of the myth of the 'self-regulating market' which still remains valid today:

> To allow the market mechanism to be the sole director of the fate of human beings and their natural environment, indeed, even of the amount and use of purchasing power, would result in the demolition of society. For the alleged commodity 'labour power' cannot be shoved about, used indiscriminately, or even left unused, without affecting also the human individual who happens to be the bearer of this peculiar commodity. In disposing of a man's [sic] labour power the system would, incidentally, dispose of the physical, psychological, and moral entity . . . attached to that tag. Robbed of the protective covering of cultural institutions, human beings would die as the victims of acute social dislocation through vice, perversion, crime, and starvation. Nature would be reduced to its elements, neighbourhoods and landscapes defiled, rivers polluted, military safety jeopardized, the power to produce food and raw materials destroyed. Finally, the market administration of purchasing power would periodically liquidate business enterprise, for shortages and surfeits of money would prove as disastrous to business as floods and droughts in primitive society.
>
> (Polanyi 1957: 73)

In the British case, there is growing evidence that a decade and a half of politically directed deregulation has led to an increasingly flexible labour market but has also led to growing social polarisation – as might have been anticipated. The research evidence in this volume indicates clearly that there have been major changes in the manner in which work and employment are organised. It also shows that there are persisting differences in national cultures which suggest that global trends are reinforced, deflected, obstructed and interpreted differently according to established institutional practices.

16

Although the chapters in the book have, albeit in rather different ways, all emphasised the *persistence* of the social in the workings of corporations, organisations and labour markets, a sensitivity to the *changing* nature of this relationship has also been generally found. One indication of the extent of change in recent decades is that the proportion of the British population of working age who are full-time tenured employees has fallen from 55.5 per cent in 1975 to 35.9 per cent in 1993 (Gregg and Wadsworth 1995), reflecting the growth of participation in post-compulsory education, earlier retirement and the expansion of non-standard employment. In any case, the low level of protection 'enjoyed' by employees in Britain means that: 'British employers face relatively few constraints on their ability to exploit external flexibility' – that is, recruitment and layoffs (Beatson 1995: 58). In the short term at any rate, therefore, we have not found grounds for optimism. Increasing precariousness and insecurity for a substantial minority if not the majority of employees would seem to be likely. We have argued, therefore, that we must look to the active reform of social institutions.

The possibilities of reform are linked to the growing interest in comparative work in economic sociology which we noted in the first paragraphs of this introduction. Given our emphasis upon the significance of the 'societal' at the national level, we would not suggest that a standard set of solutions can be simply located and applied independently of national and local contexts, and indeed, despite the particular nature of the UK experience, national systems of regulation still have an important impact, as is demonstrated by the chapters in this volume. Nevertheless, as we have also argued, increasing globalisation and internationalisation have signified the need for new institutions. International cooperation, through bodies such as the EU, might be used to bring a measure of coherence. It would have to be admitted that, to date, such attempts have not met with any great measure of success – as the Conservative government's opting out of the Maastricht protocol has demonstrated (Hall 1994) – but nevertheless, this does not remove the imperative of continuing to attempt to develop them (Sengenberger and Campell 1994).

We are not suggesting that it is possible simply to revert to the kinds of welfarist (or 'corporatist') deals which were achieved in many countries during the high water mark of the postwar consensus (Therborn 1983), and which have often been described as the implementation of social 'citizenship' (Marshall 1963). In many instances, these deals were linked to the contours of the occupational structure.[4] Citizenship rights were closely tied to employment. This close association still persists at both the national and international levels. For example, Meehan (1993: 147) has argued that 'in so far as citizenship has a Community (EU) dimension, citizens are citizens-as-workers'. However, in institutional terms, the formulation of 'citizen-as-worker' rights has rested upon the male breadwinner model of family and employment, and women have gained access to many of the rights of social citizenship as mothers and/or wives. Thus women have not only maintained social reproduction but also, in part through their dependent status, become increasingly available for more 'flexible' forms of paid work.

There are a number of pressures, from both the political right as well as amongst 'communitarians', for a return to the male breadwinner model. However, as we have argued, there are a number of other reasons, as well as the likelihood that women will wish to retain the rather modest gains they have achieved in respect of employment, which suggest that the universal 'standard employment' model is unlikely to be the norm in the future. Postwar social provision was constructed in relation to a standard employment model, but there is no necessary reason why these provisions cannot be renewed and adapted so as to be more appropriate to changing forms of 'work' and employment.

In a nutshell, we would argue that at the level of the family and household, the development of institutions to reflect and incorporate changes in both households and employment patterns would require, first, the material recognition of caring work for what it is – work. This does not mean that the household will cease to take responsibility for its members, rather that, as discussed in our first section, we must extend the boundaries of our conceptualisations of 'work', and this must be reflected in other social institutions. In some countries (Norway, for example), caring work within the household gives entitlements to pension rights for the carer. Caring work can also be provided outside the household, generating new occupations. Household and non-household provision are not mutually exclusive. Second – and this is obviously a related point – the employment conditions of non-standard work should be 'normalised' as far as is possible. That is, such employment should be associated with national insurance benefits, transferable pension rights, and so on.

Our final point also returns to debates within economic sociology. Arguments, such as those of Offe, Beck and Bauman, concerning the decline of the 'work society', and the replacing of employment and 'production' by 'consumption' as a major source of social identity, etc., have been implicitly constructed in relation to what we have loosely described as a 'Fordist' model of work and employment relations. As the 'standard model' of employment changed, so employment and work themselves were effectively downgraded as a framework for analysis and source of causal explanation. This rejection was premature. Work and employment remain as the most important determinants of 'life-chances' for the majority of the population. However, it is necessary to recognise that, as work and employment change, so will the manner in which these life chances are constructed, and our economic sociology should reflect these facts.

NOTES

1 More than 150 papers were presented at the conference, and this collection does not aim to be representative of the conference as a whole. There are therefore important topics – most notably, changes in employee representation, and unemployment – which are not addressed in this book.

2 The 1989 conference was organised at the University of Durham by the founding editor of WES, Richard Brown, together with Lydia Morris (Review Editor) and Peter Brannen.

3 Many criticisms can justifiably be made of such binary characterisations – that Ford did not actually organise his factories along 'Fordist' lines (Williams *et al.* 1992); that supposedly 'post-Fordist' economies are in fact bastions of mass production (Sayer 1989), and so on.

4 In the UK, this was recognised by Marshall (1963) in his identification of the importance of 'industrial citizenship' – the recognition of trade unions and collective bargaining – to 'social citizenship'. In the case of state welfare, the structure of 'corporatist' welfare states such as Germany and France was closely linked to employment (Esping-Anderson 1990). 'Universalist' (or Nordic) welfare states embrace all 'citizens' and are not as closely tied to paid work. However, Nordic welfare states were initially constructed on a model of social insurance linked to employment (Liera 1992) – as was the British – and (particularly in the case of Sweden and Denmark) policies of gender equality have been explicitly tied to increasing levels of paid employment amongst women. Thus paid work remains as the major route to welfare benefits.

REFERENCES

Bauman, Z. (1982) *Memories of Class,* London: Routledge.

Beatson, M. (1995) 'Progress towards a flexible labour market', *Employment Gazette* February: 55–66.

Beck, U. (1992) *Risk Society: Towards a New Modernity,* London: Sage.

Blauner, R. (1964) *Alienation and Freedom: The Factory Worker and his Industry,* Chicago: University of Chicago Press.

Brown, R. and Morris, L. (1990) 'A decade of change?', *Work, Employment and Society,* special issue, May.

Crompton, R. and Jones, G. (1984) *White-Collar Proletariat: Deskilling and Gender in the Clerical Labour Process,* London: Macmillan.

Davidoff, L. and Hall, C. (1987) *Family Fortunes,* London: Hutchinson.

Deem, R. (1990) 'Gender, work and leisure in the eighties: looking backwards, looking forward', *Work, Employment and Society,* special issue, May.

Durkheim, E. (1984) *The Division of Labour in Society,* Basingstoke: Macmillan.

Elias, P. and Gregory, M. (1994) 'The changing structure of occupations and earnings in Great Britain', Employment Department Research Report series no. 27, May, Coventry: Institute for Employment Research, University of Warwick.

Employment Gazette (1994) Historical Supplement no. 4, October.

Esping-Anderson, G. (1990) *The Three Worlds of Welfare Capitalism,* Cambridge: Polity.

Esping-Anderson, G. (ed.) (1993) *Changing Classes,* London, Sage.

Granovetter, M.S. (1985) 'Economic action and social structure: the problem of embeddedness', *American Journal of Sociology* 91 (3): 481–510.

Gregg, P. and Wadsworth, J. (1995) 'A short history of labour turnover, job security and job tenure, 1975–93', *Oxford Review of Economic Policy* 11 (1): 73–90.

Hall, M. (1994) 'Industrial relations and the social dimension of European integration', in R. Hyman and A. Ferner (eds) *New Frontiers in European Industrial Relations*, Oxford: Basil Blackwell.

Harrop, A. and Moss, P. (1994) 'Working parents: trends in the 1980s', *Employment Gazette* October: 343–51.

Hartmann, H. (1976) 'Capitalism, patriarchy and job segregation by sex', in M. Blaxall and B. Reagan (eds) *Women and the Workplace*, Chicago: University of Chicago Press.

Harvey, D. (1990) *The Condition of Postmodernity*, Oxford: Basil Blackwell.

Hochschild, A. (1983) *The Managed Heart*, Los Angeles: University of California Press.

Horrell, S. and Rubery, J. (1991) *Employers' Working Time Policies and Women's Employment*, London: HMSO.

Humphries, J. (1982) 'Class struggle and the persistence of the working-class family', in A. Giddens and D. Held (eds) *Classes, Power and Conflict*, Basingstoke: Macmillan.

Jenkins, C. and Sherman, B. (1979) *The Collapse of Work*, London: Eyre Methuen.

Liera, A. (1992) *Welfare States and Working Mothers*, Cambridge: Cambridge University Press.

Marshall, T.H. (1948, reprinted 1963) 'Citizenship and social class', in *Sociology at the Crossroads*, London: Heinemann.

Meehan, E. (1993) *Citizenship and the European Community*, London: Sage.

Offe, C. (1985) '"Work" – a central sociological category?', in *Disorganized Capitalism*, Cambridge: Polity.

Pahl, R. (1984) *Divisions of Labour*, Oxford: Blackwell.

Polanyi, K. (1957) *The Great Transformation*, Boston, MA: Beacon Press.

Rodgers, G. and Rodgers, J. (1990) *Precarious Jobs in Labour Market Regulation: The Growth of Atypical Employment in Western Europe*, Geneva: International Institute for Labour Studies.

Ross, A.M. and Hartmann, P.T. (1960) *Changing Patterns of Industrial Conflict*, New York: Wiley.

Rowntree Foundation (1995) *Inquiry into Income and Wealth*, York.

Rubery, J., Horrell, S. and Burchell, B. (1994) 'Part-time work and gender inequality in the labour market', in A.M. Scott (ed.) *Gender Segregation and Social Change*, Oxford: Oxford University Press.

Sayer, A. (1989) 'Postfordism in question', *International Journal of Urban and Regional Research* November/December: 667–95.

Sengenberger, W. and Campbell, D. (eds) (1994) *Creating Economic Opportunities*, Geneva: International Labour Organisation.

Siltanen, J. (1994) *Locating Gender: Occupational Segregation, Wages and Domestic Responsibilities*, London: UCL Press.

Therborn, G. (1983) 'Why some classes are more successful than others', *New Left Review* March/April: 138.

Ungerson, C. (1983) 'Why do women care?', in J. Finch and D. Groves (eds) *A Labour of Love*, London: Routledge.

Watson, G. (1994) 'The flexible workforce', *Employment Gazette* July: 239–47.

Williams, K., Haslam, C. and Williams, J. (1992) 'Ford-vs-"Fordism": the beginning of mass production', *Work, Employment and Society* 6(4): 517–55.

Womack, J.P., Jones, D.T. and Roos, D. (1990) *The Machine that Changed the World*, New York: Macmillan.

Part I

REGULATION, DEREGULATION AND CORPORATIONS

2

THE LABOUR MARKET OUTLOOK AND THE OUTLOOK FOR LABOUR MARKET ANALYSIS

Jill Rubery

Institutional economists are accustomed to relying on the existence of stable, slow changing and fairly transparent institutions to provide the building blocks for their analysis of labour markets and employment systems. Much has been made of the role of social norms (Wootton 1955), custom and practice (Brown 1972), family organisation (Humphries 1977), collective bargaining institutions, rules and practices (Clegg 1970), customary skill divisions and differentials (Turner 1962; Routh 1980), training and education systems (Maurice *et al.* 1986) and company culture and history (Sisson and Purcell 1983) to explain how and why labour market structures are resistant to rapid change, embody values which extend outside the market or exchange nexus and cannot be reduced to crude notions of supply and demand.

Even the traditional market economists have been getting in on the act; Bob Solow, the growth theory Nobel prize winner, published a book which declares, perhaps a little late in the day, that the labour market is a social institution (Solow 1990). The proclamation comes a little late for two reasons; on the one hand most people always knew it to be so and find it somewhat surprising, except to those accustomed to economists' modes of thought, that it has taken an eminent social scientist so long to recognise the pervasive importance of notions such as fairness in the employment relationship. It is late for another reason. Just as the neoclassical economists appear to be latching on to the notion of institutions, norms and values in labour markets, those very norms and values and associated institutions appear to be crumbling and fragmenting, perhaps heralding the final advent of that elusive competitive or market based labour market.

The problem for institutional economists, as has been hinted at already, is that these changes are taking away the customary tools of the trade, the known social values and customs through which the fusion of social and labour market structures can be readily analysed. Most institutional analyses of labour markets view the labour market as structured not only by

23

stable and slow changing institutions but also by mutually reinforcing institutions. The reinforcement and reproduction of social structures within the labour market can be regarded as providing clear cut ammunition with which to attack the notions of market-driven wage and employment systems; labour markets reproduce social hierarchies which are relatively impervious to the short run variations of market demand and supply changes, and labour markets thus can easily be demonstrated not to be simply economic but socially-embedded economic systems. This mutual reinforcement applies not only to the social and the economic – for example the convergence between occupational and social status, or between male breadwinner status and access to full-time employment at a living wage – but also to the organisational and the economic. Thus organisations with abilities to control their markets and to pay above average wages are also assumed to provide high pay and secure employment contracts. The French *regulation* school has extended this analysis of the fusion between institutions and labour markets into an historical analysis of the compatibilities between micro systems of wage determination and macro social and economic conditions (Boyer 1979).

Part of the argument to be developed here is that this insistence on the mutual reinforcing nature of institutions, on the cosy one to one relationship between labour market and social structures or between organisational and labour market hierarchies, has been one of the major weaknesses of the institutional economics tradition, denying it a dynamic and analytical contribution to the study of economic and social change. These critiques of the inherent functionalism of much institutional and segmentation theory analysis of labour market structures have long been made by the current author (Rubery 1978). Segmentation processes have been assumed to lead to a mutually reinforcing division between good jobs and bad jobs and between high skills and low skills. The current author has challenged the basis for this assumption, questioning whether bad jobs actually do require low skills or good jobs high skills; and whether indeed firms actually do have to pay high wages to secure a stable labour force if they rely on disadvantaged workers with few alternative employment opportunities. Moreover, institutions introduced to provide protection and shelter have almost by definition also created groups who are excluded from these areas of protection. Thus the creation of shelters in the labour market has also simultaneously created the conditions which could be used to undermine these sources of protection; the male breadwinner and the family wage system creating the second income earner; the· craft system creating the non-qualified worker or the apprentice. Thus the system of protection also creates the potential seeds of its own destruction. This critique of functionalist segmentation analysis is introduced here primarily to make clear that, in pointing to the fragmentation of institutions and the dissolution of institutional structures, there is no intention to hark back to a golden age

24

where there was a neat and uniform relationship between organisational, social and labour market structures and institutions.

THE DESTABILISATION OF SOCIAL AND ECONOMIC RELATIONSHIPS

Nevertheless, even with these health warnings, the changes that are taking place in labour market institutions can still be regarded as representing a major dislocation of the interrelationships between the social and the economic, perhaps undermining the usefulness of an institutionalist and/or segmentation approach. These changes certainly constitute, in the French sense, the heralding in of a new *'rapport salarial'* (Boyer 1979).

Three areas of change can be identified to illustrate the magnitude of the pace and range of changes taking place.

First, there is the loss of occupational identities. This process has gone further than that of the decline of the craft worker and has extended to a whole raft of occupations and professions, including, for example, the civil servant, the health professional or the bank manager. These occupations were previously defined by a long established set of mutually reinforcing institutions which shaped not only the social standing and the employment statuses accorded to such jobs but also the work ethic and the job content. Now civil servants are to be privatised and the public service ethos undermined through the twin effects of privatisation and performance-related pay, where performance is equated with cost saving and not public service, and the 'job for life' associated with civil service employment is about to be transformed into the 'job for as long as you are not undercut at the next tender'. Health professionals have to introduce managerial and market-related skills into their portfolio of caring and technical skills and to consider moving to more profitable trusts rather than up a professional career ladder to improve their economic well being; and the bank manager's job has been reduced to a form of salesperson, with rewards increasingly tied to commissions on sales under the guise of performance pay. All these occupations and many others have seen the dismantling of the tried and tested, and well-known employment systems associated with the job, with the result that job and career choice is inhibited not only by the number of jobs available but also by lack of information on what responsibilities, rewards and security are likely to be associated with a particular career or training decision.

Second, there is the decoupling of the link between labour market position and standards of living, associated with the decline in both full-time continuous and stable employment and the decline in single earner households. Gender segregation in the employment sphere has historically facilitated the development of gender-specific wage policies which reproduce the role of men as male breadwinners and women as subordinate second income earners. Thus male trade unionists opposed the introduction of state-based child benefits as this might undermine their position in arguing for a family or living wage (Land 1980). Standards of living, or the costs of social reproduction, provide the ultimate institutionalist basis for explaining wage structures (Picchio 1981), but the translation from standards of living to wage structures requires some similarity and homogeneity in the household positions of workers within the same wage grade or group. Herein lies the historical basis for male hostility to female entry into the labour market. Gender segregation has by no means disappeared, and men in Britain are still regarded as the main breadwinners. Nevertheless, there are problems with the simple equation between man and breadwinner and woman and subordinate worker which did not trouble the employers or unions of earlier decades. There is some breaking down of gender segregation at both the top and the bottom ends of the labour market, in particular. Highly qualified women are making entry into higher level jobs. At the top end of the labour market notions of a family or a living wage were always perhaps less important legitimations of wage levels or wage claims than where wage levels were closer to basic subsistence needs. Nevertheless the growth of dual earner families has called into question the use of the notion of a family wage as the basis of assessment of fairness of, for example, a teacher's salary. References to a family wage or a living wage are still made in pay disputes but with less vigour and openness than previously; during the railway signalmen's dispute, the fairness of differentials between signalmen and cleaners was debated explicitly in terms of skill levels and not in terms of differences in income needs between signal staff and railway cleaners.

This move away from explicitly gendered notions of income needs has facilitated the government's objective of expanding low paid employment to men as well as women. The links between standards of living, family position and employment position are being constantly eroded by government policies calling for an end to the notion that pay increases should be related to price inflation, and by government policies to force unemployed people into any job that is available. All forms of wage employment are being deemed suitable for workers in all types of family circumstance or occupational history. Unemployed and disabled people are being required to consider any kind of work and not solely work for which they have been trained. In practice the new policies may force unemployed people into switching not only occupational but also gender roles, as men move from primary to secondary income provider, with the balance of income provided either by their wives or by the state, in the form of family credit. The restriction of family credit to household heads may do something to preserve the male breadwinner identity, but the social deconstruction of men as the male breadwinner among the poorest groups of society is proceeding apace. These changes may be legitimised by some as allowing the market to set wages which reflect productivity and skill and not out-dated views of social needs. Wage structures, from this perspective, are treated as independent of social structures, and thus intervention, where required to alleviate poverty, should be directed at income distribution through tax and social benefits and not through change in wage structures which would apparently distort the operation of the efficient, if hidden, hand of the market. These arguments are fuelled by the growth of single parent families and the trend to dual income families which potentially deny any role for notions of family wages or normal living standards in the wage determination process. The fragmentation of the social structure may provide new scope for the reassertion of the independence and fairness of market determined wages.

The final example of changes that are taking place which call into question institutionalist analysis of labour markets relates to organisations and organisational policies. Segmentation theory, and indeed industrial relations theories of management strategy (Sisson and Purcell 1983), have relied upon the possibility of classifying firms into strategic and non-strategic actors, into good and bad employers or into primary and secondary sector firms. However, rapid changes in the employment strategies of even the companies with the most famous reputations for maintaining a long-term coherent employment policy unaffected by short-term market trends – for example, the redundancies at IBM and the high street banks, the downsizing of privatised public utilities – all throw into doubt the validity of organisation-based analyses of labour market structures. These changes raise the possibility that no organisation is now able to plan a coherent employment policy in the face of international competitive pressures. The changing nature of competition has undermined the notion that oligopolistic firms face stable and predictable markets, upon which they can build stable and long-term employment strategies. As a consequence of this destabilisation of markets for major as well as minor players in the market place participants in the labour market may be less able to distinguish which firms represent the good or the bad employers of the future.

These developments place major question marks under many institutionalist theories of labour markets. One of the most influential models of this type, which in fact provided a building block for much of the segmentation literature, is Lester Thurow's (1976) job competition model which he juxtaposed against the traditional wage competition model. The argument put forward by Thurow was that most investment in human capital took place within organisations and not prior to employment. Investment in education was important more for individuals competing for scarce jobs with good employers who would then invest in the training of their employees. Thus workers acquired human capital in order to position themselves favourably in the job market queue. Employers for their part were concerned to attract the best possible applicants, measured in terms

of both potential productivity and likelihood of retention within the organisation, to maximise returns on investment in training. Firms that intended
to invest significantly in training of employees needed to position and keep
their vacancies at the top of the job market queue. Their investments were
long term and thus their positioning of the remuneration and promotion
package on offer was also long term. They would not risk making short-
term adjustments through changes in the quality of the job terms on offer
to meet varying labour market conditions as this might jeopardise their
reputation as employers and thus affect the long-term supply of good
quality applicants. Workers competed for entry to jobs with known and
fixed pay and reward characteristics and wages were not subject to short-
term adjustments.

This model was widely hailed as a plausible, if a somewhat simplified
account of how labour markets functioned in say the 1970s. The plausibility
of this model is subject to severe criticisms today; first of all, many companies
which prided themselves on their reputations as good employers offering
high pay and job security have abandoned these policies in part or in
total; second, there has been a declining belief, fuelled by these first set of
developments, in the likelihood of obtaining a job for life, or even for a
reasonable period; third, in the increasingly opaque labour market,
where pay is related not only to organisations and to job grades, but also to
individual performance assessments, there is likely to be little actual knowledge of the set of pay and promotion prospects on offer. Thus the matching,
which is critical to Thurow's theory, between an employer's employment
practices and potential recruits' assessments of the benefits accruing from
employment in the firm is likely to have been undermined (or indeed may
never have existed). Employers may not be able or willing to deliver what
they promise (thereby leading to uncertainty over how to value current
known benefits), and for their part employees lack knowledge of what is on
offer or how it compares to offers from equivalent companies and may in
any case remain justifiably sceptical of the employer's ability or willingness
to deliver a long-term employment package. This critique of Thurow in fact
applies to all internal labour market and efficiency wage theories which
assume knowledge of labour market conditions by internal employees, and
also full understanding and knowledge of firms' employment policies.
In the absence of these conditions the supposed strategies of paying above
market rates or providing better promotion chances to retain labour are
unlikely to work. These conditions might be regarded as implausible under
most conditions, but particularly so in the fragmented and opaque labour
markets of the 1990s.

INTERNATIONAL COMPETITION AND LABOUR MARKET ORGANISATION: DO INSTITUTIONS STILL MATTER?

The changes that are occurring in the UK labour market are neither accidental, nor inevitable or predetermined. In some cases the specific institutional forms which are being undermined had already passed their 'sell-by date'. Thus, for example, the craft worker and the male bread-winner were 'institutions' whose time was clearly up. Many of the trends are too general across countries and associated with long-term changes in both social organisation and capitalist production for country or policy specific arguments to provide sufficient explanation.

However, international trends are not the result of autonomous and inevitable market forces, but themselves the result of actions and counter actions pursued by active agents, who may nevertheless build upon and legitimise their actions by reference to policies pursued within other countries or by the apocryphal global corporations (Rubery 1992; 1994). In practice, distinguishing between developments necessitated by funda-mental changes in the nature of production and exchange and those which can be attributed to specific political objectives and choices is not necessarily helpful or indeed possible. Such distinctions tend, by definition, to promote the notion of the hidden hand of market forces or requirements and thus may obscure the roles of institutions and political choices in the transformation of markets and production systems. Country-specific societal or institutional systems do not adjust in an automatic or predetermined fashion to external pressures or stimuli, even when responding to apparently similar international or global developments. The potential for different trajectories even within an internationally integrating economy has been demonstrated within the flexibility debate, where the need for change or for flexibility has been argued to result in the search for positive or long-term flexibility in some countries and for short-term or negative flexibility in others.

Within Britain it is important to recognise the significant role of government policy in the dismantlement of institutions, albeit justified with reference to the so-called need for adjustment to new market conditions. This has been described by Will Hutton (1994) as a policy to eliminate 'all intermediary institutions between state and individual' in the interests of driving down the price of labour. What has been significant about government policy and action in the UK has been the desire not to replace and reform outmoded labour market and social institutions with new institutional structures more suited to current social and economic needs, but explicitly to fragment and dissolve any visible social and labour market institutions which might overtly provide a check on the supposed operation of market forces and the autonomy of firms. The move to a post-pluralistic system of organisation, and away from explicit group structures with shared norms and values and shared interests has been a policy pursued with extreme vigour since 1979. The dismembering of group interests thereby deflates any claims to fair wages or fair employment conditions based on custom and practice, or to long-term employment contracts and relationships, placing the individual worker much more explicitly vulnerable to the discretionary policies of both the employer and the state. The employer is advised to pay no heed to notions of customary differentials, the going rate of wages or even the change in the retail price index, while the state denies any notion that unemployed people should have reasonable expectations of remaining in the same job stratum or occupational group from whence they came, or that the unemployed person's reservation wages may be related not solely to actual employment opportunities but also to social needs.

Hutton identified this levelling down of the labour force through the fragmentation and the dismemberment of institutions as akin to a neo-Marxist policy in which unfettered competition between capital would lead to the destructive search for low wage solutions to economic crisis. The collapse of sustained strategies by organisations, coupled with the fragmentation of the institutions which provided some shelter through collective action and shared norms from the competitive market, might suggest that we should all agree that institutionalist economics has had its day. Wages and employment conditions are being increasingly driven by the dynamics of the production system, and the notion that wage structures and employment forms are fundamental elements in social organisation and social order is being sidelined.

Two main arguments can be brought into play to suggest an alternative perspective or a different reading of the situation. The first is that social institutions, and in particular those related to the standard of living still matter. The second is that despite the problems that organisations face in maintaining coherent or consistent policies, they still exercise discretion in their employment strategies and choices. Decisions by firms, which are only partially influenced by external or market based criteria, are thus probably of increasing importance in the labour market.

In stressing the efforts of the government to clear the path of any institutions which protected workers from destructive cost cutting competition, the reduction in the influence of institutions on the labour market may be exaggerated as those institutions which in fact aid and abet the capitalists in their search for low wage solutions also need to be considered. Thus the move towards low wage employment conditions in the UK has been aided by a whole set of institutions which provide the basis through which low wage labour is supplied to the labour market. These include the continuation of the male breadwinner system of social organisation, thereby providing employers with a large supply of cheap female part-time labour; the social security system which, by topping up wages through the family credit system, provides the basis for those with household dependants to enter low wage or part-time jobs; the education system which has expanded the supply of young people available to work for 'top up' wages; early retirement schemes and redundancy pay offs which have provided a supply of older workers for part-time or self-employment; the tax and social security system which has encouraged the growth of self-employment, as an easier route to tax avoidance than direct employment; the introduction of youth training schemes paying low allowances which has provided the basis for adjustment downwards of all youth wage levels to match the new institutions. Institutions not only provide protection against the so-called hidden hand of market forces by creating uniform labour market standards, but also act to create a segmented labour supply which facilitates the development of a wide range of employment systems and practices within the labour market.

The competitive labour market within the Marxist tradition, as invoked by Hutton, differs from the neoclassical model by the absence of a mechanism to bring about full employment and a market clearing wage. However the Marxist framework for analysing pay determination involves two elements; pay levels are forced down by the forces of competition on the one hand, but this suppression of wages is also constrained on the other hand by the socially necessary costs of reproduction, including the 'historical or moral element' (Picchio 1981; Botwinick 1993). The interplay of these two elements perhaps provides a more satisfactory analytical framework for understanding the current transformations of the labour market than either the competitive Marxist or the competitive neoclassical labour market model. Employers and indeed the state may be seeking to reduce or constrain the historical or moral element in wages but they do so, at least in part, through drawing upon sources of labour – perhaps akin to the layers of the reserve army – whose social reproduction costs are borne partially by the state or family networks. Thus the institutional determinants of the standard of living remain key elements in the analysis of the transformation of the employment system. One of the most important contributions of the feminist debate, centred around such issues as the family wage, was the pointing up of the destabilising and negative effects as well as the protective and stabilising effects of labour market institutions. Trade union organisation and wage bargaining organised around the concept of a family wage (Humphries 1977; Barrett and McIntosh 1980: Rubery 1978) both protected the historical and moral element in the wage and at the same time contributed to the creation of classes of labour that were deemed available for work at below subsistence levels. Such supplies of labour were supplemented by policies such as the Speenhamland system which explicitly subsidised the employers of low paid labour (Picchio 1981). The relative balance of advantage between institutions which create shelter and enclaves for some workers, while potentially exposing the remaining workforce to unprotected wages and conditions, may change over time (as well as obviously between labour force groups at any point in time), but the exclusionary and thus discriminatory elements of systems of worker protection may be capable only of modification – through renewal of institutions – and not elimination.

It is not only in the formation of labour supply conditions that we can see the continued role of institutions, but also in the actual policies and practices pursued in labour markets. Far from firms following market trends and acting as wage takers, which would be the expected outcome of a true development of a market based labour market (even if such a market would need a strong institutional framework for it to function), we witness instead increasing discretion in the hands of organisations to adopt whatever employment practices and policies suit their needs. The market in skilled labour – in the sense of the opportunities for external mobility – is restricted by the growth of firm-specific skills. These changes are legitimised in management practice by the development of firm and individual specific pay systems, whereby the value of a worker is seen to be a joint product dependent upon his or her specific performance within a particular organisation and job position. Even within a neoclassical approach, as soon as the productivity of a worker is organisation specific, whether or not workers receive close to their actual productive contribution, becomes dependent upon their relative bargaining power compared to the employer, and is no longer the outcome of labour market forces of exchange.

Organisational-specific labour markets provide the basis for a dominant role for organisations in the structuring of labour markets. The multiple objectives of firms and their different capacities to plan for the future, together with the organisational specificity of their labour forces, guarantees diversity of practice. Trade unions have been removed from their functionalist role, identified by Adam Smith, of ensuring a fair rate for the job across labour markets. Instead labour markets have been allowed to become fragmented and opaque, with both employers and employees increasingly losing access to information on norms and practices outside their immediate employment relationship. This means that even where firms aim to develop coherent and long lasting employment systems and practices they may be unable to do so because of lack of information relating to their external environment on which to plan and develop their policies; and because the employees of the firm not only may lack information about but also may lack confidence in the firm's pay and employment package. Thus, while the prospects of long-term security and pay promotion may have been attractive in the past to potential recruits, there may be now more emphasis on maximising current rewards and rejecting deferred reward systems as too risky, thereby placing in jeopardy firms' plans for long-term investment in the training and development of their workforces. Thus the processes, which in principle have given firms much more room for manoeuvre in the labour market, have at the same time constrained the opportunities for organisations to develop orderly and coherent employment policies and practices because of the loss of information on both sides of the labour market. Labour market wide institutions often serve to remove much of the uncertainty and risk from firms' employment policies, by providing protection against poaching (Marsden 1986) and guarantees of common cost levels between competitors. Freedom to set pay or determine training, without either information or guarantees concerning the actions of competitors, de-stabilises and further fragments labour markets as firms seek to trap skilled employees within the organisational labour market.

Thus the argument that we are making here is that far from the decline of institutional forces in the structuring of the labour market, we are witnessing instead the relatively unfettered and unconstrained actions of organisations, that is unfettered and unconstrained either by coordinating regulations and institutions or by the controls imposed by a labour market. This high degree of discretion is likely to lead not to the homogeneous outcomes expected within market-based theories but to the diversity and heterogeneity predicted by segmentation theories where diversity on the demand side (in terms of type of organisation, technology, product market position, competitive strategy) interacts with diversity on the supply side (in terms of demographic and social groups with different relation-ships to and expectations of household standards of living) to create complex and heterogeneous employment systems.

THE NEED FOR COORDINATING LABOUR MARKET LEVEL INSTITUTIONS AND STANDARDS

It is through labour market based institutions which provide a coordinating role that labour standards are established, trends toward heterogeneity are modified and uniform rules and prices introduced. It is these forms of institutions that have been most subject to destruction since the 1980s. Many of the institutions which have been subject to destruction in the British labour market were designed to protect the historical or moral element in pay or to guarantee the social reproduction of labour, both in the sense of providing a stable income linked to a stable and increasing standard of living, and in the sense of providing a level of income which may ensure the continued reproduction of skills. The reproduction of skills can take place either at a labour market or at an organisational level, but it arguably requires the prospects of job and income security attached either to an occupation or to an organisation to encourage a new generation of workers to acquire skills and those with the relevant skills not to seek alternative employment. Orderly functioning of labour markets and of broader social structures does seem to require coordinating institutions to provide stability and transparency. These needs extend outside of the labour market itself to all elements of social and economic life. Stable employment and pay levels are essential not only for the reproduction of skills but also for the whole functioning of, for example, the housing market, the consumer credit system, the pension system, the taxation system and the social production and nurture of children. Stability and transparency are being undermined by the increasing precariousness of jobs, the increase in the number of jobs which do not provide for acceptable living standards, and the increasing opaqueness of the labour market, as pay is linked supposedly to organisational and individual performance, but in practice to discretionary decisions at the organisational level. These changes in the labour market are threatening or have already threatened all these broader social systems, including notably the housing and the credit systems, with the increasing number of defaults and indebtedness and the consequent failure of the housing market to operate, let alone 'clear'. The likelihood of instability in the social reproduction system is already present as turmoil in the labour market prevents the orderly adaptation to a new system of resourcing the upbringing of children.

As we have argued, the breakdown of the orderly system does not imply the ending of the role of institutions. We may have to work harder to identify the relationships between institutions and the labour market than was the case in the past, and to work harder at developing a dynamic analysis of the role of institutions in the transformation of labour markets. This role can be both negative and positive. There is no automatic process whereby there is a renewal of institutions to meet current social, organisational and economic needs. For example, the absence of jobs providing men with a living wage has not led to greater opportunities for women employees to escape from wage structures designed around subordinate second income earners. The counterpart to the decline of the full-time standard employment contract offering a family wage should be a renewal of institutions more appropriate to the increased economic independence of women – and thus abolition of jobs offering below adult subsistence wages. Instead these outmoded institutions have been extended and reinforced by the extension of neo-Speenhamland systems and the expansion of the number of economically dependent young people seeking partial employment or partial income support, as well as by the continuation of the development of low wage part-time jobs for women. Moreover, more people are being forced through changes to unemployment regulations as well as changes to employment structures to accept jobs designed to exploit second income earners but who themselves, men, women and young people, are in need of full subsistence support. Here we can witness perhaps the long-term interdependence between institutions and social attitudes and labour market organisation, as these groups are being encouraged to lower their expectations of what constitutes a fair or reasonable standard of living. The interplay between employers seeking low wage labour and employees seeking wage income to cover their costs of reproduction is resulting in a widening of the range of customary or expected income standards. Thus institutional arrangements structure the conditions under which labour is provided, but these institutional arrangements, including social attitudes and expectations, are themselves conditioned by experience in the labour market, leading to adjustment over time in expected standards of living and the social acceptance of social exclusion. These processes take place under the guise of the hidden hand of market forces, but employers are operating in labour markets where wage levels associated with particular types of jobs are influenced by the historical pattern of social organisation and indeed by current institutions of income support through the state and the family. This reverses the argument of current Conservative dogma – that the structure of wages is deemed to be prior to and uninfluenced by welfare or other social policies and practices.

The purpose of this analysis of the problems of analysing labour markets under current and future conditions has been to underline that the re-organisation of the labour market is not being driven by inevitable market forces, and that instead there are still choices that have to be made as to how labour markets are organised. Trends towards flexibility, fragmentation, precarity and individualisation are not the inevitable concomitants of the late 1990s – as is evidenced by the highly varying degrees to which these are present in relatively successful capitalist societies. They may be in practice the likely outcome if there are no serious political attempts to rethink and replace labour market institutions which have either outlived their usefulness or have been destroyed under recent political struggles within the labour market. Thus to predict or describe trends towards internal labour markets, functional flexibility or precarious work has no relevance without a simultaneous analysis of the political conditions under which labour market structures evolve. The path of development is contingent and not determined by either capitalist or social requirements. Arguments that stress the inevitable development of new forms of work more suited to new forms of social organisation are as misguided as those that stress the inevitable collapse of institutions in the face of the hidden hand of market forces. To demonstrate irrationality, contradictions and incompatibilities is insufficient as reactions to these problems may be as likely to intensify as to resolve the contradictions. Indeed to suggest that the decline in long-term and secure full-time employment will lead to people adapting to more flexible participation patterns, including the taking of voluntary leaves from the labour market, is no better than utopian nonsense (Hewitt 1993). As the number of secure jobs decreases so the competition to obtain and maintain such a position increases, forcing workers into ever longer hours of work, often unpaid, just to signal to employers that they are the most suitable worker for the job. Thus a reduction in the availability of work is more likely to lead to an increase than a decrease in the available supply of labour time. These perverse adjustment effects make the development of coordinated responses to changes in labour market conditions even more imperative.

Thus the aim of this analysis is to put back on the agenda the need for an institutionalist approach to labour market analysis and thereby to point to the possibilities of reconstructing and re-regulating labour markets. This approach rejects first the fatalistic or pessimistic view of the inevitable collapse of stable employment and also the optimistic rationalist perspective that there will be an inevitable, if long-term, trend towards a fairer distribution of work and the evolution of new work patterns to meet new life styles. Instead we need to find an intermediate ground where serious discussion about how to build new institutions can take place, while recognising the very long time it took to build institutional systems of protection and shelter in the past, and that rebuilding and renewal of institutions may this time be an equally long project. This rebuilding and renewal requires the transformation and abolition of existing but outdated or inefficient institutional influences. Thus, for example, pay structures and social security benefit systems need reform to remove from their construction the deeply embedded notions of female economic subordination; training systems need reform to remove the degree of discretion from employers in the form and level of training provided; and benefit systems need reform to eliminate the simplistic assumptions of simple family structures and continuous and lifelong employment paths.

An important part of the rebuilding and renewal should be to re-establish universal labour market standards which then reduce the influence of other social and economic institutions on the operation of the labour market. Segmentation literature has long demonstrated that segmentation is the normal outcome of labour market systems and that deregulation is more likely to result in heterogeneity than homogeneity. The heterogeneity may take different forms than in the past, with greater mobility between segments, and greater diversity in the groups found in the bottom segments, as primary jobs are converted to secondary jobs, or primary workers displaced into unemployment and forced into secondary type work. Perhaps the major change that is taking place in the labour market is that previously advantaged groups are sharing in the risks of instability, unemployment and low income previously faced only by secondary sector workers. However, sharing the risks of segmentation does not remove the inefficiencies, the unfairness or the uncertainties, or indeed improve conditions for those in the secondary sector.

36

Labour markets thus need institutions designed to increase their coherence and efficiency and to decrease the segmentation through the provision of minimum standards and transparent and stable employment practices. One issue is where such institutions should come from and what form they should take. The increasing fragmentation and destabilisation of the employment system means that it is probably not possible or appropriate to seek changes solely through collective or voluntary actions as these actions would result in only partial coverage, leading to incentives to employers to move into the unregulated sector, thereby destabilising the basis for collectively agreed standards. However labour standards simply imposed by law, whether national or pan-national (i.e. European), are unlikely to be effective unless they enjoy collective legitimacy or are enforced through collective mechanisms. There is thus still the need to build up collective organisation and a collective consensus around what constitutes appropriate labour market institutions and labour market standards. Unfortunately it is probably more difficult to establish a collective consensus in favour of redistribution towards the poor than it is when policies are acting to redistribute income towards the rich. This is because the rich have power to resist change, while the disenfranchising of disadvantaged people of their rights to employment and reasonable living standards in the 1980s and 1990s has gone effectively unchallenged. The more widespread destabilisation that we are witnessing today perhaps for the first time provides some glimmer of hope that a new consensus could be built around the need to rebuild our labour market institutions. Campbell and Sengenberger (1994) have referred to labour standards as reflecting 'accumulated learning and, as such, are a sort of inter-generational pact. . . . Many standards are responses to massive and pervasive social damage from market failure or uncontrolled economic behaviour which became visible in the firm itself, in the wider labour market, or at a later point of time' (1994: 422). From this perspective the 1980s and the 1990s can be seen as a period where there has been a massive loss of social capital and social learning and it will require a subsequent experience of 'pervasive social damage' before there is renewed collective consciousness of the need for intervention and standards. That social learning may be more rapid if the social damage affects the middle as well as the working classes, and indeed even the upper classes. However, the processes of renewal are both so long term and so uncertain that it would be foolhardy to support further destabilisation in the hope of bringing about a broader social consensus in favour of radical renewal of labour market institutions; such a position could be likened to proposing a third world war in the hope of recreating the social consensus after 1945. In these circumstances it is hard to do anything other than to defend existing labour standards and institutions against further deregulation and fragmentation, even in the full knowledge that these institutions require renewal and indeed may be preventing a

37

widespread realisation of the nature of changes wrought in less protected segments of the labour market. This may result in the worst of all possible worlds, leading to the incremental but slow dismantlement of existing institutions without the development of a widespread movement for change and renewal. But the descent into further labour market anarchy and destabilisation has consequences for the social and economic structure that are potentially too great to be either predictable or controllable.

REFERENCES

Barrett, M. and McIntosh, M. (1980) 'The "family wage": some problems for socialists and feminists', *Capital and Class* 11.

Botwinick, H. (1993) *Persistent Inequalities*, New Brunswick, NJ: Princeton University Press.

Boyer, R. (1979) 'Wage formation in historical perspective: the French experience', *Cambridge Journal of Economics* 3(2): 99–118.

Brown, W. (1972) 'A consideration of "custom and practice"', *British Journal of Industrial Relations* X(1): 42–61.

Campbell, D. and Sengenberger, W. (1994) 'Labour standards, economic efficiency and development: lessons from experience with industrial restructuring', in W. Sengenberger and D. Campbell (eds) *Creating Economic Opportunities: The Role of Labour Standards in Industrial Restructuring*, Geneva: International Institute for Labour Studies, ILO.

Clegg, H. (1970) *The System of Industrial Relations in Great Britain*, Oxford: Blackwell.

Hewitt, P. (1993) *About Time: The Revolution in Work and Family Life*, London: Institute for Public Policy Research/Rivers Oram Press.

Humphries, J. (1977) 'Class struggle and the persistence of the working class family', *Cambridge Journal of Economics* 1(3).

Hutton, W. (1994) 'Tories' neo-Marxism fragments society', *Guardian* 9 May.

Land, H. (1980) 'The family wage', *Feminist Review* 6: 55–77.

Marsden, D. (1986) *The End of Economic Man*, Brighton: Harvester Wheatsheaf.

Maurice, M., Sellier, F. and Sylvestre, J.-J. (1986) *The Social Foundations of Industrial Power*, Cambridge, MA: MIT Press.

Millward, N., Stevens, M., Smart, D. and Hawes, W. R. (1992) *Workplace Industrial Relations in Transition*, Aldershot: Dartmouth.

Picchio, A. (1981) 'Social reproduction and the basic structure of labour markets', in F. Wilkinson (ed.) *The Dynamics of Labour Market Segmentation*, London: Academic.

Routh, G. (1980) *Occupation and Pay in Great Britain*, London: Macmillan.

Rubery, J. (1978) 'Structured labour markets, worker organisation and low pay', *Cambridge Journal of Economics* 2(1): 17–37.

Rubery, J. (1992) 'Productive systems, international integration and the single European market', in A. Castro, P. Mehaut and J. Rubery (eds) *International Integration and Labour Market Organisation*, London: Academic.

Rubery, J. (1994) 'The British productive regime: a societal specific system?', *Economy and Society* 23(3): 335–54.

Sisson, K. and Purcell, J. (1983) 'Strategies and practice in the management of industrial relations', in G. Bain (ed.) *Industrial Relations in Britain*, Oxford: Blackwell.

Solow, R. (1990) *The Labour Market as a Social Institution*, Oxford: Blackwell.

Thurow, L. (1976) *Generating Inequality*, London: Macmillan.
Turner, H. (1962) *Trade Union Growth, Structure and Policy*, London: Allen & Unwin.
Wootton, B. (1955) *The Social Foundations of Wage Policy: A Study of Contemporary British Wage and Salary Structure*, London: Allen & Unwin.

3

TOWARDS THE TRANSNATIONAL COMPANY?

The global structure and organisation of multinational firms

Paul Edwards, Peter Armstrong,
Paul Marginson and John Purcell

The most important source of international economic exchange is no longer the flow of trade between countries but the multinational company or MNC (UNCTAD 1993). According to the influential views of Robert Reich (1991) – subsequently Secretary of Labor in the Clinton Administration in the USA – a global web of companies is replacing the nationally specific firm. Observers in the labour movement have expressed concern at the ability of the transnational to switch production between sites and to seek out countries with low labour costs. In addition to well-known debates on the impact of the MNC, there has been widespread discussion of the internal organisation and dynamics of such firms. Key issues, again heavily discussed, include the ways in which integration and co-ordination are achieved and the degree of centralisation which is appropriate (Brooke 1984).

Though the management of people tends either to be neglected or to be treated in a descriptive and prescriptive manner in much of the debate, a range of contributions is beginning to identify an analytical agenda. As one review puts it, even the literature which talks of international human resource management 'ignores many of the most challenging questions and theoretical implications for modern employment relations that flow from the expansion of international economic, political, technical and organizational interdependence' (Kochan *et al.* 1992: 310). MNCs' behaviour in relation to labour will be shaped by the regulatory systems of nation states, with the interplay of national and global trends being a key question; there may be different approaches to labour depending on firms' organisational structure and policies of diversification (Marginson 1992); and the balance of centralisation or decentralisation is not just a technical question but is likely to reflect internal political bargaining and to result in instability and uncertainty (Ferner 1994). Prescriptive texts see the transfer of managers as an important vehicle for the development of a global strategy, but research highlights the limited extent to which this is done and the costs and difficulties of developing an international cadre (Scullion 1992; P. Edwards *et al.* 1993).

The purpose of this chapter is not to repeat what is becoming a well-established debate but to focus on one specific issue: the supposed evolution of the firm from being nationally specific, through stages variously labelled multinational and polycentric, to the true transnational enterprise. This issue underlies some of the more specific topics such as international managerial mobility, for it considers how far firms are developing the global orientation which is necessary before managerial mobility becomes a serious question. It also links the debates on MNCs directly to those on production globalisation. Though, as we shall see, discussion on the evolution of the MNC has neglected the point, the links are evident. The more that firms adopt a truly global perspective, the greater is the possibility that they act as bearers of 'best practice' and thereby contribute to the globalisation of production. Perhaps the central point is that we need to know what trans-nationality actually implies: if firms are indeed moving in a transnational direction, what are their key attributes, and what are the implications for the ways in which labour relations are handled?

The 'transnational solution' has been canvassed most thoroughly by Bartlett and Ghoshal (1989). They contrast it with three prior approaches to cross-country operations. What they term *multinationals* build a strong local presence in each country. Such firms stress the ability to operate in each local market and thus tend to be decentralised groupings with little strategic direction from headquarters. *Global companies* have a more centralised and global-level approach to markets; the head office has a strong role in laying down policy for subsidiaries. *International companies* exploit parent company skills through world-wide adaptation rather than centralised imposition; they have a more federal structure in which the centre co-ordinates rather than instructs. All these structures are felt to have difficulty in handling the growing complexity of global markets.

The fourth type, the *transnational*, is seen as the coming solution to this problem. As writers such as Hedlund (1986) also argue, firms need to move away from hierarchical organisation towards a more flexible struc-ture. The transnational is characterised by differentiated contributions from each national team, with knowledge being shared and responsibility dispersed. Instead of centralised command, responsibility is devolved, and co-ordination is attained not through instruction and monitoring but through co-operation, team work and shared values. A key example of this form, which is admitted to be rare, is Asea Brown Boveri (ABB) under the charismatic leadership of Percy Barnevik (Bartlett and Ghoshal 1993). There is supposedly horizontal networking through *ad hoc* task groups which transfer knowledge between decentralised operating units that

41

enjoy considerable financial autonomy. The transnational solution is seen more as an approach, or a frame of mind, than as a clear structure. There are clear resonances with many other arguments, notably those associated with flexible specialisation and 'post-Fordism', about the importance of replacing rigid bureaucracy with more flexible and less hierarchical forms. The model of the transnational provides a useful case study for the consideration of such wider topics.

There are some critics of the transnational model. Hu (1992) has argued that there are really very few transnationals: most firms are rooted in a particular national base on which they depend for their basic operating style, and national financial regimes prevent the rise of the truly stateless corporation. For Hu, perhaps only ICI met the transnational model. The subsequent de-merger of the firm might well raise issues about the firm's continued global integration. Porter (1990) similarly argues that firms gain competitive advantage from their location in specific national contexts.

A further issue concerns different routes towards globalism. The usual image of globalisation, as found for example in Reich's (1991) work, is one of a firm which seeks careful integration. Even though trade may be in services or problem-solving, rather than physical goods, and even though it may involve many different legal entities, the global firm is seen as a seeker of economies based on the exploitation of a key skill or competence, rather than as a financial engineer shifting capital in the pursuit of short-term profit. Other literature on business strategy (notably Hill and Hoskisson 1987) shows, however, that in addition to this 'synergistic' approach, firms may also seek 'financial' economies using loose direct controls and penalties on subsidiaries which fail to meet financial targets: here, central rules and procedures are eschewed.

As argued elsewhere, at least four ideal types of MNCs can be identified. These are financial control (for example, Hanson); the integrated international company, such as ICI; the decentralised network, like ABB; and the federation as practised by inernational management consultancies (Ferner and Edwards 1995). Each type is 'global' in its approach, but with different patterns of control and authority relations.

The relationship of this theme to the Bartlett–Ghoshal model is two-fold. First, firms can adopt a global perspective but without necessarily becoming a multi-centred, networked, power-sharing 'transnational'. Second, they may not have abandoned the administrative controls and data collection and monitoring of older models of the MNC. As we shall show, globalism is certainly an active trend, but routes to it are more varied than is often thought, and hierarchy and accountability remain strongly in evidence. The wider implication is that any shift to post-Fordism may be slow, patchy, and less of a break from the past than is sometimes claimed.

This chapter pursues three particular issues. First, just what do MNCs look like? The literature has proposed various ideal types, and it is often implied that firms more or less approximate to one or other type. Yet empirical attempts to assess this assumption are rather rare. A subsidiary question here is how far a firm's organisational arrangements follow from its world-wide structure. Thus it is assumed that firms which are structured around international divisions, rather than around territorial units, will have a more global strategic focus. The tightness of these links requires study.

The second issue is the 'country of origin' effect: do MNCs share fundamental features, as much of the literature on transnationality implies, or do those based in one country differ from those in others? It has, for example, long been felt that American-owned firms are more formalised and centralised than European MNCs (Roberts and May 1974). More recently, a 'European' approach, sometimes further differentiated into Northern and Southern, or Germanic and Latin, has been identified (Leeds et al. 1994). It is not the aim here to debate in detail these rather vague national stereotypes. But we are in a position to assess some aspects of the debate. In particular, as against the view that MNCs from different countries can be distinguished in ideal-typical terms, we show where MNCs display common features and in what respects they differ.

Third, what are the implications for management's approach to labour issues? Early work, notably that using the New International Division of Labour paradigm, argued that MNCs could freely shift production around the globe in the search for cheap labour. A wide array of research has questioned this view: firms are less omniscient than is sometimes thought; they do not necessarily seek the cheapest labour; and location decisions are often driven by a concern to be close to key markets rather than by labour costs (Cohen 1991. ch. 8; Ramsay 1991; Marginson 1992). It remains the case, however, as Ramsay stresses, that MNCs are enormously powerful. They may be less able to move production around the globe than is sometimes supposed, and they may not have a deliberate policy of marginalising unions. But their decisions may in the long run still press them in one direction rather than another. Arguments made elsewhere in relation to the labour process debate apply exactly: managers may not deliberately de-skill, but the long-run effects of their actions may still have this result (Armstrong 1988). In the same way, policies in the MNC need not be deliberate and explicit for them to have a substantial impact on labour, and, though market considerations are important, the *ceteris paribus* tendency towards seeking cheap labour may well encourage drift, albeit slow and qualified, towards certain parts of the globe.

This chapter uses the Second Company Level Industrial Relations Survey (CLIRS2), together with illustrative case study evidence, to address these issues. It begins by describing briefly existing models of MNCs and the ways in which the present evidence addresses them. It then introduces the data and how they may be used. Research findings are presented in two main areas: the degree to which firms fit existing stereotypes, together with the question of whether they are evolving in a particular direction; and the implications of globalism for management control systems and the management of labour.

MODELS OF THE MULTINATIONAL

Many models of the MNC have been proposed. In earlier work (Marginson *et al.* 1993) we reported initial tests using Perlmutter's (1969) still influential model of ethno-, poly- and geo-centric firms. We developed a series of measures and created an index for each type. The key result was that firms did not appear to cluster around the three types. Instead, they were distributed approximately normally along each dimension. Other work (P. Edwards *et al.* 1993) has used case study evidence to assess some of the other extant typologies. Firms were found to display various characteristics simultaneously: for example, they were centralised in some respects and decentralised in others. The implication is not that typologies are worthless, for they identify important tendencies; the error is to assume that these tendencies are necessarily opposites.

The typologies in question are, however, difficult to apply empirically, and some judgements as to the features which an ethnocentric, say, should display were rather arbitrary. In the present analysis, we therefore take the Bartlett–Ghoshal model, which is undoubtedly the most influential of its type, as the starting point. Leong and Tan (1993) report a test of it. They presented statements aimed at capturing the essence of the four types of MNCs to 131 senior executives and asked them to choose one; they correlated the resulting categories with statements about the organisation of the company and the use of skills and resources. As expected, the transnational type was selected least often, by 18 per cent of the sample. There were many of the expected links with other aspects of firms' reported behaviour. A rather basic difficulty in this study, like several others in the field (e.g. Roth *et al.* 1991), is that it reports attitudes and beliefs. It does not focus on concrete practice such as the existence of key institutions within firms or the use of various forms of pay systems. All we learn is that managers who describe their firms in certain ways, and ways defined for them at that, also tend to believe other things. The present study, by contrast, was much more concerned with practice and the existence of certain arrangements and institutions, as distinct from managerial belief. For example, are data collected by head offices, how often are there meetings between managers across the globe, and is there a department for the training and development of managers engaged in international operations?

Precisely because of this, there are also two constraints. First, it is difficult to find measures which will differentiate between all of Bartlett and

Ghoshal's types. The transnational is particularly hard to define in terms of its organisational structures. It will also have some features in common with global firms but is supposed to differ from them more in the quality of its internal dynamics than in its structure. Given that transnationality is claimed to be an attitude of mind or approach, one might ask whether the definition is clear enough to be anything other than self-fulfilling: any firm alleged to be a transnational but lacking the returns in terms of growth and market power can be dismissed as not truly a transnational. There are parallel problems with differentiating between *international* and *global* types, for they are both relatively centralised and co-ordinated.

We thus differentiate between what we term *nationally* and *globally oriented* approaches. The former covers the Bartlett–Ghoshal multinational type. In particular, firms here should retain a strong identity with their home base and have a relatively loose set of linkages with overseas operations. Global firms will be more co-ordinated, more likely to practise international management development, and more likely to collect data from subsidiaries. Now, it might be argued that we are able to measure differences only between a type of limited interest, the old-fashioned nationally oriented firm, and all other MNCs. The point, however, is that it has yet to be shown that this type is indeed in the minority. In relation to global firms, moreover, we can show which features were more common than others and thus begin to establish whether the different routes to globalism discussed above are in fact in evidence.

We need to assemble a series of measures which are likely to indicate the degree to which a firm adopts one of these two types of organisation. The limitation – and this is the second constraint – is that our survey was not designed with this sole aim in view, so some indices are indirect while there may be dispute about others. As discussed, moreover, the two types should not be seen as stark opposites, for elements of national and global focus can co-exist. Rather than try to place firms in pre-defined boxes, we are concerned to explore just how far they have all the features which would indeed place them in one of the boxes. A certain orientation can be seen as a tendency, which may exist to varying degrees.

DATA SOURCES

The survey

CLIRS2 is a representative sample of large companies operating in the UK. The survey population was companies employing 1,000 or more people in the UK, with at least two UK sites. Public services were excluded. Initial telephone screening was conducted of all companies meeting these criteria. The survey used stratification by size, sector of operation, and whether the firm was UK- or overseas-owned. In each firm, personal interviews were conducted with two respondents: the senior executive responsible for personnel and industrial relations, and a senior finance executive. Interviews were completed in 176 firms, between February and August 1992.

The overall response rate, defined as pairs of completed interviews obtained as a proportion of interviews plus refusals, was 28 per cent. This reflects the difficulty of obtaining two interviews with senior managers. Difficulties were particularly great in relation to the finance manager: 66 per cent of refusals were by this manager, 28 per cent by the personnel respondents, and 6 per cent by both. None the less, the response rate is comparable to those of other surveys in the management accounting field (e.g. Drury *et al.* 1993; Hill and Pickering 1986). Extensive checks were undertaken to assess non-response bias. The sectoral breakdown was very similar to that of the population. There were some differences by size and ownership, which can be controlled for using weights as indicated below. But the key issue is whether non-respondents differed from participants in their control of subsidiaries. This was checked using information from the 812 (of the original 975) firms who provided complete responses at the screening stage. The personnel respondent was asked about the degree of centralisation of policy, using a four-point scale. There was no substantial difference on this question between those who later participated in the full questionnaire and those who did not.

Differences between sample and population were dealt with by weighting according to size and ownership. All data reported here are weighted. The figures can be taken as representative of the population. Of the 176 companies, 101 (unweighted; 104 weighted) were MNCs, of which 58 were UK-owned and 43 were overseas-owned. It is with this group that this chapter is concerned.

In addition to the main survey, a small follow-up study was conducted at the European head offices of overseas-owned firms. The aim here was to allow for the fact that, in the case of British firms, we were studying the headquarters of the whole organisation, whereas this was not the case with our interviews at the UK head offices of non-British firms. Of the 43 overseas-owned firms, interviews were conducted at 26 (15 with European headquarters and 11 with headquarters elsewhere). In view of the small size of this group, we do not make systematic use of the data on them but we report, where relevant, the basic information from them. Analysis of these 26 firms shows that there was no systematic bias between replies at the UK and at the European head office levels, which offers further confirmation of the validity of the UK-level responses (A. Edwards 1993).

Case studies

Case study work, undertaken with Anthony Ferner and Keith Sisson, throws light on the dynamics underlying the quantitative data from the survey (P. Edwards *et al.* 1993; Ferner and Edwards 1995). We refer here to two British-based manufacturing firms. 'Components' is a long-established firm in the engineering sector. During the 1980s it expanded its international activities, particularly in North America. It was trying to become a global player in its specific areas of expertise, and was thus seeking 'synergies' across its national businesses. 'Process' was a longer-established MNC in the chemicals industry. It was arguably further down the road towards trans-nationality, while still facing tensions between a territorial and a global orientation.

GLOBAL STRUCTURE

Measures of globalism

Our first task was to develop concrete measures which could be expected to differentiate between the nationally and globally oriented ideal types. The logic here is essentially descriptive and classificatory: using the ideal types as benchmarks, how many firms have the expected characteristics on each empirical index? We can then proceed to the second step, namely, the exploration of the correlations between the empirical measures. We identified seven features of the structure of firms, together with the same number of aspects of internal organisation. These are listed in Table 3.1.

The most obvious measures are the first two structural indices. On the former, following Porter (1986), we asked finance managers whether the world-wide enterprise was structured along multi-domestic lines (with the explanation, 'i.e. national subsidiaries are the most important line of organisation') or global lines (also suitably explicated). Evidently, nationally-oriented firms would choose the first and globally-oriented ones the second. As the table shows, multi-domestic organisation remains common, with half of firms saying that national subsidiaries were the most important line of organisation.

We asked, second, about five forms of trading relationships between parts of the enterprise, which have been summarised into three in the table: no internally administered relations; some form of networking or administration; and integrated production systems. Nationally-oriented firms would choose the first. This is one of the few dimensions on which the Bartlett–Ghoshal types of global and transnational firms can be distinguished from international ones. International firms should display some kind of networking, while the global and transnational types would be expected to display an integrated production system. Approaching half the

Table 3.1 Measures of global orientation

(Row percentages)	Orientation	
	National	*Global*
Structural characteristics		
1 World-wide enterprise organised primarily along lines of:[a]	Multi-domestic 51	Global 33
2 Trading relations between parts of enterprise	No internally administered relations: 45	Network/ admin: 43 Integrated: 13
3 Upward reporting in Accounting and Finance	Indirect 70	Direct 29
4 Financial reports from business unit level?	No 53	Yes 47
5 Market penetration as measure of performance?	No 63	Yes 38
6 Profits turned over to global HQ?	No 43	Yes 57
7 Communication globally using PCs?	No 41	Yes 60
Organisational characteristics		
1 Board members responsible for different business functions?	No 23	Yes 77
2 Board members responsible for different territories?	Yes 61	No 39
3 Frequent meetings between personnel managers?	No 66	Yes 34
4 Centralisation of managerial pay?	No 65	Yes 35
5 Frequent international managerial movement?	No 46	Yes 54
6 Policy on managerial movement?	No 57	Yes 43
7 Training and development department for managers in overseas subsidiaries?	No 73	Yes 27

Note: [a] The first question asked whether the enterprise was organised on multi-domestic or global lines or both; if both, respondents were asked which was the more representative. The figures in the table combine these replies. In the remaining 16 per cent of cases, neither was considered more representative.
Base: All multinational companies, UK HQ interviews (N=104).

firms had no form of administrative links between the parts of the world-wide enterprise. At the other extreme, 13 per cent claimed to have a system of integrated production. The closeness of this figure to Leong and Tan's (1993) attitudinal evidence, suggesting that 18 per cent of MNCs are transnationals, is instructive.

The third measure shows whether there was an indirect rather than a direct reporting relationship within the finance function between the head office and operating subsidiaries. The former should be associated with nationally-oriented firms, because territorial units would be relatively autonomous. More integrated firms would have direct links with their operating units so that performance could be monitored.[1] Over two-thirds of firms said that reporting was indirect.

This third measure asked about upward reporting. Fourth, we addressed the downward monitoring by the head office of subsidiaries. A global firm would be expected to monitor down to the level of the business unit, while a nationally-oriented one would seek less detailed reports. There was a roughly even split between the two types of firms.

The fifth measure indicates whether market penetration is used as an index of the performance of subsidiaries. The rationale is that global companies are supposed to adopt a strategic vision: market penetration should index the extent to which a firm sees its markets in such a way, whereas a multi-domestic firm will be more likely to see its operations as extensions of its domestic activity with less strategic concern. As can be seen, the nationally-oriented approach predominated here.

Finally, we have two less demanding measures of globalism: are profits turned over the headquarters, and is there a system of world-wide communication using PCs? Globally oriented firms would be expected to collect profits centrally, rather than leave them at territorial level, and to have systematic communication. A more global approach was evident here.

Turning to the organisational measures, the first two consider the responsibilities of members of the company's board: did they cover business divisions (with a 'yes' indicating globalism) and were there territorial responsibilities (a 'yes' indicating a nationally oriented approach)? Both approaches were in evidence, suggesting that global and national orientations can co-exist. The third measure, the frequency of meetings of personnel managers, has obvious implications.

On pay systems for managers of subsidiaries, the fourth measure, we assume that global firms adopt a relatively strategic view and thus have some central direction. Nationally-oriented firms are more likely to leave pay policy to local conditions. The latter approach clearly predominated.

Finally, we have three measures of managerial mobility and career development: do managers move between subsidiaries; is there a policy of doing this; and is there a department with responsibility for the training and development of managers in subsidiaries? Globalism, indicated by affirmative replies, is arguably easiest on the first and most difficult on the last. As the table shows, this seems to have been the case.

These basic figures suggest that there is indeed evidence of globalism. A third of companies are organised primarily along global lines, and more than half have some degree of international production integration, but it seems to be much more evident in some aspects of firms' operations than others. We now consider this directly.

Relationship between measures

We examined the degree of association between each structural measure and each organisational measure. The level of association was small. Of the twenty-one inter-correlations among the structural measures, only five were significant. In particular, the third measure was related to four of the others. For example, indirect reporting relationships were common where firms were organised on multi-domestic lines and where there were no administered relationships.

Of the twenty-one organisational inter-correlations, eight were significant. The clearest pattern was, not surprisingly, a linkage among the last three measures of career mobility and planning. Thus firms with frequent managerial mobility tend to have training and development departments. There was also a link between all three of these measures and the frequency of meetings of personnel managers.

We also counted how many global characteristics firms had on the structural and organisational measures. One might expect a large number of structural features to be reflected in organisational arrangements. In fact, there was no association.

The implication is that firms do not fit into the ideal types of nationally or globally oriented approaches. These types represent extreme tendencies, and very few firms seem to display all the characteristics that might be expected of them. Three points follow. First, the assumption that typologies used in management textbooks have direct counterparts in the real world is mistaken. Second, though globalism is in evidence, it does not seem that it comes in self-contained types. Third, we have shown in just what respects firms have indeed adopted a global orientation. Such an approach is most common in: giving board members responsibility for business functions; computerised communication; turning profits over to global headquarters; and in the movement of managers globally. In all other respects, fewer than half the firms met the definition of globalism.

Determinants of globalism

If we treat our measures as indices of different dimensions of a global approach, how far do they show that some types of firms are further down the global route than others? Findings here underline the aspects of variability and uncertainty identified above.

Perhaps the most useful measure is *the length of time* for which a firm has been operating as an MNC. The clear expectation in the Perlmutter and Bartlett and Ghoshal models is that their types are evolutionary: firms should move from the ethnocentric or multinational stage towards a global and eventually a transnational approach. For our UK-owned firms we have information on the time during which they had a 'substantial presence' (defined as accounting for at least 10 per cent of world-wide employment) overseas. On only one of the structural measures, and three of the organisational ones, was there an association with this measure of age. Using our alternative measures of ethno-, poly- and geo-centricity (Marginson *et al.* 1993: 50–2) produced a similar result. There thus seems little evidence of any evolutionary logic driving firms forward.

This may seem surprising in the light of accounts of corporate restructuring in firms such as ABB and IBM. Yet first, these are the firms which always appear in the managerial texts. It appears that there are many more MNCs which do not follow the example. If they are in the lead in the move towards transnationality they have a thin straggle of followers. Second, MNCs have been around for a very long time and they do not yet seem to have become truly global. For example, Ford, established as a major MNC since the 1920s, announced in 1994 that it was to re-organise on a global basis, with the design of certain types of cars being centralised in one world-wide operation. The fact that it has taken Ford so long to reach this point suggests that globalisation is a slow process. Third, it is also an uncertain one. The idea of the 'world car' has been widely promoted, at least from the 1970s, but Ford's early moves in this direction failed. Differences between national markets and problems of co-ordination suggest that there are forces pulling MNCs apart as well as drawing them together.

Case study findings illustrate this point. In Components some national subsidiaries had sufficient power within the firm to resist moves towards standard company-wide systems; for example, the French operation withstood the application of standard Anglo-American job evaluation systems. Age is also a poor proxy for organisational stability. We show elsewhere that our survey firms had experienced a dramatic degree of change over the previous five years (Marginson *et al.* 1995a). For example, of the whole 176 firms in the sample, 65 per cent had experienced a significant merger or acquisition, while 63 per cent cited the closure of existing sites. Both case study firms had also been involved in a series of acquisitions and divestments. In some cases, new businesses were integrated into existing structures whereas in others they were kept at arm's length, the different approaches reflecting the degree of commonality between businesses and also accidents of history and geography. This constant change meant that there was little time to integrate one business before a new re-structuring was undertaken. MNCs seem to be in a state of flux, rather than of evolution to a common end point. Yet, and here the aspect of drift is important, they may be heading in certain, albeit different, directions: Components was self-consciously set on a course of being a world-class manufacturer in specific products; Process had already attained a degree of sophistication and was looking for further means of developing 'synergies'.

A second possible influence on globalism is the *size of the firm*. We have data on only 82 of the 101 MNCs. There was a strong tendency for firms organised on global lines to be larger than the multi-domestics: the mean sizes were 46,000 and 12,000 employees respectively. Similar links between a global orientation and size were evident in relation to two of the structural indices (S5 and S7) and two of the organisational ones (O2 and O6). There was thus some tendency for globalism to be associated with size, but the lack of association on several variables also suggests that small size need not preclude a global orientation.

Third, *business structure* may be important. The model of the global firm in the literature is one of an integrated global web. We asked financial managers to say whether the world-wide enterprise was a single business (with 90 per cent of sales from one business); a dominant business (70 per cent from one business); a related business (businesses are in related fields but none contributes 70 per cent to overall sales); or a conglomerate. The distribution across these categories was 29, 13, 39 and 20 per cent. Globalism would be expected to be lowest in the last category. In the event, there was little association with our measures of globalism. This is consistent with the point about financial economies made above. The literature expects globalism to be associated with integrated webs. It can also, however, be attained through a conglomerate structure.

Fourth, the *country of ownership* may be important. As shown in Table 3.2, four of the measures of structure showed a relationship to ownership. As against the view that American firms are highly centralised, direct reporting was most likely in European-owned firms, while the US-owned were less likely than either UK- or European-owned firms to have reporting from the business unit level. They were, however, more likely to have a PC network. Finally, on market penetration, there was a clear tendency for this to be targeted least by the UK-owned firms: overseas-owned firms were more likely to target market penetration than were British-owned firms. These differences were underlined by sharp contrasts on five of the eight organisational measures. As the table shows, overseas-owned firms as a group were twice as likely as the British-owned to hold meetings of personnel managers, to have a policy of managerial mobility, and to have a training and development department. The European-level interviews confirmed this result. In short, there were some differences of structure, the most notable being the absence of the targeting of market penetration by British

Table 3.2 'Global' response by country of ownership

(Column percentages)		UK-owned	Overseas-owned			European HQ
			USA	Europe	All	
N		65	19	19	39	26
S1:	Global lines mentioned	45	49	65	57	
S2:	Network/integrated	50	57	68	63	
S3:	Direct reports	26	23	43	33	
S4:	Reports from business unit level	50	29	52	42	
S5:	Targeting of market penetration	29	42	63	53	
S6:	Profits to global HQ	63	48	48	48	
S7:	Communicate using PCs	51	83	64	73	
O1:	Business functions mentioned	81	81	59	70	
O2:	Territories not mentioned	44	23	39	31	
O3:	Frequent personnel mgt meetings	22	73	38	55	72
O4:	Pay centralised	35	29	48	39	77
O5:	Frequent movement	39	83	66	74	58
O6:	Policy of movement	27	70	69	69	
O7:	Training department	19	36	38	37	88

Note: N gives the weighted number of cases, except for the European HQ interviews, where no weighting was undertaken.
Base: UK HQ and European HQ interviews.

firms. Managerial organisation differed more sharply, with overseas-owned firms being substantially more 'advanced' in their human resource policies than their British counterparts.

Conclusions

The model of the global and transnational firm assumes that there is one route to globalism, namely, that through synergistic economies. Our results suggest that there are also other means to this end, and hence that globalism has a number of forms. Moves towards globalism seem to have been patchy and uneven. Globalism has various dimensions, and there was little evidence that these were most developed in older firms.

This is not, however, to argue that there is no such thing as globalism. As we show elsewhere, companies organised along global, rather than multi-domestic, lines were likely to hold regular meeting of personnel managers from different countries and (an item not discussed here) to have a world-wide personnel policy committee (Marginson *et al.* 1995b: 10). Some currents towards globalism are evident, but they are more varied and indeterminate than current models of the MNC imply. As we now show, it also has some distinct consequences.

CONCOMITANTS AND CONSEQUENCES OF GLOBALISM

We consider the concomitants and results of globalism under three heads. These are the monitoring of subsidiaries; the degree of autonomy of subsidiaries (and the control systems to which they were subject); and globalisation and labour (i.e. the implications in terms of trade union recognition).

Monitoring of subsidiaries

One source of power for the MNC is its ability to allocate resources. If a plant is performing poorly, funds can be re-directed to other parts of the globe. Before this power can be exercised the centre needs the relevant information. We asked personnel respondents of all MNCs whether data were collected on eight issues, and managers in UK-owned firms and at European level about the uses made of these data. Table 3.3 shows the replies.

On data collection, 70 per cent of MNCs collected at least some

Table 3.3 Collection and use of data on labour indicators by headquarters

(Column percentages)	UK HQ					European HQ
	All	UK-owned	Overseas-owned			
			USA	Europe	All	
Data collected						
Negotiated pay settlements	32	37	26	24	25	58
Overall labour costs	50	43	69	54	63	85
Industrial action	18	23	13	9	11	58
Numbers employed	64	60	67	76	72	92
Absenteeism	13	17	4	4	4	23
Labour turnover	25	29	22	13	17	69
Managerial pay packages	53	49	71	48	60	58
Labour productivity	34	27	34	55	44	54
Any data collected	70	64	85	74	79	92
Uses of data[a]						
As input into investment decisions	14 (22)					54 (59)
As input into divestment decisions	14 (22)					42 (46)
To evaluate business unit managers	45 (70)					54 (59)
Personnel evaluation/information	38 (59)					89 (97)
Comparisons between operating sites	36 (56)					73 (79)

Note: [a] Figures in parentheses show the percentage of firms collecting any data which make a given use; other figures are a proportion of all firms.
Base: UK-owned companies and European HQ interviews.

information. More than half of them collected information on managerial pay packages and numbers employed. The rate of data collection was higher in the overseas-owned than in the UK-owned firms. (The very high rate of data collection at European level is notable, though the fact that there was indeed an office, and a personnel function, at this level may tend to exaggerate the extent of this.)

Case study material puts this result in context. Though our case firms were both large, diversified organisations, they continued to see the control of headcount as important. This may seem surprising given their general emphasis on devolution. The explanation was that numbers employed were a significant component of overall costs and that they indexed how well a subsidiary was using its resources. In Process, for example, selling a certain volume of goods was estimated to require so many staff; a subsidiary would not be able to hire more workers unless it could show a clear need for them.

As reported elsewhere (Marginson et al. 1994), we considered which sorts of firms were most likely to collect data. Organisation along global lines and the integration of production were associated with data collection, but the strongest link was with one of the organisational measures, the presence of frequent meetings of personnel managers. There was no significant effect of country of ownership once these influences were allowed for. The implication is that frequent meetings and data collection are probably jointly determined, but that a global orientation in terms of business structure also plays a part.

As to the use of the data, it was very common for the data to have some specific use. For example, 70 per cent of UK-owned firms collecting data used them to evaluate business unit managers. Operational evaluation of data was most common where meetings of personnel managers were most frequent and where there was a training and development department.

Again, we can draw on case study evidence. In the firms considered here, the direct comparison of the productivity and labour cost performance of plants in different countries was rare. There were two main reasons. First, many products were highly specialised, often being made at only one site. In such instances, there were no meaningful comparisons to be made. Second, firms simply had to be in certain markets to be close to their customers and to exploit the size of the market; this was particularly true of the need to be in North America. Given that it was impossible to move from a market, the idea of making cost comparisons was academic. Other firms do make direct cost comparisons, and use these in reaching decisions on investment decisions. This has been found by Mueller and Purcell (1992) in the car industry, by Frenkel (1994) in the case of a US-owned pharmaceuticals firm and by Coller (1994) in a food company. In the last case, managers at underperforming plants were put under pressure to adopt certain approved policies of functional flexibility. The explanation may be that such firms make standard products such as soaps and packaged food at various locations; direct comparison is meaningful. **Process** by contrast concentrated on more specialised products where cost was less critical. It may be, therefore, that the allocative use of cost data tends to occur in certain sorts of firm, namely, those producing standardised goods in competitive markets.

Two conclusions may be drawn. First, the collection and use of data were associated with a global orientation. Second, in line with different routes towards globalism, even highly global firms, like **Process**, do not always collect or use cost data, but in more standardised markets the use of labour performance measures seems to be important.

Degree of autonomy of subsidiaries

Apart from labour relations data, what other means are used to monitor and control subsidiaries? We asked about the indices of financial performance that head offices collected, and about how far down the organisation these reporting relationships went. As Table 3.1 shows, half the firms in the sample required reports from the level of the individual business unit. Given that they were often large, divisionalised firms, in which the logic is that head offices do not become involved in this level of detail, the figure is rather high.

In Table 3.4 we present this information in more detail and also indicate the extent of financial reporting from overseas subsidiaries. The table shows a high level of data collection, particularly on profit or the standard accounting indicator of return on investment (ROI).[2] The table shows a higher level of reporting among overseas-owned than among UK-owned firms. This might be attributed to UK firms' closer interest in their operations in the UK, as compared with overseas; but the difference remained even when operations within the UK were compared. In addition to these data on overseas operations, we have information on the reporting regime more generally: for example, in the vast majority of firms business unit managers were expected to attend frequent meetings to review progress.

Financial regimes thus set important constraints on local autonomy. Case material again illustrates this point. One American site of **Components**, for example, had been making losses for some time; its financial status was reviewed closely in the UK (and alongside this, in line with above remarks, went a total ban on recruitment without approval from the UK). Another site had recently been acquired by the company; managers in it spoke with surprise of the detailed reports that they had to submit and the number of meetings with higher level managers to review these reports. In **Process**, these demands were less evident but there was one strongly market-driven pressure, namely, the need to develop and sell products in a shorter time span.

Table 3.4 International collection of financial data

(Column percentages)	UK-owned	All overseas-owned
Per cent collecting reports on		
Profit or ROI	71	91
Market penetration	29	51
Number of indicators used		
None	23	5
1–3	45	38
4 or 5	33	57

Base: UK HQ interviews.

Alongside financial controls went a wider set of controls in terms of culture and expectations. Thus managers in both companies were asked how they prevented local managers from going their own way, for example by meeting 'bottom line' financial requirements by cutting training or investment. The general answer was that the culture prevented this: managers met each other frequently, people reached general manager positions only if they accepted the company way of doing things, and there were frequent review and audit processes. Beyond this, there were some clear standard models of behaviour. In **Process**, these were part of the firm's long-established tradition as an MNC, but new approaches included the use of a company-wide system for the identification and development of 'managers with potential'; and there was an annual review system to ensure that subsidiaries were implementing development systems. In Components, there was concern about undue fragmentation in marketing, with sales teams from many different divisions going to one customer; there were moves towards sales teams targeted at each customer. Even ABB may be more subject to central direction than is sometimes suggested. On the model of the task force, 'the *creation* of the task force and the definition of its role were the result of the intervention of a higher-tier manager rather than of "spontaneous" generation' and there is strong emphasis on the corporate mission and the firm's 'policy bible' (Ferner and Edwards 1995: 239).

In short, co-ordination was greater than might appear at first sight, although this was often through expectations and understandings rather than formal mechanisms. Such expectations can change rapidly. This perhaps makes the MNC less predictable than it is often pictured; it is a connected structure, but the form of the connections is imprecise and variable.

Globalism and labour

We posed a series of questions to personnel respondents in British-owned firms about their approach to unions and the impact of labour policies.

Replies on five key items are summarised in Table 3.5. European-level respondents were asked about the first two.

The first asked about general policy on dealing with unions. Given the very different national regimes governing union recognition, we offered a complex array of policy statements. In fact, as the table shows, over half the respondents in the UK-owned firms, and just under half of the European-level interviewees, chose the simple option of its being general policy not to bargain with trade unions at all. Analysis among the latter group (Maeland 1993: 68) showed, not surprisingly, that it was firms based outside Europe which were most likely to oppose unions.

Second, we asked whether avoiding countries with a union presence affected locational decisions. While two-thirds of the sample said that it was not important at all, it is still noteworthy that around a third of UK and European interviewees gave this factor some weight. Third, when asked about the general direction of the distribution of employment, a slightly smaller proportion said that there was a drift away from coverage by collective agreements.

The last two questions concerned pay policy. One image of the MNC is that pay is left to local conditions with little central direction, except that there may be a policy of paying rather above the going rate. According to Enderwick (1985: 95), MNCs pursue such a policy in order to attract high

Table 3.5 Approaches towards unions and pay bargaining in overseas sites

(Column percentages)	UK-owned	European HQ
Policy towards unions is		
General avoidance	53	46
Some acceptance	47	54
Effect of employment distribution on % of workers covered by collective agreements		
Reduce	28	35
No change	72	62
Increase	0	4
Locational decisions take account of wish to avoid unions?		
Yes	33	
No	67	
Pay determination		
Involves HQ decision/veto	57	
Left to national mangement	43	
Policy is to pay wages		
Above local average	29	
Around average/no account taken of local rates	71	

Base: UK-owned companies and European HQ interviews.

quality labour. We again asked a detailed question about the role of head-quarters. For purposes of analysis, we can take as 'centralised' situations in which headquarters decided pay increases, laid down a range, or monitored and could veto settlements; other arrangements are 'decen-tralised'. In fact, some central direction of pay policy occurred in over half the firms, suggesting more co-ordination than might have been expected. This did not, however, involve a policy of paying above the local rate (which was mentioned by fewer than a third of the sample).

We may, for UK-owned firms, correlate these measures with our indices of globalism. A picture emerges of worsening prospects for unions as globalism advances. Table 3.6 shows the key correlations. Where companies were organised on multi-domestic lines, 40 per cent avoided unions – a figure which rose to 63 per cent where global lines were predominant. Further, more integrated trading relations were associated with union avoidance. Similarly, those stressing market penetration (S5) were more

Table 3.6 Links between union avoidance and globalism measures

(Row percentages)	Policy to TUs		Trend of employment		TU avoidance in location decisions?	
	Avoid	Accept	Less TU	No change	Yes	No
S1: Multi-domestic/global						
Multi-domestic	40	60				
Global	63	37				
Both	80	20				
S2: Trading relations						
None	55	45				
Admin/network	65	35				
Integration	100	0				
S5: Market penetration?						
No	35	65	53	47	59	41
Yes	60	40	17	83	22	78
O3: Frequent meetings?						
No			22	78	27	73
Yes			46	54	54	46
O5: Managerial movement						
Rare	64	36	20	80	20	80
Frequent	40	60	45	55	60	40
O6: Policy on movement?						
No			22	78	24	76
Yes			43	57	56	44

Note: Only statistically significant relationships are reported. Overall, of the 42 correlations between 14 measures of globalism and 3 indices of approach to unions, 14 were significant.
Base: UK-owned companies.

than twice as likely as other companies to say that avoiding unions was of some importance in locational decisions; a drift away from unionised settings was most likely in companies with advanced organisational systems for management development (O3, 5 and 6).

Again, case material supports the picture. Both Process and Components had long recognised unions in Britain and generally did so in overseas territories. Their general policies would be of dealing with unions where local conditions suggested or required. Thus both had acquired unionised operations in the USA, and followed standard French and German practice in collective agreements. Yet if they had the chance to avoid unions, they took it. Components had re-located one of its unionised American plants to a non-union state. In Process, a new site had been opened in a non-union setting. Though union avoidance was not the major aim, with the location being chosen for its tax concessions and other reasons, the effect was none the less to shift the organisational centre of gravity away from the traditional unionised locations. More generally, the assumption of managers in both companies was that unions had rather little role to play.

There was thus a general trend for the more globalised firms to move away from union recognition. It is true that the trend was limited: not all measures of globalism were involved, and the overall importance of union-isation in locational decisions was small, but small and uncertain trends are still significant, particularly when there seem to be few moves in the opposite direction. We have mentioned mechanisms within companies leading them to operate in non-union situations where the chance arises. The possible development in the opposite direction builds on the fact that these companies do not simply head for low-cost labour. They need to be in certain markets, and for some of their high technology products they need a highly educated and skilled work force. Process has located a major new plant in the north of Italy for both these reasons, rather than go to a lower-cost area.

If nation states or the EU strengthen the rights of unions and workers, there is unlikely to be an immediate flight of capital. There are thus some possibilities for countering the drift away from unionisation, though their prospects look poor. This is not the place to review this issue in detail, but the recent conclusions of Sadowski *et al.* (1994) are illuminating. In respect of German industrial relations, they argue that the EU laws have had little effect and, in particular, that 'social dumping' is little in evidence. However, German unification and wider competitive pressures have had a clear effect, for example in promoting a search for flexibility and cost cutting. 'The ability to compare industrial relations performance across sites', conclude Marginson and Sisson (1994: 48), 'is enabling trans-nationals to exercise more general pressures on pay, benefits and working conditions'. The need for a skilled work force, and to operate within national labour relations systems, are certainly constraints. As Humphrey (1994: 342) notes in relation to Japanese firms in Brazil, there has been to date a relatively peaceful introduction of Japanese methods. This reflects the rights of unions in the labour system and shortages of educated labour. However, these conditions may be changing so that managements 'can develop the evaluation and control systems needed to increase pressure on workers'. The MNC is not all-powerful, but its effects are still profound.

CONCLUSIONS

We identified three issues that this chapter would address. First, in relation to the nature of the MNC, the multinational emerges as a more complex and variegated species than it has often been portrayed. The various dimensions of globalism did not correlate very closely with each other, and there was little evidence that the longer-established multinationals had moved furthest in the direction of globalism. We have identified at least two routes to globalism, based on synergies and on financial economies; these represent, moreover, tendencies which may be present within one firm. While Process, for example, was well-practised in such synergistic activities as international management development, the company also had to meet financial requirements. We would argue that the balance between these two forces operates at a general level within all MNCs. Thus we have underlined the reporting relationships and control systems which were widespread in MNCs. Even the networked companies such as ABB are likely to retain these, and they also have other mechanisms, notably cultural expectations, to manage integration (Ferner and Edwards 1995). Among the generality of MNCs, there is certainly a global approach, but it rests on coercive comparisons and financial controls at least as much as on decentralised networks.

In terms of wider debates on re-structuring and flexible specialisation, hierarchy and centralised control have yet to be abandoned. New forms of organisation are not only rare but also share important features, notably the meeting of targets and the pursuit of the corporate vision, with older bureaucracies.

Second, in terms of country of ownership, the most striking differences were between UK-owned firms and those based overseas, with any distinctive American or European approach being less apparent. American-owned firms did not appear to be particularly centralised, either in terms of their financial reporting or the autonomy granted to subsidiaries. Perhaps, as MNCs based elsewhere have developed, and American-owned ones have become less imperialistic and more sensitive to local conditions, the old model of the heavily centralised American firm loses some of its validity. By contrast, UK-owned firms collected fewer items of financial information than did other firms and yet they also granted less autonomy. A policy on managerial mobility, and a department to handle it, were also rare among the UK-owned firms. This suggests a picture of relatively undeveloped systems, with a lack of local autonomy being used as a substitute for financial systems which provide data to head offices while also allowing subsidiaries freedom to operate.

As for the impact on labour relations, three findings stand out. First, there was the quite widespread general antipathy towards unions, together with a clear drift away from countries that are heavily unionised. Second, globalism within the firm did seem to heighten these tendencies. Third, however, the comparison of unit labour costs and the making of direct productivity comparisons between plants was associated with a certain sort of globalism, namely that based on relatively standard products. There are quite strong forces within large MNCs tending to weaken unions; it would need a substantial effort to counteract them.

Overall, therefore, there seems to be some drift towards globalism, although this is along various tracks and bargaining within MNCs suggests that the process has many uncertainties. Pressures from the internationalisation of production are likely to grow. The challenge for research is to move beyond the models which have dominated the literature in the past towards an understanding of, first, the nature of globalisation, second, the main routes which firms can follow in response and, third, the implications for the ways in which they organise themselves.

ACKNOWLEDGEMENTS

The survey reported in this chapter was funded by the Economic and Social Research Council (ESRC) and the Employment Department; the case studies were undertaken in the Industrial Relations Research Unit, University of Warwick, also funded by the ESRC. An earlier version of the chapter was presented at the 'Work, Employment and Society in the 1990s' conference: we thank participants, and also the editors of this volume, for their comments.

NOTES

1 It could be argued that globally-oriented firms will also practise indirect reporting, through international business units. Conceptually, however, if a firm is serious about the idea of synergy it should be expected to have some more direct linkages with individual units. Empirically, we find that the measure was correlated with others in such a way as to support the interpretation in the text.

2 This apparently conflicts with the finding that, in relation to *business units* in the UK, only 37 per cent of firms targeted ROI (see Marginson *et al.* 1993: 15–28). The question discussed in the text asked about the reporting of 'profit or return on investment', whereas our later and more detailed question specified return on investment alone and also asked whether indicators were given

to 'business unit managers as *specific targets*'. Within the UK, 33 per cent of firms reported both, 23 per cent neither, and 40 per cent only the specific measure. This confirms that the earlier question was picking up a less detailed financial control device.

REFERENCES

Armstrong, P. J. (1988) 'Labour and monopoly capital', in R. Hyman and W. Streeck (eds) *New Technology and Industrial Relations*, Oxford: Blackwell.
Bartlett, C. A. and Ghoshal, S. (1989) *Managing Across Borders*, London: Century.
—— (1993) 'Beyond the M-form: toward a managerial theory of the firm', *Strategic Manangement Journal* 14, winter special issue: 23–46.
Brooke, M. (1984) *Centralization and Autonomy*, London: Holt, Rinehart & Winston.
Cohen, R. (1991) *Contested Domains*, London: Zed.
Coller, X. (1994) 'Managing flexibility on the food industry', paper to Industrial Relations in the European Community Network conference, Dublin, July.
Drury, C., Braund, S., Osborne, P. and Tayles, M. (1993) *A Survey of Management Accounting Practices in UK Manufacturing Companies*, ACCA Research Report 32, London: Association of Certified and Corporate Accountants.
Edwards, A. (1993) 'Perceptions of control: a comparison of the perceptions of managers at the European and UK headquarters of foreign-owned firms in Britain', MA thesis, University of Warwick.
Edwards, P. K., Ferner, A. and Sisson, K. (1993) 'People and the process of management in the multinational company', *Warwick Papers in Industrial Relations* 43, Coventry. Industrial Relations Research Unit, University of Warwick.
Enderwick, P. (1985) *Multinational Business and Labour*, London: Croom Helm.
Ferner, A. (1994) 'Multinational companies and human resource management', *Human Resource Management Journal* 4(3): 70–87.
Ferner, A. and Edwards, P. (1995) 'Power and the diffusion of organizational change within multinational enterprises', *European Journal of Industrial Relations* 1(2). 229–57.
Frenkel, S. (1994) 'Patterns of workplace relations in the global corporation', in J. Bélanger, P. K. Edwards and L. Haiven (eds) *Workplace Industrial Relations and the Global Challenge*, Ithaca, NY: ILR Press.
Hedlund, G. (1986) 'The hypermodern MNE', *Human Resource Management* 25(1): 9–36.
Hill, C. W. L. and Hoskisson, R. (1987) 'Strategy and structure in the multi-product firm', *Academy of Management Review* 12(2): 331–41.
Hill, C. W. L. and Pickering, J. F. (1986) 'Divisionalization, decentralization and performance of large United Kingdom companies', *Journal of Management Studies* 23(1): 26–50.
Hu, Y-S. (1992) 'Global or stateless corporations are national firms with international operations', *California Management Review* 34(2): 107–26.
Humphrey, J. (1994) '"Japanese" methods and the changing position of direct production workers: evidence from Brazil', in T. Elger and C. Smith (eds) *Global Japanization?*, London: Routledge.
Kochan, T., Batt, R. and Dyer, L. (1992) 'International human resource studies', in D. Lewin, Olivia S. Mitchell and Peter D. Sherer (eds) *Research Frontiers in Industrial Relations and Human Resource Management*, Madison, WI: Industrial Relations Research Association.
Leeds, C., Kirkbride P. S. and Durcan, J. (1994) 'The cultural context of Europe', in P. S. Kirkbride (ed.) *Human Resource Management in Europe*, London: Routledge.

Leong, S. M. and Tan, C. T. (1993) 'Managing across borders', *Journal of International Business Studies* 24(3): 449–64.

Maeland, H. N. (1993) 'The role of personnel at European headquarters in foreign-owned multinational companies', MA thesis, University of Warwick.

Marginson, P. (1992) 'European integration and transnational management–union relations in the enterprise', *British Journal of Industrial Relations* 30(4): 529–46.

Marginson, P. and Sisson, K. (1994) 'The structure of transnational capital in Europe', in R. Hyman and A. Ferner (eds) *New Frontiers in European Industrial Relations*, Oxford: Blackwell.

Marginson, P., Armstrong, P., Edwards, P.K. and Purcell, J. with Hubbard, N. (1993) 'The control of industrial relations in large companies', *Warwick Papers in Industrial Relations* 45, Coventry: Industrial Relations Research Unit, University of Warwick.

Marginson, P., Armstrong, P., Edwards, P.K. and Purcell, J. (1994) 'Managing labour in the global corporation', paper to International Research Conference on Corporate Change, Sydney, August.

Marginson, P., Edwards, P.K., Armstrong, P. and Purcell, J. (1995a) 'Strategy, structure and control in the changing corporation', *Human Resource Management Journal* 5(2): 3–27.

Marginson, P., Armstrong, P., Edwards, P.K. and Purcell, J. (1995b) 'Extending beyond borders: multinational companies and the international management of labour', paper to International Industrial Relations Association Tenth World Congress, Washington, DC, May–June.

Mueller, F. and Purcell, J. (1992) 'The Europeanization of manufacturing and the decentralization of bargaining', *International Journal of Human Resource Management* 3(1): 15–34.

Perlmutter, H.V. (1969) 'The tortuous evolution of the multinational corporation', *Columbia Journal of World Business* 4(1): 9–18.

Porter, M. (ed.) (1986) *Competition in Global Industries*, Boston, MA: Harvard Business School Press.

Porter, M. (1990) *The Competitive Advantage of Nations*, London: Macmillan.

Ramsay, H. (1991) 'The Community, the multinational, its workers and their charter', *Work, Employment and Society* 5(4): 541–66.

Reich, R. B. (1991) *The Work of Nations*, New York: Simon & Shuster.

Roberts, B.C. and May, J. (1974) 'The response of multi-national enterprises to international trade union pressure', *British Journal of Industrial Relations* 12(3): 403–16.

Roth, K., Schweiger, D. M. and Morrison, A. J. (1991) 'Global strategy implementation at the business unit level', *Journal of International Business Studies* 22(3): 369–402.

Sadowski, D., Schneider, M. and Wagner, K. (1994) 'The impact of European integration and German unification on industrial relations in Germany', *British Journal of Industrial Relations* 32(4): 523–37.

Scullion, H. (1992) 'Strategic recruitment and the development of the international manager', *Human Resource Management Journal* 3(1): 57–69.

UNCTAD (United Nations Conference on Trade and Development) (1993) *World Investment Report 1993*, New York: United Nations.

4

FRAGMENTS OF INDUSTRY AND EMPLOYMENT

Contract service work and the shift towards precarious employment

John Allen and Nick Henry

It has frequently been noted that the shift to services in the advanced industrial economies involves a widening and deepening of the social (and relatedly technical) division of labour. As far back as the 1920s, Allyn Young, with a nod in Adam Smith's direction, observed that the social division of labour depends upon the extent of the market and that greater specialisation leads to productivity increases which, in turn, stimulate economic growth. The greatest advantages delivered by an expanding division of labour among industries are to be had by using labour in 'roundabout' or indirect ways. Put another way, specialisation may secure more efficient, possibly cheaper, ways of doing things, as well as providing novel, more innovative ways of doing them (Young 1928). Today, this is the language of subcontracting, externalisation or outsourcing, where firms – both manufacturing and services – tend to concentrate on their 'core' activities and buy in what else they require to keep the operation going.

As is well known, private sector services are among the main beneficiaries of this growth in subcontractual relationships, with both prestigious services, such as finance and commercial services, and less prestigious services, such as cleaning, catering and security, expanding of late. Not all the expansion in these industries, however, amounts to the creation of new jobs. Much of it has involved a transfer of 'in house' jobs to outside contractors or, in the UK, an increasing shift from public to private sector firms (Rees and Fielder 1992): in other words, a shift in the lines that divide labour, rather than straightforward growth in employment.

In this chapter, we wish to explore how a shift in the division of labour divides labour. Our focus is one-sided, in that we look at the consequences of the growth of subcontracting in the three less prestigious industries mentioned above (contract cleaning, contract catering and contract security) in two of the most dynamic locations in the south east of England in the late 1980s and early 1990s – high-tech Cambridge and the City of

London.[1] Our argument, in brief, is that what is new about the growth of these industries is not so much the absolute increase in job numbers, but rather the transformation of the employment relations experienced by those who have been pushed out of secure employment or who are entering the bottom end of the labour market for the first time. More significantly, we argue that this transformation is part of a wider political and economic shift in the nature of employment relations in the UK, a shift which could be said to be leading towards a new employment regime based upon *precarious employment.*

How such a regime is secured, however, is an open-ended question. It is not enough to will it politically. There is no ineluctable path along which firms and their workforces will travel. Whether or not there is a move towards looser practices on hiring and firing workers will vary across industries and occupations, as will the degree to which workers find themselves working as contract labour. In the case of the low status cleaning, catering and security industries, where much of the work is perceived to be of the kind that anyone can do, the shift to a new regime appears to be under way, but it is largely through the changing *corporate geography* of the large contract firms that the relations of precarious employment are secured.

The findings are based upon a series of interviews at the corporate, supervisory and operative levels in a number of the largest firms in the contract cleaning, catering and security industries in the UK. In all, 81 semi-structured interviews were conducted across 20 companies, with the initial interviews carried out at the corporate level and subsequent interviews conducted at various levels in the internal hierarchies of each firm. In particular, interviews were undertaken with employees at the bottom end of the hierarchies (e.g. security guards, catering assistants and cleaners) in which detailed discussions of the nature of their employment and work were recorded. In a number of instances, where the largest firms had operations in both Cambridge and the City of London, interviews were conducted with management and members of the workforce at both locations. This enabled us to study the response of the contract service firms to the different forms of economic growth at each location, as well as to record potential differences in employment relationships and labour market practices.

In the first part of the chapter, drawing upon the work of Ulrich Beck (1992), we look at what this shift to a new employment regime may entail and the way in which the contract service industries have been held up as an example of the direction of change in the United Kingdom. A variety of ways in which jobs and employment may become precarious are highlighted. Following that, we show how the ability to secure precarious employment practices is assisted in a number of different ways through the *fragmented* organisational structure of the leading operators in the contract service industries. In particular, we draw attention to the manner in which formal and informal work practices co-exist within large corporations as a means of 'getting the work done' and, at the same time, maintaining an atmosphere of pervasive insecurity. Finally, and in contrast, this same fragmented structure is shown to pose a geographical problem for the large firms in that the distance between sites undermines their ability to hold their organisational and employment practices in place.

A NEW EMPLOYMENT REGIME?

It would be misleading to claim that a new employment regime was in place in the UK. None the less, it is interesting to note that the political debate on jobs which has worked its way across Europe has, as its focus, the balance between employment protection rights and labour market flexibility. While it was the rate of unemployment in EU countries which sparked the debate, the issue and indeed, for some, the resolution of the jobs question has become the balance between the protection and de-regulation of workers' rights. This is not so much a concern with the flexibility of the labour process or the tasks that people do, therefore, as with the ease and cost of hiring and firing workers. It is flexibility of employment, not work, which is the central issue.

Ulrich Beck, in *Risk Society* (1992; German edn 1986), was among the first to recognise that it was the employment regime put in place over the post-war period in the advanced industrial nations which would be at the heart of future discussions. The 'lifelong full-time work' which characterised the so-called 'golden age of capitalism' well in to the 1970s was, in his terms, becoming destandardised.[2] By this, he meant that the essential characteristics of employment during this period – standard contracts covered by collective bargaining agreements, the concentration of work in large factories or office sites, and the expectation (for men anyway) of regular, permanent employment – were beginning to shatter. In its place, a new employment regime was said to be taking shape based upon less secure, individualised contracts, the geographical dispersal and organisational fragmentation of the workplace, and a greater flexibility in hours worked as well as in the length of employment. The overall result of this, according to Beck, is an explosive growth in employment insecurity.

Others have commented on particular aspects of such an employment scenario; what is novel about Beck's account is that he considers what he refers to as the 'Taylorism of employment relations' to be part of a wider set of changes in modern society, from a rather straightforward, wealth-orientated industrial society to one characterised by risk and uncertainty in a number of spheres. With the old assurances around jobs, family and especially the environment said to have disappeared, Beck is prone to exaggerate the general state of 'risk' in our midst and while few, we suspect, would subscribe to the whole package, (or, indeed, to Beck's risk scenario as being about to shape the future of, say, the modern European economies), the focus upon the precariousness of modern life is a provocative one. What Beck's employment scenario lacks in geographical sensitivity and national detail, therefore, it makes up for in the spectre which it presents. The idea of employment risk becoming regularised is unsettling and it strikes different chords in different European countries. In our view, within the modern economies of Europe, it is in the UK economy where the greatest resonance with this risk scenario is discernible, not, we should add, as a completed shift but as a direction of change and, as yet, only within certain industries and occupations.

What is interesting in the UK context is the barrage of central government policies and initiatives in the 1980s and 1990s which have as their aim the dismantling of various forms of employment protection and the loosening of 'rigidities' in the labour market. The list is extensive and includes the abolition of the wage councils, the weakening of unfair dismissal protection rights, the undermining of trade unions' abilities to organise effectively at the workplace and beyond, as well as the push to privatise or contract-out public services (Deakin 1992; Deakin and Wilkinson 1992; Standing 1989). Taken together, it is not altogether unrealistic to suggest that the various policies and initiatives add up to an underlying economic strategy: one that places low waged, unregulated labour at the forefront of solutions to resolve the 'jobs question' in the UK and, in consequence, to improve the overall competitiveness of the national economy. Whether successful or not as a strategy, it is important to note, however, that it is directed towards resolving the *formal* employment question. The package of measures is not designed, either intentionally or unintentionally, to push labour outside the formal labour market towards the informal sector. On the contrary, its deregulatory thrust is aimed – in our view – at promoting a formal employment regime which is based on both the experience and widespread influence of precarious employment practices. Indeed, the option of informal employment practices becomes less attractive to employers the more the state intervenes to remove the regulations which govern the employer–employee relationship (Pahl 1984).

Precarious employment

Notwithstanding the volume of legislative change, its impact should be measured by both its actual and its pervasive influence within an economy. In actual terms, we need look no further than the public sector and the changes in employment relations which have already taken place. Whether it be the de-nationalisation of public utilities or the contracting-out of public services, both programmes have resulted in the erosion of employment rights and cost-cutting exercises (Cousins 1988; Fevre 1989; Rees and Fielder 1992; Pulkingham 1992). As to the extent of the legislative impact, while it is difficult to gauge the effect upon private sector firms, it is interesting to note that the contract service industries (in particular, cleaning and security) have frequently been cited by Employment Ministers of successive Conservative governments as positive examples of new employment relationships.

In fact, it is not altogether surprising that the privatisation programme and the contract service industries should figure prominently in any new development in employment relations, as they both represent situations where a transfer of jobs from one employer to another takes place. It is this act of transfer which creates the possibility for a reshaping of employment relations, without provoking an altogether damaging response from labour, even where it is the same workforce that moves with the contract to fill the jobs; the EU's Transfer of Undertakings (Protection of Employment) regulations are both a testament to this possibility and a recognition of labour's vulnerability to the practice of contracting out. Beck recognises this possibility, and also the fact that the subcontract relationship in general represents an extension of the social division of labour which makes it easier for the contract firms to implement employment and work changes (Beck 1992: 147–8). It is in this sense that the division of labour divides labour *within* a social class (Sayer and Walker 1992: 255).

In the labour-intensive contract service industries, for example, a number of ways in which employment has become formally precarious emerged from our interviews at the corporate, supervisory and operative levels of some of the largest firms in the contract cleaning, catering, and security industries in the country. In total, the UK workforces of the firms included in the study amounted to some 85,000 employees, the vast majority of whom, over 90 per cent in the case of the industry leaders, were below professional and (central or regional) managerial level. While we obviously cannot claim that the employment experiences of this predominantly operative workforce are identical, the majority of guards, cleaners and catering staff involved would have been exposed in one way or another to the following practices.[3]

In the first place, the process of tendering introduces an element of formal insecurity. The lengths of contracts vary, although few last beyond three to four years. Job security is, therefore, often limited to the length of the contract. Part of the terms and conditions of a contract may, however, involve a repackaging of jobs and hours with the subsequent loss of redundancy rights, sick pay entitlements, and various fringe benefits this may entail. In many cases, this is accompanied by a wage reduction which, as one contract cleaner found who had been passed from the public sector to a private contractor and then on again to another contractor as the contract changed hands: 'there is nothing you can do about it because they more or less say, well, if you don't want it, go'. Equally insidious, therefore, is the degree of arbitrariness that enters the employment relation when a contract is up for renewal or is put out to tender for the first time. Whether the contract is moving from 'in house' to subcontractor, or from one private contractor to another, the workforce has no automatic right to re-employment. Individual workers are subject to the will of the client who has put the work out to tender, and to the discretion of the incoming management.

In contract cleaning, for instance, it is custom and practice to pass a workforce from one private contractor to another, on the understanding that the company losing the contract will be unable to place them. There is also a question of trust involved, whereby clients may wish to seek continuity of employment for some if not all of their cleaners. However, if a client should wish to terminate the employment of the existing workforce, then that option is always available. With contract security, the firm that has lost the contract will attempt, if at all possible, to place its long-standing guards on other sites which it holds in a region, although some may be retained by the incoming contractor for their knowledge of specific buildings. The rest will be placed in a central pool to cover absentees (and paid a retainer to turn up at the regional centre) or made redundant. For the successful company, again, the client has the power of veto over who is and who is not taken on under the new contract. In contract catering it is more difficult to generalise, although it would appear that incoming contractors attempt to re-engage a significant number of the existing workforce to maintain a working knowledge of catering within the operation. (In each industry, however, the site management are unlikely to be re-engaged at the end of a contract.)

Overall, what is striking about employment on a contract basis within these industries is that it is both regular *and* insecure. It is regular in the sense that, for many, there is continuity of employment between contracts, despite the instability and high turnover among some groups of workers, and the frequency with which contracts can change hands (in one NHS hospital, for example, the cleaners had experienced three changeovers in four years). It is insecure in the sense that the particularistic relationships exercised by clients and incoming management reproduce a job which is formally precarious. As one black contract security guard noted of a client's supervisor : 'if they come across and say we don't want you here any more, that is it, off you go . . . someone might not look the part, or not do something, and most contracts are like that, and if I came in this morning, they could say "you are out".'[4]

Another way in which the vulnerability of contract employment is compounded is through the actual identity of the workforce and the lack of visibility attached to their work by clients. Working under a different employer from that of the majority of a workforce (in effect, working in someone else's workspace) tends to create a social distance between the client's work and the contract work. The representation of contract work as marginal or peripheral to the 'real work' carries with it a potential indifference on the part of the client and their workforces to the rights and futures of contract workers.[5] If the same functions were performed 'in house', the guards or catering staff would share the same corporate identity as the rest of the firms' workforces, and indeed they would also very likely share the same rights and benefits, as regards holiday entitlements and sick pay for example.

Also, in part because of the social distance between the two workforces within the same space, contract work tends to lose its visibility. In the case of cleaning, much of this is, of course, done either before or after the so-called 'working day' of 9 to 5 and is therefore unseen. Where contract cleaners are employed on a full-time basis, however, *they* rather than the work they perform tend to be unseen. They tend to occupy different spaces within a building from the client's workforce, are frequently asked to take their breaks at different times, and move about a building in a variety of different ways. In like manner, the majority of contract catering staff remain unseen for much of their working day, with only the counter staff or waiters visible to the client's workforce, and then often as an unacknowledged presence. Contract security work never stops; it takes place throughout the day and night, and yet only the outline of the guards is visible, regardless of the hour: 'people', as one guard commented, 'completely look through you'. In the daytime, they monitor the entrances and exits to a building, yet their presence is often remote from that of the client's workforce: in part as an intended feature of security work, but also because of the social distance that a contract identity bestows (see Allen and Pryke 1994).

Contract service work in cleaning, catering and security is precarious, therefore, not simply because the practices of clients and contract management are in line with the present UK government's attempts to create a new employment regime, but also because contracting-out divides labour in ways that compound their vulnerability. While the transfer of work (and frequently of the workforce too) from one employer to the next creates the possibility for a reshaping of employment relations, it takes the imposition of a peripheral contract status to help secure it. Risk here, at the bottom end of service labour markets, is experienced as a regular feature of employment life, encompassing the expectation of instability, insecurity and vulnerability. Moreover it is important also to stress the formal, nominally permanent nature of this type of contract employment. While a number of the larger firms interviewed employ labour on a casual or temporary basis, they do not do so in sufficient numbers to warrant generalisations about the emergence of a casualised contract workforce, in London at least.

71

Within contract cleaning, much of the work is performed on a regular basis, implying a form of tacit permanency. Likewise in contract security, 'floater' guards are employed to cover unanticipated shortages across sites and part-timers are used to cover weekend shifts, but on a regular, quasi-permanent basis. Temporary workers are also used for one-off events within catering, and to cover gaps created by sickness and holiday leave, but the overwhelming number of workers are employed on a regular basis. We should be wary, therefore, about identifying work characterised as vulnerable or insecure, such as part-time work or contract labour, with a movement towards casualisation. On the contrary, we appear to be witnessing a segment of the new working poor whose regular employment is formally precarious (see Allen and Henry 1995).

It is not just the divide between contract and non-contract labour which helps to secure a risk-fraught pattern of employment, however. The structure and organisation of the leading contract service firms also helps to secure the employment relations of precarious work.

FRAGMENTS OF INDUSTRY

Beck (1992) among others has drawn attention to the geographical dispersal and fragmentation of the workplace into smaller units (Shutt and Whittington 1987; Sayer and Walker 1992). Peter Dicken and Nigel Thrift (1992), in response to Richard Walker's (1989) critique of 'corporate geography', have spelt out the ongoing significance and changing nature of the large corporation. At issue is the very concept of the large industrial organisation in the wake of changes which point to flatter, less centralised, more dispersed forms of production. Acknowledging the multitude of organisational forms to be found in large corporations, Dicken and Thrift go on to elaborate the paradoxical character of today's big firms. They are larger, more centralised than ever before, yet leaner and less centralised in their style of management. They are more powerful than hitherto, yet capable of orchestrating labour and production across increasingly dispersed sites. Not all large industrial organisations are said to look like this, though clearly they consider this profile to be akin to the leading edge of organisational change.

Interestingly, most of the major operators in contract cleaning, catering and security in the UK resemble this profile (nearly all of these were included in our study). Largely on the basis of a rapid acquisition of companies in the 1980s, a handful of leading firms dominate each industry and orchestrate labour across a multitude of sites. One of the three firms which dominates the UK's contract cleaning market, for example, is a Danish-based multinational with its European head office in London. In the mid-1960s it was one of a number of small Danish cleaning companies; today, it is the world's largest cleaning company with 120,000 employees in

Europe, North America and Brazil, including a workforce of 12,000 spread across numerous sites in the UK alone. Another market leader is a subsidiary of a UK industrial services multinational, with just under 10,000 employed on the cleaning side of its operations. Within contract security, the largest firm in the UK is a Netherlands-based multinational of Swedish parentage which operates in thirty-six countries worldwide with a workforce of just under 7,000 in the UK, of which 4,000 are in contract guarding. The company employs over 35,000 in total, with major interests in both west and east Europe, as well as in Argentina and India. Close behind, in terms of UK market share, is another multinational security firm which operates in twenty-two countries. It has a total workforce of 30,000 spread across all its divisions, with over 3,000 guards in the UK, of which just under a third are in London and the south east. Finally, in contract catering, three UK based multinationals hold 80 per cent of the market. Two of the three are, also, the third and fifth largest contract caterers in the USA, as well as major players in the European league. In the UK, these two companies employ 52,000 between them (which perhaps should be set alongside the 40,000-odd who comprise the whole of British Steel's workforce), across thousands of sites.

Apart from their size, however, since the 1980s the management structure of many of these firms has altered too, with flatter, more mobile forms of management put in place. Increasingly, therefore, the big contract services firms in the UK are taking on the characteristics of the large corporations referred to by Dicken and Thrift. Yet there is a twist, in so far as the contract 'giants' are not as substantial as they appear. At the risk of exaggeration, they are *hollow* (rather than 'hollowed out') entities who formally organise workers on somebody else's site. They are multi-site operations, yet they do not own the sites. They are mass service firms in terms of employment, yet they possess few tangible assets other than perhaps the offices which house their 'lean' management. One of the leading contract catering firms referred to above, for instance, employs 22,000 workers across 3,300 sites in the UK, yet hardly has a kitchen which it can call its own. Their major asset is, in fact, difficult to conceptualise and even harder to capitalise: it is the value created by customer loyalty – the goodwill of a client to renew a contract and release a further stream of profits.

In sum, the big contract service firms are hollow corporations composed largely of *fragments*, with each site isolated from every other and with no interdependent division of labour (as in many manufacturing industries) to integrate the sites across space. There is some movement of people between sites to gain experience in the contract catering business, but none to speak of in contract cleaning or security. More than that, the workforce in each fragment is relatively isolated from central operations and, as noted earlier, they are distant socially from the majority of people on the client's site. 'You are on your own', as one unit manager in cleaning candidly observed, 'this is your contract, this is your building'. While the centre of operations in these large service firms may be formal, dynamic and strategic, the sites are scattered, loose, unpredictable workplaces.

As a result of this particular organisational form, the large contract services firms are structured by what may be referred to as a *tension* between, on the one hand, the objective of orchestrating workers across a multitude of sites on a legal basis and, on the other, the need for the work to be done at each site regardless of formal regulatory requirements laid down by the state. Where the former characteristic points to the *formal* organisation of work and employment by the large service firms, the latter points to the possibility of *informal* employment practices entering the world of contract work. The very fact that these industries are composed of fragments implies that this tension will be felt more sharply the larger the organisation. The boundary between formal and informal activities has the potential, therefore, to be drawn *within* the firm, at some blurred point(s) between the centre and the virtually semi-autonomous sites scattered across towns and cities (Portes *et al.* 1989). The leading operators in the respective industries, however, attempt to resolve the tension between the formal/informal worlds of work in different ways through social relations *in* production specific to each industry.

Social relations in production

Social relations in production refer to the authority relations that, in the case of the contract services, get things done at the workplace – they deliver the product (Burawoy 1979). It involves the co-ordination of clusters of workers across and within sites, as well as the motivation and control of the workforce. Moreover, it is the exercise of these relations of authority and power across the fragments of these industries which *secures* precarious employment practices.

In contract cleaning, for example, within the big firms the site supervisor or unit manager is responsible for the organisation and control of work. At the risk of caricature, their power is almost akin to that of a contract gang-leader in the nineteenth century. They are responsible for the formal monitoring of wage sheets, attendance, and sick pay entitlements where applicable, plus the supervision of health and safety standards and the training of new workers in the use of machinery and cleaning materials. Unit managers are also largely responsible for recruitment, often through word-of-mouth and social networks among the existing workforce. The right to dismiss is limited in formal terms, although in practice it rests with the unit manager. If the unit manager suggests that someone has not been doing the job properly, and a replacement is available, then the manager's word is likely to be accepted by the centre. Alongside the formal dimension, therefore, there is the arbitrary power wielded by managers which gives them a wide remit of personal authority. In some cases, this power is used to reinforce the formal vulnerability of the workforce; on other occasions it will be used to introduce the possibility of working informally, and thus avoiding regulatory practices covering taxes, social benefits and so on. This is more likely to involve the use of undeclared labour (perhaps through the use of 'family teams' where one member covers for another, or a 'second jobber') than it is to involve unrecorded cash payments.[6] The former practice is simply a means of ensuring that the cleaning gets done that day. In the language of industrial sociology, it offers the employer numerical flexibility.

At the centre of operations, the regional or divisional headquarters, the key consideration is the winning of market share; that is, retaining and increasing the number and size of contracts. Central to this process is the cost of labour and the conditions under which it is employed; of secondary significance, perhaps of remote significance, is the co-ordination of labour and who actually does the cleaning work and, to some extent, what employment practices are used to ensure that it gets done. In an industry composed of fragments, the centre may well collude in the use of informal labour practices, although stopping well short of any type of systematic fiscal fraud. This, then, is one way in which the tension between the formal and the informal sides of the cleaning industry may be resolved – that is, towards the informal end.

Within contract catering, the lead operators also rely heavily upon their unit managers to ensure that a daily service is delivered. Like their counterparts in cleaning, they are responsible for a wide range of administrative and practical tasks and, indeed, are the lynchpin between centre and site. Their power, however, appears to be more circumscribed than that of unit managers in contract cleaning. The visibility of the operation (as opposed to the workforce itself), the tangibility of the product and the acknowledgement of skills among the workforce (from chef to 'cook-mums') combine to limit both the personal power of the unit manager and the potential to introduce informal working practices into the operation. There is also a high degree of integration across sites; but it involves the co-ordination of food sales, rather than the co-ordination of labour.

In contrast to both the cleaning and security industries, the large firms in contract catering reap their profits from the economies of scale realised through food sales. All sites are on-line so up-to-date information is available on sales, thus enabling the large companies to switch between suppliers to obtain discounts on volume or on special items. The cost of labour and the conditions under which it is employed are, therefore, of relatively less significance to central operations. This is not to suggest that they are of minimal significance; it is merely to draw attention to the fact that the tension between the formal side of the catering business and the less predictable, fragmented world of catering work is not as taut as in those contract industries which rely on the costs and conditions of labour to deliver a competitive advantage. Nonetheless, the workplace fragments help to ensure that the contract workforce lacks the employment security enjoyed in many other service industries.

Finally, in contract security there is an overt attempt among the large firms to avoid employment practices across sites spilling over into informal agreements and arrangements, largely because they wish to differentiate themselves from what they perceive as the 'unregulated' sector of the industry. In consequence, the tension between a formal centre of operations, responsible for ensuring that sites are staffed, and the diversity and remoteness of the sites themselves is experienced sharply. The ethics of security work – integrity, honesty, reliability and so forth – are difficult to monitor, and trust is formally suspended through the close surveillance of guards by electronic technology. For example, at night in particular, the presence and the movement of guards is monitored through regular telephone checks and the logging of 'walks' registered on computer at regional operational headquarters. In practice, however, the attempts to control a workforce at a distance by various technologies has little to do with the quality of work itself and more to do with the number of bodies 'in place'.

The regional centre is largely indifferent to how the work is done (unless a client complains), but scrupulous about tasks and bodies. Contracts are won and lost on the number of guards employed, the hours worked, the cost of labour and the types of task specified. Many clients buy security as an insurance requirement, rather than as protection for their premises, and the question of costs translates directly into the number of bodies employed and the rate per hour. What helps to drive down the cost, however, is in part the relative isolation and powerlessness of guarding work. Even site supervisors have little opportunity to shape the day or influence the pattern of work on site. Things get done or, more accurately, nothing happens on site simply because there are sufficient bodies placed at each fragment. The cost of labour is also driven down by the fact that there are no regulatory barriers to entry in the security industry. Unlike elsewhere in the rest of Europe, anyone can set up a security company in the UK. The prospect of being tainted by association with the informal practices of small security firms is thus sufficient to maintain a strong form of self-regulation among the 'blue chip' security firms.

THE DILEMMAS OF FRAGMENTATION

The fragmented structure of contract service firms is not wholly to their advantage, however; it holds both advantages and disadvantages to service firms, especially the larger ones. The very distance between sites, which helps firms maintain a workforce under conditions of employment insecurity, may also hinder their ability to deliver a profitable service. Indeed, the competitive advantages of size enjoyed by the larger firms may be undermined by the costs imposed by the distance between sites, especially if they resolve the tension between the formal and informal dimensions of employment thrown up by the fragmented structure of the contract industries in a formal manner – as tends to be the case in contract catering and security. It is interesting to look at the dilemmas faced by the large contract service firms when they attempt to 'slot in' fragments in places like Cambridge, as opposed to the concentration of sites and contracts in London.

The nature of the Cambridge 'high-tech' phenomenon is well known and characterised by the continuous turnover, as well as the rapid growth, of large numbers of very small establishments (Keeble 1989; Massey and Henry 1992; Segal et al. 1985). Even if many of these establishments do not actually fit the popular image of starting up in garages and garden sheds, few require contract services on any scale. Moreover, the extreme fragmentation, not to mention the fragility, of this growth has posed considerable problems to the large contract service firms. Faced with contracts which are varied, small and in constant flux, the leading operators have been unable to co-ordinate and integrate these particular fragments of industry in a form which their size allows. Distance has reduced their competitive advantage.

In contract security, for example, one of the elements of the product provided by the leading contractors is that of an immediate response or 'back-up' facility. Mobile supervisors are on hand to provide further assistance to static guards on particular sites if required. Should guards fail to follow the procedures of control laid down by the centre, such as regular, hourly contact, then a mobile supervisor is likely to be despatched to investigate. Yet the provision of this element of service is dependent upon the combination of individual contracts within an operating 'district'. Such a combination has proved difficult for the lead operators, given the diverse nature of demand from the 'Cambridge Phenomenon', and one response has been to expand the size of the 'district' covered by a mobile supervisor. However, the companies then face a 'friction of distance effect', as the ability to respond quickly is reduced because of the distance covered. The inability of the lead operators to overcome this effect became apparent through the growth of a locally-based contract security industry (in all some twenty-five, mostly small firms) which outmanoeuvred the (multi)nationals and led to reduction of the latter's presence in the region.

In this example, the question arises as to how local security companies can provide a mobile supervisor to co-ordinate activities across sites more effectively than the lead operators. One answer is that, in some cases, they do not provide this element of service or they do so on an ad hoc basis (for example, you ring up an off-duty colleague if you have a problem). Put another way, they represent a different slice through the formal/informal work boundary. Each of the large security companies provides a standardised product delivered through formal relations of control which include a high-level back-up facility of mobile supervisors and regular contact with the guards. Indeed, these are formal requirements laid down by the industry's own regulatory body, the British Security Industry Association (BSIA), which was set up and is presently dominated by the lead security companies.[7]

Central to the 'service requirements' of the BSIA is the vetting of all personnel over the previous twenty years – an expensive and time-consuming exercise. Just as smaller and local companies find their own solutions to 'back-up', however, so they are less likely to undertake formal vetting procedures of all employees. In Cambridgeshire, for example, one local company employed only ex-service personnel (which in their view nullified the need for vetting) while another had 'informal' relations with the local police concerning the vetting of prospective employees. In other words, those companies which do not belong to the BSIA are able to introduce a variety of 'informal practices', including little or no vetting and even employment 'off the cards', primarily because of the lack of legally-binding regulation. This is a clear cost advantage in an industry described earlier as one in which contracts are won on the basis of the number of 'bodies' in place, rather than the quality of the work. Often branded by the lead operators as 'cowboys', these local firms retort that they provide as good a service as their larger competitors, albeit of a different form which does not necessarily meet the requirements of an industry association dominated by the major players.

This implies that the 'formal' requirements 'imposed' upon the lead operators in the contract security industry, which were introduced to win large, national and blue-chip contracts from in-house (such as the major public service contracts like the Ministry of Defence or a number of established finance houses in the City of London), actually serve to limit their competitiveness and represent costs in relation to the more 'informal' practices of smaller, local companies. As a result, the leading contract security companies have largely failed to win many of the security contracts for Cambridgeshire firms.

Contract caterers face a similar dilemma. As the critical requirement of any catering 'unit' is its insertion into a standardised system of food sales to deliver profits through volume discounts on food supplies, the nature of demand generated by the high technology firms of Cambridgeshire is problematic for the leading firms. In these small, research-based companies, the few contracts requiring staff restaurants have been won by the lead companies. Yet the majority of high technology companies require catering more attuned to business lunches and buffets – a demand which may vary greatly in terms of the numbers of guests provided for and the number of functions in any one period of time. In such circumstances, the critical ability to dictate volume and the type of food sold is severely weakened. In consequence, the advantages of a large organisation are lost and, as with security, the region has witnessed the growth of a locally-based contract catering industry to meet this particular type of demand. Over eighty small caterers, many of them home-based, have grown up in the region which are able to provide business lunches and buffets, to cater for either a handful of people or two hundred, with relative ease.[8] Indeed, the option of calling on the informal local labour markets of the villages of Cambridgeshire, through the flexible employment of an army of mothers with young children, provides cost savings in contrast to those lost from food sales by the leading operators.

In contract cleaning, the overcoming of distance has taken a further twist. The unit manager can introduce informal working practices. In this way, the response of some of the leading operators to the cost competition gained through the use of informal practices by local companies is the option to use such informal practices themselves. (Such a path is not open to the lead contract security companies.) As in many other places, the leading contract cleaning operators are to be found competing successfully for contracts in Cambridgeshire, in part through a particular resolution of the formal/informal work tension. Many of the local cleaning companies of significant size in Cambridgeshire have been acquired by the lead operators as part of the process of gaining market share. With less need to integrate such 'fragments' in an exclusively formal manner, the risks of non-renewal of contracts are minimised.

Above all, the fragmented structure of the large contract service firms provides both advantages and disadvantages to these companies in their use of space. Principally, while they are able to make geography work for them in terms of securing certain employment practices, the multitude of sites and their virtual isolation may also impose 'friction of distance' effects. Whether or not these effects are overcome, however, is dependent partly upon the manner in which the tension between the formal and informal organisation of work is resolved in the different contract service firms.

CONCLUSION

The growth of contract labour since the mid-1980s in the UK labour market carries with it a number of consequences for the nature of work and employment in the UK's cities and regions. In a broad sense, it signals the potential unease felt by many that a 'job for life' is a less than viable prospect. For those in low paid work at the bottom end of the labour market, the imposition of a contract status has already divided them from others more secure in the labour market, as well as driving down wages to a level which heralds talk of a new working poor. At present, there is limited evidence of those with tradable skills higher up the income scale having experienced the uncertainty of precarious forms of employment, although the lack of predictability around careers and the erosion of job-holding have permeated an increasing number of workplaces, including that of the professions. Much, of course, depends on how far one sub-scribes to the general direction of change signalled by Ulrich Beck (1992), that risk and uncertainty have increasingly permeated all walks of life (including work and employment) and the extent to which risk 'divides' in the ways that wealth and education do.[9]

Regardless of the extent of a 'risk society', however, what this chapter has tried to outline is that the precariousness of employment is not simply about employment rights, nor wholly about government attempts to de-regulate the labour market in the UK. The picture is a more complex one, involving a number of related shifts in the fragmentation of both labour markets and industrial organisations. In one sense, the large, multinational contract service firms represent an extreme version of such shifts, with their dispersed workforces and hollow structures. However, the extent to which other workers find themselves as contract labour or, indeed, experience a sense of precariousness through its introduction at their workplace will be a measure of just how far the UK has moved towards Beck's risk-laden society.

NOTES

1 The findings presented here form part of a larger ESRC funded programme of research based in the Faculty of Social Science at the Open University. The aim of the programme was to examine the form of growth laid down across London and the south east of the UK in the latter half of the 1980s and early 1990s. We wish to acknowledge the funding received from the ESRC to conduct the research on the contract service industries (R000233008).

2 For an assessment of the 'golden age' of the post-war economic boom, see Marglin and Schor (1990), and also Armstrong *et al.* (1991).

3 In one of the leading support service firms in the UK, for example, of its 8,500 staff only 500 fell into (central and regional) managerial categories. The rest comprised mainly cleaners, some guards, and site supervisors. Likewise, in the security sector, the company with the second largest market share in the UK has 3,000 basic guards out of a total UK workforce of 3,300. The remainder comprised mobile supervisors, contracts managers as well as district managers, and a small number of HQ staff. In the case of one of the largest contract catering firms in the UK, its central HQ staff totalled only 22 – out of a UK workforce of 22,000! None of these companies was atypical in our study.

4 See Allen (1995) for an account of the ethnic divisions of labour in the low paid contract service industries in London, and how ethnic identities cross-cut the class and gender characteristics of contract service occupations.

5 As one contract vending operator commented: 'You felt that you were part of the company when you worked [in house], well you were part of the company

and you felt like part of the company and it was a completely different feeling than it is now working for an outside caterer. I mean we always class ourselves really as working for [the in-house company, the client] and you still feel in a way like you work for them, but now you don't get included really in anything that's going on [here]. It's separate'.

6 It is often overlooked that some 3 million people in the UK do not earn enough to pay income tax, so the issue of tax avoidance is not an automatic reason for undertaking informal work. Also, around one-third of all part-timers remain outside of the national insurance nets because of their low earnings (see Hakim 1992 and Hewitt 1993).

7 Initially little more than a trade association, since the 1980s the BSIA has recently taken on a 'regulatory' role, with existing and prospective members inspected as to whether or not they meet certain 'service requirements'. This function has come about due to the persistent refusal of central government to create a legislative framework to oversee the industry, despite the pleas of many of its leading members. These pleas reach a peak during the furore which regularly accompanies the 'exposure' of security companies run by convicted criminals – a sharp illustration of the formal and informal tension which exists within the industry.

8 The number and size of many of the contract service firms operating in Cambridgeshire in catering, cleaning and security was obtained through a postal survey conducted in 1992. In total, 212 establishments were identified from Yellow Pages and local authority business lists. Subsequently, 30 of these establishments proved to have 'gone away' and 71 returns were received giving a response rate of just under 40 per cent.

9 See Ruskin (1994) for a constructive critique of Beck's account of a 'risk society'.

REFERENCES

Allen, J. (1995) 'Precarious work and shifting identities: contract labour in a global city', in A. Martens and M. Vervneke (eds) *Social Polarization of the European Cities*, Lille: Anthropos.

Allen, J. and Henry, N. (1995) 'Growth at the margins: contract labour in a core region', in C. Hadjimichalis and D. Sadler (eds) *Europe at the Margins*, Chichester: Wiley.

Allen, J. and Pryke, M. (1994) 'The production of service space', *Environment and Planning D: Society and Space* 12(4): 453–75.

Armstrong, P., Glyn, A. and Harrison, J. (1991) *Capitalism since 1945*, Oxford: Basil Blackwell.

Beck, U. (1992) *Risk Society: Towards a New Modernity*, London: Sage.

Burawoy, M. (1979) *Manufacturing Consent*, Chicago, IL: University of Chicago Press.

Cousins, C. (1988) 'The restructuring of welfare work', *Work, Employment and Society* 2(2): 210–28.

Deakin, S. (1992) 'Labour law and industrial relations', in J. Michie (ed.) *The Economic Legacy 1979–1992*, London: Academic.

Deakin, S. and Wilkinson, F. (1992) 'European integration: the implications for UK policies on labour supply and demand', in E. McLaughlin (ed.) *Understanding Unemployment: New Perspectives on Active Labour Market Policies*, London: Routledge.

Dicken, P. and Thrift, N. (1992) 'The organization of production and the production of organization', *Transactions, Institute of British Geographers* 17(3): 279–91.

Fevre, R. (1989) *Wales is Closed: The Quiet Privatization of British Steel*, Nottingham: Spokesman.

Hakim, C. (1992) 'Unemployment, marginal work and the black economy', in E. McLaughlin (ed.) *Understanding Unemployment: New Perspectives on Active Labour Market Policies*, London: Routledge.

Hewitt, P. (1993) *About Time: The Revolution in Work and Family Life*, London: Institute for Public Policy Research/Rivers Oram Press.

Keeble, D. (1989) 'High-technology industry and regional development in Britain: the case of the Cambridge phenomenon', *Environment and Planning C: Government and Policy* 7: 153–72.

Marglin, S. A. and Schor, J. B. (1990) *The Golden Age of Capitalism: Reinterpreting the Postwar Experience*, Oxford: Clarendon Press.

Massey, D. and Henry, N. (1992) 'Something new something old: a sketch of the Cambridge economy', *South East Programme Occasional Paper Series no. 2*, Faculty of Social Sciences, The Open University, Milton Keynes.

Pahl, R. (1984) *Divisions of Labour*, Oxford: Basil Blackwell.

Portes, A. Castells, M. and Benton, L. A. (eds) (1989) *The Informal Economy: Studies in Advanced and Less Developed Countries*, Baltimore, MD: Johns Hopkins University Press.

Pulkingham, J. (1992) 'Employment re-structuring in the Health Service: efficiency institutes, working patterns and workforce recomposition', *Work, Employment and Society* 6(3): 397–421.

Rees, G. and Fielder, S. (1992) 'The services economy, sub-contracting and the new employment relations: contract catering and cleaning', *Work, Employment and Society* 6(3): 347–68.

Ruskin, M. (1994) 'Incomplete modernity: Ulrich Beck's Risk Society', *Radical Philosophy* 67: 3–12.

Sayer, A. and Walker, R. (1992) *The New Social Economy: Reworking the Division of Labour*, Oxford: Basil Blackwell.

Segal, Quince and Wickstead (1985) *The Cambridge Phenomenon: The Growth of High Technology Industry in a University Town*, Cambridge: SQW.

Shutt, J. and Whittington, R. (1987) 'Fragmentation strategies and the rise of small units: cases from the north west', *Regional Studies* 21: 13–23.

Standing, G. (1989) 'The "British Experiment": structural adjustment or accelerated decline?', in A. Portes, M. Castells and L. A. Benton (eds) *The Informal Economy: Studies in Advanced and Less Developed Countries*, Baltimore, MD: Johns Hopkins University Press.

Walker, R. (1989) 'A requiem for corporate geography: new directions in industrial organization, the production of place and uneven development', *Geografiska Annaler* 71B: 43–68.

Young, A. (1928) 'Increasing returns and economic progress', *The Economic Journal* 38: 527–42.

5

THE SOCIAL ORDER
OF THE SHIP
IN A GLOBALISED LABOUR
MARKET FOR SEAFARERS

Tony Lane

A small German ship docked in July 1994 at Mostyn, a tiny North Wales port on the Cheshire Dee estuary. Within hours of arrival the ship's cook, a Kiribatian, and the mate, a German, were found dead in the ship's hold where the timber cargo had de-oxygenated the atmosphere. The particular circumstances of this case apart, what was a seaman from a small group of South Pacific islands (Kiribati was once known as the Gilbert Islands) doing aboard a small German ship trading in European waters? We might equally ask what were five Tuvaluans (Ellice Islanders) doing aboard the German-owned, Antiguan-flagged, North Sea trader, *Janne Wehr*, when she called at Felixstowe in November 1992, fortunately in this instance without recorded incident to the crew? Answers to such seemingly esoteric questions call for an account of the contemporary labour market for seafarers and the wider, global structures which enfold it.

GLOBALISATION, FLAGS OF CONVENIENCE
AND DEREGULATION

While the detailed concerns of this chapter focus on the construction and functioning of the social order of the ship when crews are drawn from a global labour market, the ultimate aim is to contribute to the debate on the processes and structures of globalisation. After a glance at the globalisation debate, the chapter surveys the causes and consequences of the globalisation and accompanying deregulation of shipping since the mid-1970s. The analysis of a large sample of the crews of the world's ships will show that the ability of industry's unregulated labour market to provide competent crews is questionable. It will then be argued that widespread and growing anxiety about crew competence which has been prompted by the financial penalties of marine pollution and fuelled by the advance of environmental politics, has led to an emergent process of re-regulation of the world's first wholly global industry.

The choice of the shipping industry as an example might seem a little idiosyncratic since the industry is an almost unmapped wilderness in the sociology of economic life. Sociologists have almost invariably been far more interested in what were the archetypally modern industries – those with large establishments, intricate organisations and mass workforces. However, as contemporary industry tends in new and different directions there are good grounds for bringing this important if little-known industry nearer centre stage. The case for doing so rests primarily on the fact that since the mid-1970s the shipping industry's labour market for crewing deep-sea ships has become global.

The term 'globalisation', as used here and elsewhere, is less a concept and more a useful means of assembling under one roof a range of phenomena which seem to be related, even if the structures and the institutions of the ensemble are resistant to consensual theorisation. 'Globalisation' refers to the advancing economic integration of all world regions into a dynamic mesh of trading, production, distribution and financial relationships which constantly challenges the regulatory role of the nation state.

The globalisation process has, of course, attracted the attention of a large number of theorists, analysts and investigators who are not nearly so disparate as a first reading might suggest. Whether the approach is oriented toward theorising a world-system (Wallerstein 1979; Chase-Dunn 1989; Froebel *et al.* 1980; Henderson 1989) or with theories of the firm and international trade in an age of multinational corporations (Kindleberger 1970; Vernon 1971; Barnet and Muller 1975; Hymer 1975; Hood and Young 1979), they are all inevitably drawn at some point, if with varying weight of emphasis, to the role of the nation state. Implicitly or explicitly, in one form or another, the same question is invariably asked: 'If there is irrefutable evidence of an increasingly integrated global economy but scarcely any of an emergent global political state, doesn't this suggest the emergence of an economic system threatening to outrun and subvert the sovereignty of the nation state?' *This* question informs all contributions to the globalisation debate.

The creation of flags of convenience (FOC) and the abolition or absence of restrictions on the movement of capital were the preconditions for globalisation of the shipping industry. Flags of convenience provided national identities essential to international trade but without the regulatory requirements and practices characteristic of nations with indigenous shipping industries.

Setting aside earlier developments in the inter-war years, the introduction of FOC has gone through two distinct stages. The first period was 1946–70 when US and Greek shipowners began to build up very large fleets under the Panamanian and the Liberian flags. American owners, enjoying free movement of capital, could escape US wage rates, US taxation and the legal requirement of building ships in high-cost US shipyards. Greek owners, who had gone abroad to London and New York during the war and taken their ships with them, were not anxious to take their businesses back afterwards to a politically unstable Greece (Carlisle 1981; Harlaftis 1988).

Shipowners in Japan and the maritime nations of Europe experienced stringent restrictions on the export of capital in the first period of FOC development. They were also operating under supportive domestic fiscal regimes and in a mainly buoyant world market for shipping services where crew costs were not normally a source of competitive disadvantage. The Japanese and German governments, for example, were encouraging native owners to rebuild their fleets, while in Britain and Norway shipping made significant contributions to the balance of payments, and shipowners had correspondingly powerful political connections (Sturmey 1962).

The squeeze on Japanese and European owners came after the 'oil shocks' of the mid-1970s and the slowdown in the rate of growth of world trade. Twenty years later, in the mid-1990s, freight rates generally show no sign of recovering to the equivalent levels of the 1950s and 1960s, despite a boom in the dry bulk trades in 1994–5. In the meantime, fiscal regimes in Japan and Europe have become less friendly, although compensation could be found in the relaxation of exchange controls which make it easy for those shipowners deciding to stay in the industry to flag their ships abroad.

The second stage of development of FOC began when a procession of Japanese and European owners flagged their ships in foreign countries from the mid-1970s, and at a growing rate in the 1980s. By so doing they could avoid the regulation of domestic labour markets and significantly cut employment costs (Yannopoulos 1988). Once flagged out, owners could reduce crew size, retain key nationals but on a self-employed basis, and hire the balance of the crew through manning agencies in low-wage countries.

The flagging out process became easier and more attractive as an expanding number of small states offered their flags as 'refuges'. By the mid-1990s there was a well-established market for flags as minuscule island states discovered a useful source of revenue for a minimal outlay.[1] 'Flags' were regularly advertised in the shipping press, consultancies offered advice, computer software and printed guides were published and 'flag' representatives touted for custom. By the mid-1990s the shipping daily newspaper, *Lloyd's List*, was resigned to the industry's reincarnation as a living theatre of the absurd, irreverently reporting attempts by Barbados to establish itself in the flag market:

> Students of strange maritime facts will be entranced to discover that last week saw the Barbados Ship Register improbably opening its doors – in Des Voeux Road, Hong Kong. London-based Barbados Principal Registrar Captain Alan Morris, who some might recall did

much the same job for the Bahamas bunting until he swapped ensigns a few years ago, was in Hong Kong last week commissioning [a] local surveyor . . . to represent the Caribbean haven. The appointment of a local registrar went down well with the HK shipping community, who turned up in some numbers to listen to Capt Morris lucidly provide 101 reasons for registering their ships in another island in the sun.

(Lloyd's List 15 May 1995)

The growth of FOC fleets, the development of new flags and the decline of the nationally flagged fleets is illustrated in Table 5.1. However, the decline of European and Japanese fleets did not mean that nationals of these countries ceased to be shipowners. A survey of FOC fleets as early as 1978 identified 53 per cent of FOC tonnage as owned in the USA and Greece, 17 per cent in Hong Kong, 9 per cent in Japan and a further 9.4 per cent in Germany, Italy, Switzerland, Canada, the UK, Norway and the Netherlands combined (UNCTAD 1978: 11). By 1992, UNCTAD reported that Japanese owners were the second largest users with 17 per cent of the total FOC fleet.

Recent reports in the shipping press have underlined the use of FOCs by Russia and the Ukraine while the People's Republic of China has been flagging out ships for many years. In these latter cases, however, the rationale is different from that of OECD-country owners. China used the Somalian flag briefly in the 1970s, and the Panamanian flag subsequently,

Table 5.1 Selected flag of convenience and national fleets, 1978 and 1992 (million gross tons)

FOC fleet	1978	1992
Bahamas	0.1	20.6
Bermuda	1.8	3.3
Cyprus	2.6	20.5
Liberia	80.2	55.9
Panama	20.7	52.5
Singapore	7.5	9.9
St Vincent	0.01	4.7
Vanuatu	0.0	2.1
Malta	0.1	11.0
National fleets		
France	12.2	3.4
Germany	11.2	5.4
Greece	34.0	25.7
Italy	11.5	7.5
Japan	39.2	25.1
Norway	26.1	2.0
UK	30.9	4.1

Source: Lloyd's Register of Shipping

so that it could trade its ships into such countries as the USA where own-flagged ships were barred (Lauriat 1977). In the 1990s Croatian ships use the Panamanian and St Vincent registers as a means of evading local political difficulties; Russia and the Ukraine use several flags as a means of gaining access to Western capital markets. Western banks will take mortgages on Russian ships only if ships are registered in a country with a legal regime enabling quick and certain repossession in the event of default. Most FOCs are able to satisfy banks in this respect by offering mortgage document-holding facilities.

Approximately half the world's deep-sea labour force of 1.25 million, almost all of whom are male, is impermanently employed aboard FOC ships where the permutation of nationalities can vary from voyage to voyage. By the late 1980s the ILO estimated that the Philippines had 90,000 seafarers employed on foreign-flag ships, South Korea had 50,000 and India 20,000 (ILO 1990: 57). Other Asian nationals, such as Bangladeshis, Myanmarians (Burmese), Sri Lankans, Indonesians and Chinese from the People's Republic, together with smaller numbers of Malagasys, Maldive Islanders, Western Samoans, Tuvaluans and Kiribatis are also commonly employed on FOC ships. Nearer home in the Atlantic region, Portuguese and Cape Verdeans are widely employed, if not in large overall numbers. In the 1990s the political transformations in Eastern Europe have brought substantial numbers of Poles and Croats into the labour market and somewhat smaller numbers from Estonia, Latvia, Romania, Russia and the Ukraine.

The modal ship trading internationally has a crew of at least three nationalities and crews of four 'or five nationalities are common (see pp. 92–95). The existence of an irregularly employed, polyglot, internationalised workforce poses one set of theoretical questions for sociological analysis that is of more than intellectual interest: how can a functioning social order be established in such unpromising circumstances? Other questions are raised by the fact that these internationalised crews frequently work aboard ships whose nationality is not their own and which for all practical purposes is fictional: what happens to political rights and obligations where there is no state to enframe them?

Standard workplace analyses of social relations have usually been able to assume that, whatever the drama, it was enacted by participants who, by virtue of their common nationality, had some understanding of the formal and normative rules of engagement and of the various institutions of state and civil society which framed their action. These assumptions are utterly redundant in the case of FOC regimes. As one shipping economist with first-hand knowledge of the industry said of FOCs:

> Most FOC countries do not have the necessary mercantile services
> or consulates abroad to enable them to enforce their maritime

regulations. Thus, shipping firms operating tonnage under FOC are practically free to maintain their own standards so far as the numbers, qualifications and terms of employment of officers and crew members are concerned. It should be added that when, during the 1970s, the Liberian authorities attempted to impose some regulations, several firms shifted their tonnage from the Liberian flag to other FOC and quasi-FOC flags.

(Metaxas 1985: 27)

A leading ship manager who was familiar with running ships under FOC said that they were 'designer flags embroidered to suit owners' requirements' (Spruyt 1990: 47). The same view was put more bluntly by Paul Chapman, a recent secretary of the New York-based ecumenical organisation, The Center for Seafarers' Rights:

> Seafarers on [FOC] ships are working in a lawless environment. Without flag state enforcement the ship's operators are free to take the law into their own hands. In effect, life on board is no longer controlled by a sovereign nation, but by a sovereign shipowner.
>
> (The Sea November/December 1991)

The ability of shipowners under FOC administrations to run their ships as they please makes it impossible to make any detailed generalisations about FOC fleets. An early attempt by the ILO to investigate conditions aboard Panamanian ships (in 1949) found a very wide variation in practices and conditions aboard the 30 ships inspected, observing that the 'crews on many Panama ships were engaged on the basis of Italian, Greek, British or other laws or collective agreements' (ILO 1950: 24). Unsurprisingly in these circumstances, the committee found:

> the conditions of safety and employment in the ships it saw depended largely on the owners, agents and masters. There are owners who, because of their national traditions or their sense of responsibility, see to it that their ships are seaworthy and comply with good standards of safety and employment conditions. There are others who are apparently irresponsible and looking solely for quick profits and are prepared on that account to take risks as to the safety of passengers and crew and apply the lowest standards of employment that the crew (often in the grip of circumstances and prepared to to accept any job rather than be unemployed) will tolerate.
>
> (ILO 1950: 28)

Any investigation of the fleets of regulated nationally flagged fleets at this or any other time would also find wide variations within them – but at or above a common and regulated standard. Such a base line was absent in the Panamanian fleet in 1949 and has never been established in other FOC

88

fleets at any time since. Every critical comment to be found in the ILO report of 1950 has been regularly repeated ever since.

In the matter of the shipboard social order, what could be made of the case of the ship *Good Faith*, a 9,000-ton general cargo carrier flying the Liberian flag, with a crew of twenty-four made up of twelve nationalities, when she called at a UK port in 1993? The ship had a Dutch master and Filipino chief engineer, the other officers being Croatian, Polish, Indian and Ghanaian. The ratings consisted of three Cape Verdeans, three Chileans, four Filipinos, two Portuguese and one each from Croatia, Ecuador, Germany and Togoland. If this is an extreme case – and it is – it nevertheless highlights some interesting questions.

Here is a workplace which in international law is part of the national territory of Liberia, except that Liberia is no more than a piece of land divided between warlords and their followers. In any case, the Liberian registry which administers Liberia's maritime code is run by a private firm based in Reston, Virginia. *De facto*, this ship is stateless and, given the literally murderous conditions in Liberia, the concept of civil society in that desperate country is not even a joke in poor taste. In short, and in this aspect of the crew's circumstances, the *Good Faith*'s social order is free of any external regulation apart from that of the owner. What about internal regulation? There is bound to have been 'something' there, for without whatever it is the ship could not function. Whatever 'it' is, it can hardly have had any language-cultural basis since among the twelve nationalities there were nine different languages. Communication will certainly have been in English but if this is the *lingua franca* of seamen generally it was, on this ship, no one's native language. Yet the ship functioned in the sense that it had crossed oceans safely, collected and delivered cargoes without reported incident and, for the two years following, went unmentioned in casualty reports.

Among crews drawn from the same national society, construction of the social order of the occupation has made it normally straightforward for a collection of complete strangers to be able to take a ship safely to sea (Aubert and Arner 1958). This may also be true for ships' crews of several or even many nationalities, because nationality in itself makes little difference to the contours of the ship's socio-technical division of labour. Lists of crew showing the hierarchical and technical arrangements of rank from ships of a large number of nationalities are easily assimilable into a common set of categories. In the case of the *Good Faith*, and making the not unreasonable assumption that among the crew was a nucleus of men with extensive seagoing experience and very few novices among the remainder, the ship was probably manned by people familiar with the social and technical division of labour, the rhythms, routines and customary rituals of shipboard social exchange. These characteristics taken together form the essential features of an occupational culture which, in the new circumstances of a global labour market for seafarers, may often provide the only prospect of a shipboard social order. Perhaps, even, the name *Good Faith* is in a limited sense neither parody nor irony.

THE INTERNATIONAL LABOUR MARKET FOR SEAFARERS

The core of the system of the older maritime nations was national collective bargaining machinery and joint supply of labour. In the new global regime both elements have disappeared. The first response by Japanese and European owners, in their attempts to remain competitive in the period of declining freight from the mid-1970s, was to cut voyage operating costs by reducing crew size. Ultimately, this strategy failed as freight rates continued to fall, and more and more owners sought cheaper sources of labour in Asia. At the end of the 1980s the intricate network of institutions formed to regulate maritime labour markets in Japan and Europe were in an advanced state of collapse. EEC employment of seafarers halved between 1980 and 1986 and exactly the same process of decline has been taking place in Japan, where it was reported in 1988:

> The Ministry of Transport in Japan has called on the country's beleaguered shipowners to step up their restructuring plans and reach agreement on the use of mixed crews. All of the big six lines except NYK have faced hefty losses in recent years and in a bid to stay afloat they have switched vessels to open registers and employed lower-cost Filipino, Korean and other Asian crews. . . .

> The Ministry of Transport has now thrown its weight behind the owners in calling for the use of lower-cost Asian seafarers on board Japanese-flag ships, despite strong opposition from the All Japan Seamen's Union (AJSU) which has seen the number of ocean-going members fall from around 23 000 in 1986 to 12 000. Concern is obviously growing at government level over the pace at which Japanese-registered ships are being transferred, especially to Panama and Liberia, and the AJSU is equally concerned that in ten to 15 years' time there will be no jobs left for its deepsea members.

> (*Lloyds List* 1988)

Six years later, in 1994, the same course of action was again being urged by the Japanese Ministry of Transport: 'Japanese shipping needs to increase the number of foreign seafarers it employs and take further cost-cutting initiatives to remain competitive in the market, a new government report says' (*Lloyds List* 21 July 1994).

The transfer to FOCs by owners from Japan and Europe has had the inevitable effect of bringing about the attrition of labour market-related institutions in their home countries. At the same time, the new labour supply nations have been establishing or enlarging a similar set of institutions – but primarily as a means of supplying labour to the world market or of providing captive labour dedicated to foreign shipowners and ship managers. Among these institutions are trade unions.[2] In 1988 the Norwegian ship management firm, Barber International, said it had signed an agreement with Portuguese seafaring unions to provide crews for ships on the Norwegian International Ship register. The total cost for a ship with twenty-two crew would be around $400,000 per annum compared with a similar crew of Norwegians which would cost more than $1 million (*Lloyds List* 4 February 1988). Later in the same year, Barber International announced it had struck another deal for providing crews for the Norwegian International Register, this time with South Korean seafaring unions. The price on this occasion was $440,000 per annum for a twenty-two person crew (*Lloyds List* 2 June 1988). By 1993, Barber International had had about four years' experience of employing Polish seafarers who were reckoned to be 'competitive with the Far East'. Satisfied with this source, Barber was signalling its commitment by setting up a joint recruitment office with Solidarity, in Szczecin (*Lloyds List* 31 August 1993)

Reports of the prices of different crew sources have become stock items in the shipping press. There is a constant need for new intelligence and anticipatory deals in an extremely fluid market and this is accurately reflected in activities of firms like Barber International. In 1993 Barber managed the crewing for a diverse fleet of 180 ships flying 14 different flags, most of them beneficially owned in Norway. Aware of owners' actual and prospective needs and preferences, the firm constantly monitors and samples labour supply options so it is always able to either match owners' preferences of crew nationality or offer alternatives. In this context 'monitoring and sampling' involves setting up the terms of crew agreements – as in the case of the Portuguese and South Korean seafarers cited above – in advance of having a buyer.

There are several hundred globally operating firms who organise crews for ships in the same manner as Barber. The International Ship Managers' Association (ISMA) handbook says its members manage a total of 1,840 ships of which approximately 1,500 fly flags of convenience. The total crew population of ISMA members' ships runs to 50,000 (*Lloyds List* 19 September 1994). Some indication of how these and other ships are actually crewed is provided by the data from a crew composition survey.

THE SOCIAL ORDER OF THE MULTINATIONALLY CREWED SHIP

Anxieties about crew competence are fuelled by the knowledge that it is common for ships to be crewed by persons of several nationalities who may normally find it difficult to communicate with each other except through intermediaries and who, in emergencies, might each panic in their own language to the detriment of everyone's safety (Donaldson 1994). Yet debates about the operational consequences of having crews consisting of several or many nationalities are unable ever to proceed beyond the stage dictated by anecdotal evidence. At the most elementary descriptive level, there are few data on crew size and structure: age, experience and certification of officers, nationality of crew members. Regarding the social order of the ship, there are no data at all.

An attempt to overcome the crew data deficiences for flag of convenience ships was made by obtaining access to Immigration Office data on ships calling at UK ports. All ships arriving at UK ports from abroad – including the EU – are required to deposit with the Immigration Office a complete list of crew. With the co-operation of the Home Office, a sample of these lists was obtained for two separate sample periods of one month each in 1992 and 1993. All crew lists for ships arriving in the sample period in Liverpool, London, Tees–Hartlepool and Felixstowe were collected and analysed.

The sample yielded a total of 1,078 ships, mustering between them 66 flags and 17,543 seafarers of 87 nationalities. Nationally-flagged ships accounted for 9,755 seafarers (55.6 per cent of the total); the older flags of convenience (Panama and Liberia) accounted for 2,372 seafarers (13.5 per cent of the total); the newer flags of convenience (fifteen of them – Antigua, Bahamas, Bermuda, Cyprus, Danish International, Honduras, Hong Kong, Isle of Man, Luxembourg, Malta, Norwegian International, Singapore, St Vincent, Tuvalu and Vanuatu) accounted for 5,416 seafarers (30.9 per cent of the total). The results of the sample can be read only indicatively. It must be stressed that the sample is not a sample of the world fleet but a sample of that portion of the world fleet calling at UK ports.

In the following discussion, the focus is on the crewing patterns found on ships with crew complements greater than ten and registered with the three largest FOCs – Panama, Liberia and Cyprus. A brief account will be subsequently given of a sub-set of ships with crew complements smaller than ten. In Table 5.2 we can see the general pattern of multinationality crews and note that between one-quarter and one-third have crews comprising four or more nationalities. In the case of one-nationality crews, the large number of Panamanian-flagged ships of this sort is due to Japanese owners' preference both for the Panamanian flag and for crews consisting homogeneously of South Koreans (seven ships) or Filipinos (four ships). Among the ships with two-nationality crews, the ubiquity of Filipino ratings and junior officers sailing with German or Norwegian senior officers is the most significant characteristic.

Nationality composition is difficult to characterise in tabular form in the case of ships having crews of three or more nationalities, although an attempt at classification has been made in Table 5.3.

Table 5.2 Crew composition by number of nationalities[a]

No. of crew	No. of ships by flag		
Nationalities	Cyprus	Liberia	Panama
1	3	9	17
2	19	11	19
3	24	7	7
4	16	6	7
5	3	2	4
6	2	1	6
7	2	–	–
8+	1	1	1
Total	70	37	61

Note: [a] The numbers of one-nationality ships have been adjusted to take account of 'political' flagging. Seven Cyprus-flag, eight Liberian-flag and ten Panamanian-flag ships with one-nationality crews have been excluded.

The data in Table 5.3 take in thirty-seven nationalities. In order to make this complexity manageable, the first term in the nationality column describes the senior officers, i.e. masters and chief engineers or master only. The second term describes the other most numerous nationality. An example is a Liberian-flag container ship with a British master, a Singaporean chief engineer, a Malaysian chief officer, a Hong Kong second engineer and the rest of the crew consisting of two Singaporeans, a Taiwanese, four Hong Kong and seven Filipinos, is entered as 'European + Filipino'.

An extreme example of the problem of classification is the case of a Cyprus-flag ship whose crew of twenty-six had nine nationalities: the four senior officers were Greek, the other officers being one Cypriot, one Egyptian, one Thai and two Filipinos; the rest of the crew were one Tanzanian, one Polish, one Pakistani, two Indians, three Filipinos and eight Egyptians. This crew is entered as 'European + LDC' since Egypt is classified by the OECD as a 'less developed country'. A similar classificatory simplification has been imposed on a group of fourteen ships under the Cyprus and Panamanian flags, where the senior officers were Italian and all other officers Croat. Eight of these ships had ratings from either Malagasy (four) or Western Samoa (four), while the other six ships had Croatian ratings as well as junior officers. These ships appear as 'European + LDC' or 'European + E European'.

In ships with East European crew members, Poles are the most common nationality, with Belgian, German and Norwegian senior officers. There are also two Russian crews with Greek and Norwegian officers, but these are unusual. Russian seafarers still sail mainly on CIS-owned ships. As far as LDC crews are concerned, there are Kiribatis and Tuvaluans with

Table 5.3 Ships' crews consisting of three or more nationalities

| | No. of crews | | |
Nationalities	Cyprus	Liberia	Panama
European + Filipino	20	10	4
European + Indian	–	1	1
European + E European	1	–	–
European + European	–	1	–
European + LDC	4	1	20
NIC + NIC	–	2	1
NIC + LDC	–	1	–
E European + LDC	3	–	–
Totals	28	16	26

Notes: NIC = Newly industrialising countries
LDC = Less developed countries.

German officers.[3] More typically, LDC crews sail with South and East European senior officers: there are Spaniards with Hondurans, Bulgarians with Sri Lankans, Poles with Maldive Islanders, and Greeks with Tanzanians, Pakistanis, Myanmarians (Burmese) and Indonesians.

Some of the examples given above suggest that multinationality extends right through the ship's hierarchy and division of labour: Table 5.4 gives confirmation. Ships' officer corps are no less heterogeneous than the corps of ratings and petty officers. Not untypical was a Panamanian-flag chemical carrier with a crew of twenty-five. The officers were Norwegian, Croatian and Filipino, the balance of the crew being Filipino.

The continuing importance of Europe as a source of senior officers has already been seen in general and is shown in more detail in Table 5.5 where the actual employment figures are given. Some 83 per cent of senior officers on Cyprus-flag ships are European, and 71 per cent in the case of Panamanian ships, but only 50 per cent in Liberian ships. In the case of Cyprus the distribution reflects the preferences of the German and Greek owners who are the main users of this flag. In Liberian ships, by contrast, the preferences of Far Eastern owners for officers from the same region can be seen. There is also evidence of the same pattern in Panamanian ships.

Finally, there follows a short account of the crews of seventy-eight FOC ships with complements of fewer than ten which were excluded from the preceding analysis. This group covers a larger selection of flags: in addition to Cyprus, Liberia and Panama there are the Norwegian International, the Isle of Man, Hong Kong, Antigua and Bermuda. These small crews are no less likely to be multinational; for example, an Antiguan-flagged ship with a crew of eight had three Germans, two Poles,

Table 5.4 Number of nationalities among officer corps

No. of Officers	No. of ships		
Nationalities	Cyprus	Liberia	Panama
1	3	9	17
2	19	13	25
3	15	12	7
4	5	5	2
5+	3	2	1

Table 5.5 Number of senior officers employed by nationality or region of origin, in crews of more than two nationalities

Origin	Cyprus		Liberia		Panama	
	N	%	N	%	N	%
N Europe	136	47	42	39	49	24
S Europe	89	28	7	6	74	36
E Europe	24	8	5	5	23	11
Philippines	23	8	18	16	23	11
India	–	–	10	9	–	–
Japan	–	–	14	13	8	4
NIC	–	–	14	13	27	13
LDC	14	5	1	1	3	1
Totals	286	96	111	100	207	100

two Indonesians and one Tanzanian. The modal small ship's crew had three nationalities and the dominant mixes were Germans and Poles (seventeen ships) or Norwegians and Poles (nine ships). Filipinos were also prominent in these ships which trade almost exclusively in European and Mediterranean trades, ten ships having German officers and Filipino ratings. There were also four ships with German officers and Tuvaluan ratings, and five with either German or Dutch officers and ratings from the Cape Verde Islands.

Notwithstanding appearances to the contrary, the labour market for small ships' crews combines old and new practices. On the one hand there are plainly examples of the modern practice where crews have been recruited *en bloc* through agencies and flown to Europe to serve out fixed term contracts – the obvious examples here are the Tuvaluans and the Filipinos. On the other hand, there is still a casual labour market in such major port cities as Hamburg, Rotterdam, Antwerp and Piraeus. This market mainly supplies ships in the shorter-sea trades but also provides last minute substitutes for larger ships short of one or two hands. Established-yet-transient seafarers from Portugal, the Cape Verde Islands, Chile,

Indonesia, Ghana and increasingly from Poland, Russia and the Baltic states are the principal contributors to this casual market. Migrant seafarer communities have been a familiar part of the waterfront districts of the larger ports of the world for several centuries. In Europe where they were once an adjunct, both socially and economically, to the indigenous docker and seafaring communities, they now form virtually the only remaining waterfront-domiciled seafaring communities.

The revealed pattern of crewing has in most cases little to do with *racial* preference even if shipowners and managers, senior officers and insurers do have ethnic enthusiasms, 'substantiated' and decorated with well-honed anecdotes. These preferences are usually *ex post facto* rationalisations of deliberate decisions made on other grounds. The overwhelming use of European, East European and South Korean senior officers reflects two calculations made by shipowners and managers; first, that it is best to have fellow nationals, or other nationals with similar cultural characteristics, in charge of one's ship on the grounds of being able to establish effective ship–shore communication; and second, with India and East Europe excepted, that the new labour supply countries have been unable to implement training and educational regimes capable of producing sufficiently skilled and experienced senior officers. The Philippines is an obvious case in point.

The Philippines has a basic educational system and English, the *lingua franca* of shipping, is widely and adequately spoken. The economy shows few signs of being able to match the economic growth of the advanced NICs in the region; accordingly, the large population should be a continuing source of cheap labour for the foreseeable future. The continuing problem with the Philippines has been its inability to run a training regime capable of producing sufficient numbers of well-trained and reliably certificated officers. This has been widely known in the industry for a number of years, but has only recently been expressed in public. In July 1994, in the context of an eighteen-month run of shipping press articles about crew competence, someone finally decided to talk openly about officer certification in the Philippines:

A dramatic fall in the pass rates recorded by the Philippines maritime training schools has followed a thorough overhaul of the previously corrupt system of examination. . . . Pass rates as high as 100% were being regularly recorded in the early 1980s by some of the 70-odd schools and, although the rates dropped to a more realistic 40–50% in 1986, by the late 1980s they were once again in the 90% and above range. Cheating, bribing and fixing in the exams were endemic. . . . It was well known for some time both in and outside the Philippines that licences could be bought, but the biggest impetus for change came in 1991 when the Hong Kong authorities refused to recognize

Philippine licences for employment on Hong Kong-registered ships.
. . . Elaborate security measures [introduced in 1992] resulted immediately in the overall pass rate falling to 15%. In May last year the pass
rates for master mariners were 12%, chief mates 17%, second mates
11% and third mates 3%. Foreign employers of Filipino seamen are
still concerned, however, that the exams, although now 'tamper-
proof and leak-proof', are still of a generally low standard.

(*Lloyds List* 28 April 1994)

The implication of this revelation is startling. If it had been well-known
for some time that the process of certification was corrupt and of a low
standard, while European and Japanese shipowners and managers were
continuing to recruit Filipino officers in growing numbers, we can
conclude only that they were complicit and compliant in recruiting officers
who in at least eight cases out of ten were corruptly certificated.

The dawning realisation that, in the medium-term, the newly-arrived,
mass supplies of labour from non-traditional sources (with poorly developed
state-regulated maritime infrastructures) could not possibly have the same
technical and experiential skills as the displaced labour from traditional
maritime nations, has led to several developments. Owners and managers
of large fleets have set up their own agencies in an attempt to find and
regularise the supply of well-trained and able personnel. In some case they
have also established training institutions and supplied key personnel from
Europe and Japan.

These labour market interventions, however, are less substantial than
they might seem. Labour supply agencies require negligible capital investment. Training is a different matter; in this respect there is a patent desire
to avoid too deep a commitment – partly because of the capital and revenue
costs of doing so, and partly because of a concern to keep future options
open should another, cheaper source of labour present itself. There is,
after all, the news that: 'Vietnamese seamen are set to replace more expensive Filipinos on Japanese-controlled flag-of-convenience ships working the
short sea trades in the Far East' (*Lloyds List* 4 March 1994). There was also a
great flurry of excitement in the late 1980s at the possibility of some 90,000
state-trained seamen from the People's Republic of China being made
available to the global labour market, the price of an able seaman being
quoted as US$40 per month compared with the (then) cheapest rate for
a Filipino able seaman of approximately US$250. Western ship managers,
anxious to be able to supply labour from this source to broaden their
market profile to prospective customers, rushed to have themselves
pronounced accredited agents. *Lloyds List* sub-editors neatly caught the
flavour of this with the headline, 'Battle hots up for control of labour
"bazaar"' (27 June 1988).

The 'bazaar' dimension of the labour market is unlikely to go away in
the absence of effective regulation. The following exchange between the

author and the personnel director of one of the world's largest ship management companies makes this point conclusively:

> TL: What about new sources of labour supply? You have elected to build up your relationships with India and the Philippines but you will be aware of the possibilities of disturbances in these labour markets that you have no control over. Wouldn't the prudent thing be to keep a pretty close eye on other sources of labour?

> X: We do. In the last year I have been in about seven other countries looking at other labour supplies apart from what we have got. Burma and Indonesia were two. China we know about but I was back there. We haven't looked at Vietnam although we have seen plenty of reports on it. I believe their English is not very good although inevitably everyone who is flogging Vietnamese will say that they do English courses just as everybody we visit in Latvia says that they employ someone to teach them English. We haven't visited West Africa. I have mixed feelings about it. But the shortages are not in ratings, the shortages are in officers.
> Latvia is all right, I was impressed by Latvia. I think the Baltic states are somewhat further ahead. We had quite a few Latvians and Estonians with us right through the 1960s but most of them had jumped out before the war. Croatia is getting expensive. You are paying a Croatian tanker master $4600 a month inclusive which is quite a lot. An Indian would be about $3500.
>
> (Interview with author, April 1994)

No doubt most owners and managers would prefer stability and continuity, but they have become so accustomed to shopping for crews that they are reluctant to make any substantial long-term investment in labour from any one source. As a managing director of a major German ship management company observed in this context: 'Everybody is frightened of the Philippines, of the world's reliance on the Philippines for seafarers', this comment being offered in tacit explanation for his firm's recent decision to diversify away from complete dependence upon Filipino ratings by replacing them with Sierra Leonese on three specialised tankers carrying hazardous cargoes (interview with author, April 1994). As long as crewing to adequate levels of competence is optional and wages reflect the global distribution of income, shipowners and managers are bound to 'experiment' with any new labour sources making an appearance. If this means optimising the balance of skills and costs by buying different sections of crews from different world regions, thereby assembling multinational crews, then of course they will do so.

Once owners and managers have been into the 'labour bazaar', taken their pick, put it on planes and finally delivered it to ships, what happens next? One answer came from a senior British officer who had written feelingly to his union (NUMAST) of his experience aboard a Liberian-flagged tanker:

> My last ship was under Liberian flag with a Korean crew, none of whom could speak any English, a Filipino 3rd officer with poor English, an Indian 2nd officer with a heavy Indian accent, a Hong Kong Chinese 2nd engineer with very poor English and a Republic of China cadet whose technical training language had been in Chinese and thus could not understand any technical terms. On this ship communications with the crew by any officer was impossible except in sign language. When the 2nd engineer was on watch communication between the bridge and engineroom was not possible and communications on the bridge between helmsman, lookouts and officers was on the most basic terms.
>
> The most worrying aspect was safety. Our fire and lifeboat drills were farcical as we often had situations where not only could none of the crew understand the officers but the officers could not understand the commands they were given nor each other. No instruction could be given in safety procedures and none of the instructional material on board was in all the languages required.
>
> (*The Telegraph* [Journal of NUMAST: National Union of Marine, Aviation, and Shipping Transport Officers] 1990, vol. 23, no. 12)

Evidence of a different kind, but no less suggestive of the possibility of a fragile social order aboard multinationally-crewed ships, was given to the Donaldson Inquiry into the loss of the tanker, *Braer*, on the Shetlands, in January 1993. In its written evidence, the Church of England's Missions to Seamen offered the following abstract of a report from the Avonmouth chaplain of an incident in February 1993:

> I was approached by two Russian engineers, the only foreigners on a Greek-owned vessel, which was otherwise completely manned by Filipinos. During their month-long voyage they had endured mounting hostility from the captain, officers and crew because they were known to be working for less pay than the former Filipino engineers. The Filipinos had realized that they would soon be losing their jobs to cheaper labour.
>
> On my advice the Russians went to the local hospital for a medical report on their injuries (they had been assaulted with chairs and threatened with knives and they feared that if they sailed with the ship their lives would have been in real danger).
>
> In the event they took their medical report to the police who visited the ship, and notwithstanding threats from the captain and the vessel's owner, who said there was no problem, the two Russians

were repatriated. As usual they were threatened with their names being placed on a blacklist.

I encountered a similar situation the following day on a ship where the crew was made up of equal numbers of Filipinos and Bulgarians, but the Bulgarians were paid less. The feeling of hostility on board was very evident.

(Missions to Seamen, 1993, Typescript of evidence submitted to Donaldson 1994)

In contrast, a programme of interviews with seafarers of varying ranks and nationalities conducted in Rotterdam in 1994 had 'getting on well together' as one recurrent theme. A Filipino second engineer said, by way of example, that on a Chinese ship there were only two Filipinos, the rest being Indonesian, 'and they cannot well speak English so I learnt their language, otherwise it was actions and signals. They were a good crew, they are laughing a lot.' Another recurrent theme is that 'getting on well together' is actually a condition qualified by the nationality of other crew members in general or of significant persons in the ship's hierarchy. Filipino officers appear to prefer Japanese senior officers, detest Koreans, like Norwegians and will tolerate Germans and British!

The quality of the experience of everyday shipboard life for officers is critically dependent upon the character, competence and personality of the senior officers. They live next to them in adjacent cabins, they share the same table in the saloon and they are personally supervised by them at work. In no respect, save sleeping, can their company be avoided easily. In these circumstances, the manner and manners of the captain or the chief engineer may be as disruptive, as unifying or as indifferent in a ship crewed by persons of one nationality as in one crewed by several or many nationalities. Ratings (paradoxically, given their place in the ship's hierarchy) are far less visible and supervised; they live and eat separately from the officers and their work frequently takes them to parts of the ship where they are out of sight. When officers join a new ship they want to know about the personal qualities of the master or the chief. Ratings, on joining, want to know about food (quantity and quality), shore leave, regular payment of wages and the availability of overtime. To the extent that the master and chief have powers or discretions in these areas, then ratings will want to know about personalities, but their prime interest is in the ship's condition and its work regime. As a Hungarian able seaman said, 'I look at the machinery. No technology means more work and more overtime' (Rotterdam interview, July 1994).

Such evidence as there is of the shipboard social order on FOC ships suggests that, in respect of the functional framework of everyday life, it does not differ in any significant way from that to be found aboard nationally-flagged ships from the older maritime nations. The functional framework merely allows the ship to arrive and depart because the crew sufficiently observe the elementary rules of living and working together. It provides the necessary, but not the sufficient, conditions for a high level of social cohesiveness and professional competence. 'Functional framework' embraces the form of the ship's hierarchy and nomenclatures of rank and includes the interchangeability of routines of maintenance, the 'calendar' of the day, the social allocations of living and eating spaces, the mechanisms of social distancing between officers and ratings, and crew judgements of what makes a good ship (Aubert and Arner 1958; Schrank 1983; Lane 1986, 1990).

The fact that we can identify elements of a global seafaring culture which enables people to coexist socially in most cases, should not be taken to mean that there are simple but nonetheless working examples of internationalism. It should hardly be news to sociologists that, given a well-articulated and common structure, people of different nationality can easily move from one example of it to another and adjust rapidly. This adjustment is at the level of mundane, everyday social intercourse where reciprocal recognition of a humanity held in common is elementary to life itself.

A functioning normative order merely enables the continuation of mundane existence. It does not follow that it produces high levels of competence and, indeed, it might be argued that it is especially unlikely to do so aboard ships with multinational crews. The British tanker master whose letter was quoted above complained, not of problems of social order, but of impaired professional competence; the Missions to Seamen padre spoke essentially of the fragility of social order and its susceptibility to fracture in the existing conditions of the global labour market; the Rotterdam interviewees spoke of 'getting on', when 'getting by' might have been more accurate.

The deeper meanings which suffuse shared values, expectations and the silent words of gesture and expression upon which social cohesion depends can be found only within a common language group or, though in a more limited way, among a linguistically differentiated group enjoying a long-running and therefore cumulative familiarity. Seafarers of different nationalities, who are discontinuously employed and arbitrarily assembled at the anonymous ordering of distant others into a series of impermament nationality permutations, are most unlikely to generate the level of cohesiveness which is a precondition of high levels of professional competence. Incidents in which the structures of events illustrate this point are a matter of recent record and regular commentary.

ENVIRONMENTAL POLITICS AND IMMINENT RE-REGULATION

The importance of the issue of multinational crews was revealed when 161 passengers and crew died in a fire aboard the *Scandinavian Star*, a Norwegian-owned, Bahamian-flagged ferry running between Norway and Denmark:

> In 1988, while the vessel was being operated as a cruise liner in the Gulf of Mexico, a fire broke out in the engineroom. When the fire was spotted, the Honduran motorman had to use hand signals to raise the alarm because he had no common language with his Filipino watch engineer. The incident was investigated by the US National Transportation Safety Board and its report revealed that the crew came from 27 different countries. The NTSB ruled that language problems between crew members had hindered firefighting efforts and it also blamed inadequate crew training. Two years later, fire again broke out on the ship now being used as a ferry. ... Evidence from crew members, backed up by the subsequent official inquiry report, showed how the same problems highlighted in the original blaze had been crucial factors in the second fire. Most of the mixed nationality crew had been taken on only one week before the disaster and few had the necessary certificates or safety training required for the ship's Scandinavian services. Language problems were, once again, blamed for preventing an effective response to the emergency. The investigators found there had been confusion between the Scandinavian officers and Portuguese and Filipino ratings and that safety notices on board the ships were not in Scandinavian languages.
>
> (*The Telegraph*, 1994, vol. 27, no. 5)

Questions of communication and multinational crewing were also raised in *Safer Ships, Cleaner Seas*, the report of the inquiry into the circumstances of the wreck of the *Braer* (Donaldson 1994: 99–102). Real and apocryphal stories, in abundant circulation among seafarers and insurers and their surveyors, were taken seriously by Lord Donaldson and his fellow assessors:

> Everyday communication is quite different from communication in a crisis. Crews which are capable of communicating with each other and others in everyday dealings may not be capable of the rapid exchanges necessary in a crisis. Everyone tends to panic in his own language; in a crisis there could be a polyglot panic, with crews speaking only in their own languages.
>
> (Donaldson 1994: 100)

Coastal pollution caused by the wreck of large oil tankers and spillages in refinery ports has surely been one of the most important factors in bringing environmental issues into public prominence throughout the industrialised world. If there was little political fall-out from the wreck of the tanker, *Torrey Canyon*, off Land's End in 1969, the *Braer* incident served to consolidate political pressures on the global shipping industry which had previously been prompted by a long string of large and small tanker accidents culminating in the stranding of the *Exxon Valdez* in Alaska in 1989.

As an example of the political potency of environmental issues in the late twentieth century, it would be hard to exaggerate the global impact of the *Exxon Valdez*. The cost to the US government, marine insurers and the Exxon Corporation of the clean-up operations, litigation and compensation is still unknown, but only to the extent of the final number of billions of dollars. This one incident, coming at a time of increasing alarm at the environmental costs of industrialisation, has had a powerful impact on shipowners and ship managers who are being increasingly squeezed by the worldwide growth of what is known as Port State Control.

There is an extensive body of international conventions ostensibly regulating ships' operations which are promulgated by the International Maritime Organisation, a UN agency without enforcing powers. Among the conventions are those covering marine pollution, safety of life at sea, and the training and certification of seafarers. However, there is no single body responsible for enforcement, and with flag of convenience states accounting for more than half the world's fleet, only nationally-flagged fleets (and not all of those, either) have the administrative capacity to require compliance. The role of enforcement has increasingly been assumed either by individual states or alliances of states. In the USA the United States Coastguard has in 1995 taken to boarding selected ships in territorial waters and refusing entry to US ports if ship and crew are found seriously deficient. In Europe the Port State Control is an inter-governmental organisation of surveyors and inspectors. These officials (usually experienced ex-merchant ships' officers) routinely board ships in port and have the power to detain those with substandard structures and equipment, or improperly or inadequately licensed officers. Inspection reports are filed on a networked database and are therefore quickly available to the officials of all contributing countries.

The European Port State Control organisation was formed in 1982 in the aftermath of the wreck of the *Amoco Cadiz*, which left a quarter million tonnes of crude oil on the Breton coast in 1978. A low key organisation until the *Exxon Valdez* ran aground in Alaska, the European organisation was allowed to become more active and has been adopted as the model for other regions of the world. The European Port State Control ship reporting system is not EU-based and the effective area of operation includes Canada and all Baltic states, and extends southwards in the Atlantic to Morocco.

Port State Control regimes are widely and sometimes enthusiastically supported by the various representative international associations of the shipping industry. A good example is INTERTANKO. This association of independent tanker owners accounts for about 70 per cent of the world's tanker tonnage and has been prominent in its support for Port State Control and, indeed, any other measure capable of enforcing compliance with international conventions. Tanker owners with newer and better maintained ships have been facing a depressed market for many years, and have been obliged to continuously find ways of cutting costs to stay competitive with the marginal operators who have run old and poorly maintained ships and been careless of their crews and international conventions. The established tanker owner has had two sources of resentment: first, that a very large and high quality investment in a young ship has been obliged to compete with a small and low quality investment in an old ship, and second, that their professional standards regarding ship maintenance and crew competence have had to be lowered in an attempt to stay in business. Among this global elite in the shipping industry, the view is now firmly established that re-regulation is in their own best interests and that environmental politics might be a force for progress. In these circumstances the question of crew competence can only continue to loom larger.

Constant cost-cutting since the early 1980s has produced a substantial shortfall in officer training in the countries best equipped to do it; an acute shortage of skilled and experienced senior officers is imminent. The managing director of one British ship management firm thought more environmental disasters would be needed before the critical lesson of crew competence was learned:

> The industry is leading itself down a path which is almost disastrous and I believe there will have to be more cataclysmic accidents, *Torrey Canyons*, *Exxon Valdezes*. The only thing that is going to get people off their backsides is something like that where the world will say that enough is enough. Then the money will be found for training high quality crews but unfortunately we will have let it go too far because the kind of experience we are talking about takes ten to fifteen years to put in place.

(Interview with the author, April 1994)

The speaker is right; nevertheless, in this most global of all industries a retreat, a rediscovery and a return to the nation state are underway. Environmental politics, conducted separately if inter-connectedly in a number of nation states, have obliged the industry to appreciate that while an unregulated global market can undoubtedly produce crews, some crews (and probably a growing number) are of doubtful competence. Other crews, through no fault of their own, are incompetent and a danger to safe navigation and the environment.

104

We have seen in this chapter how global forces will reach down and determine the life chances and experiences of the 'residents' of an industry's smallest and remotest institution. We have also seen how the effects of that reach might run back up the causal spiral and rearrange a seemingly monolithic socio-economic order. This last point is important. The debate on globalisation is marked by a pronounced and morbid fatalism, which holds that the forces governing it are so powerful as to be beyond the reach of anyone. It is possible that this paralysing pessimism derives from a grand theorising mode which delights in the bold brush strokes of epochal trends. A leavening of detailed case studies, combining examinations of macro, meso and micro structures and institutions, might reveal a less 'historically determined' process carrying within it many possibilities which remain to be realised: or not.

NOTES

1 The self-governing British dependency of Bermuda, prompted and guided by British shipowners, launched its own registry in the late 1950s when the largest user was P&O. Although never large, the registry has been a useful source of revenue. In 1982–3 the registry received $525,000 in revenue of which $415,000 was profit (*Financial Times*, 9 September 1983). Commenting on the Vanuatu registry, a *Financial Times* correspondent said: 'In a new country with only 120,000 people spread over a large number of islands, with no income or corporation tax – and the possibility that collecting it would be more expensive than the yield – and with a budget propped up by foreign aid, any extra source of revenue is extremely useful' (30 September 1981).

2 Lack of space has led to the role of trade unionism being set aside in this chapter, despite the fact that the International Transport Workers' Federation (ITF) does actually play a very important countervailing role in the labour market. The ITF engages in annual negotiations at the ILO, where a minimum wage is set, it negotiates directly with some shipowners and ship managers and is otherwise very influential. A separate essay on the ITF is being prepared for publication elsewhere.

3 A German ship management firm set up a training school in Tuvalu in the early 1980s to secure a dedicated source of low cost labour for its ships. This move, unsurprisingly, was welcomed in the islands. Through the export of labour, the government of this miniature and fragmented republic of atolls was able to secure its only source of foreign currency earnings. It is not recorded whether this has produced a positive balance of trade with Germany.

REFERENCES

Aubert, V. and Arner, O. (1958) 'On the social structure of the ship', *Acta Sociologica* 3: 200–19.

Barnet, R. J. and Muller, R. E. (1975) *Global Reach*, London: Jonathon Cape.

Carlisle, R. (1981) *Sovereignty for Sale*, Annapolis, MD: Naval Institute Press.

Chase-Dunn, C. (1989) *Global Formation*, Oxford: Basil Blackwell.

Donaldson, Lord (1994) *Safer Ships, Cleaner Seas*, Report of Lord Donaldson's Inquiry into the Prevention of Pollution from Merchant Ships, London.

Froebel, F., Heinrichs, J. and Kreye, O. (1980) *The New International Division of Labour*, Cambridge: Cambridge University Press.

Harlaftis, A. (1988) 'The Greek shipowners, the economy and the state, 1958–1974', D.Phil thesis, Oxford.

Henderson, J. (1989) *The Globalization of High Technology Production*, London: Routledge.

Hood, N. and Young, S. (1979) *The Economics of Multinational Enterprise*, London: Longman.

Hymer, S. (1975) 'The multinational corporation and the law of uneven development', in H. Radice (ed.) *International Firms and Modern Imperialism*, Harmondsworth: Penguin.

ILO (1950) *Conditions in Ships Flying the Panama Flag*, Geneva: ILO Publications.

ILO (1990) *Recruitment and Placement of Asian Seafarers*, Geneva: ILO Publications.

Kindleberger, C.P. (1970) *The International Corporation*, Cambridge, MA: MIT Press.

Lane, T. (1986) *Grey Dawn Breaking: British Merchant Seafarers in the Late Twentieth Century*, Manchester.

—— (1990) *The Merchant Seamen's War*, Manchester: Manchester University Press.

Lauriat, G. (1977) 'New flag for Peking fleet', *Far Eastern Economic Review* 95: 111–12.

Metaxas, B. (1985) *Flags of Convenience*, Aldershot: Gower.

Schrank, R. (ed.) (1983) *Industrial Democracy at Sea*, Cambridge, MA: MIT Press.

Spruyt, J., (1990) *Ship Management*, London: Lloyds of London Press.

Sturmey, S. G. (1962) *British Shipping and World Competition*, London: Athlone Press.

UNCTAD (1978) *Review of Maritime Transport*, New York: UNCTAD.

Vernon, R. (1971) *Sovereignty at Bay*, New York: Basic Books.

Wallerstein, I. (1979) *The Capitalist World Economy*, Cambridge: Cambridge University Press.

Yannopoulos, G.N. (1988) 'The economics of flagging out', *Journal of Transport Economics and Policy*, 22: 197.

Part II

THE RECOMPOSITION OF SKILLS AND EMPLOYMENT

6

THE SOCIAL CONSTITUTION OF LABOUR MARKETS

Why skills cannot be commodities

Bryn Jones

Labour markets are different. Expansion of the sphere of market exchanges is still the political and economic orthodoxy. Yet economists do concede that manifold personal, cultural, social and political factors complicate the buying and selling of labour services. Most obviously, working capacity, or labour power, or skills, are inseparable from their owner, the individual employee. *Pace* Marxism it is one commodity which is difficult for its owner to alienate. Yet, even in labour market processes where price-competitive exchanges seem more appropriate, extrinsic factors govern transactions. This chapter will attempt to show how and why skills cannot be traded solely as commodities. This is not so much because they are exceptions to market processes, but because market exchanges in general take place through sets of distinctive social institutions.

Neo-classical economics' price-clearing competitive market is empirically rare in the employment of skills. Skills are inseparable not only from individuals, but also from a complex of expectations, needs and rights attached to persons. The most complete of price competitive markets have been found to be moulded by cultural factors (Hodgson 1988: 184–5). These and other forms of dependence suggest that markets operate through general politico-cultural arrangements. Markets are recurrent exchanges of items of ostensibly equivalent values. Regularity of exchanges is possible only through politico-cultural arrangements which limit the price competitive openness of the neo-classical model. Such critical points have been known for some years. What is not currently available is a conceptual framework which offers a systematic alternative to the competitive market paradigm of neo-classical economics. The aim of this chapter is to suggest the outline for such an alternative theoretical stance by identifying a framework of 'social constitutions' which both makes markets possible and differentiates various kinds of markets.

This idea of a social constitution will be developed by drawing upon some recent theories of the social aspects of market exchanges and previous attempts to define alternatives to price-competitive models of labour markets. The gist of my argument is that the succession of alternative models – such as segmented labour markets, internal labour markets, occupational markets and so on – are incomplete and often contradictory because they retain the neo-classical paradigm as their yardstick. For closer examination of the latter suggests *either* that the price-competitive market is unsubstantiable, *or* that it exists only as a dependent variable of a more fundamental set of politico-cultural institutions of exchange. At best the price competitive market is a subsidiary derivative in a broader class of markets defined on the basis of social rather than economic conditions. Alternative taxonomies of market types which do not subscribe to the neo-classical paradigm need to begin in full recognition of the fact that a market is a social and not an exclusively economic instititution.

The historical expansion attributed to markets is, in one sense, a societal solution to problems of social order (Granovetter 1985). Market relationships maintain an appearance of apolitical action while resolving differences of power by contracts and transactions. In reality they are a submerged sphere of informal politics. However, recent developments in the field of socio-economics contradict the long-standing sociological tradition of market relationships as amoral, instrumental actions. Like other forms of political life markets are based on normative institutions which constrain and legitimise the exercise of power (Jones 1994). Norms, entitlements, and regulations in markets are more diffuse and less explicit than political constitutions. Market participants operate largely on the basis of uncodified social constitutions.

One important element of the labour market as socially constituted indicates the relevance of this approach. To participate in a market the individual needs to gain *membership* of it. Involvement in a labour market is not unlike that of a polity. One can be part of a polity without being a citizen. Enfranchisement may not be accessible to aliens or other groups, e.g. women, in many states. Consequently studies which use individual views to investigate labour markets may not be accurate, if those individuals rarely participate in labour market transactions. Studies based on the views of workers in long-term employment (see Blackburn and Mann 1979) are not likely to be an accurate guide to the social character of labour markets – because their direct participation in labour market transactions is rare. The same, paradoxically, might be said for long-term unemployed persons, who are clearly attached to a labour market, but not necessarily active 'members' of it; this point will be amplified in the following section. By contrast those likely to participate regularly in the exchange of jobs can be expected to be practising members of a labour market, as will those whose occupational groups have recognised involvement in a labour market constitution.

The second section of this chapter will illustrate this thesis with examples from two types of British labour market: the spread of self-employment in the UK construction industry, and the trend towards graduate qualification amongst British engineers in manufacturing. These are critical cases for the theory of social constitutions for they are inadequately described by both the pure economic model of the market and the alternative categories of internal, external, and segmented markets.

WHAT ARE TRUE MARKETS?

In the neo-classical description of the labour market exchanges are regulated by the price mechanism and the quantities of economic resource available to the participants. Thus the level of wages and the numbers of jobs offered by employers are reciprocally determined, and also influenced, by the scarcity or otherwise of the types of labour skills sought, and the employers' product and production costs and sales revenues. Amongst other key criticisms of this model (see Craig et al. 1985:113) is the important point that social rules may govern the supply of labour or employment offers. Even more important is the observation that local labour markets – affecting the majority of workers – exist only as a set of social practices characterised by social networks, socially-constructed identities and accepted forms of social interaction (Harris et al. 1985). Remove these 'non-economic' elements and the monetised acts of exchange, which define the neo-classical model, ccase to exist.

However, a minority of economists have recognised for some time that price-clearing market mechanisms do not function in most employment situations. The influence of collective norms in setting 'fair wage' thresholds in many jobs has been recognised (Solow 1990). More radically, Akerlof (1984) has proposed that market-clearing wage rates will not func tion in many forms of employment, because actual jobs involve exchanges closer to 'gifts' than pecuniary equivalences – the sociologically well-known phenomena of effort bargaining, 'making-out', and indulgency (Akerlof 1984; Baldamus 1961; Burawoy 1979: ch. 4; Gouldner 1964). These points are disconcerting for a full-blown neo-classical conception. Yet they are not destructive of it. They relate primarily to unionised workplaces and to the secondary stage of labour exchange – that is the formal and informal agreements about the details, pace and execution of work tasks. In the more impersonal initial stage of recruitment and hiring it is possible to claim that the core of price-competitive market forces still functions.

Ostensibly more radical challenges to the market view of labour exchanges comes from the market segmentation theories. In the Internal Labour Market (ILM) formula of Doeringer and Piore (1971), ILMs arise because firms deliberately choose internal recruitment and re-allocation rather than hiring from outside 'on the market', and because skills are firm-specific and easier to develop from existing employees. Doeringer and Piore were prepared to retain the concept of price competitive labour markets as a yardstick for these internal processes, and also retained the view that the latter were still a sub-type of the former. However, as Marsden (1986) notes, since wages are set by administrative politics, and possibly by national regulatory processes, it is difficult to regard ILMs as governed only by supply and demand for firm-specific skills (Marsden 1986: 152–62). An additional objection would be that the firm's capacity to create its own supply of labour skills for particular jobs means that wages do not need to function as market prices to attract these.

The secondary stage of the labour exchange, and the ILM phenomenon, both show that the firm encapsulates the market while retaining some of its basic elements. Related aspects of recruitment such as the 'extended internal labour market' (Manwaring 1988), in which existing employees act as informal selection and recruitment agents, confirm the predominant influence of the enterprise, beyond the internal bureaucracy in the ILM model (see also de Gaudemar 1987). However, the scope for the open, competitive, neo-classical market will be diminished even further, as skills – and hence recruitment – and reward processes become more firm-specific (Green and Ashton 1992: 292; Millward *et al.* 1992: 351–5). This empirical complication is compounded by the theoretical ambiguity of the internal–external assumption inherent in Clark Kerr's (1954) seminal statement of the phenomenon. Kerr's original designation of internal markets was wider than the bureaucracy of job transfers within firms, at the heart of the Doeringer/Piore concept. Kerr intended the ILM category to include any 'institutional' arrangement other than the neo-classical open-competitive model. Externality consisted of outsiders bidding to get into this or other employment processes (Kerr 1954: 101–2).

Analysis of labour markets as segmented in other ways than a simple internal–external dichotomy have tended to fade into broader questions about the organisation and control of the labour process on the one hand, and theories of macro-political and societal regulation on the other (Marsden 1986: 164–75). Segmentation protagonists who have stuck with the original perspective have gone on to argue that the neo-classical price-competitive model was never generally applicable since labour markets are inevitably fragmented, and separated and conditioned by differing social and political factors such as gender (Craig *et al.* 1985). However, this fragmentation and social conditioning would not seem to rule out the pre-dominance of price-regulating competition *within* the different segments. Marsden, on the other hand, manages to step more completely out of the neo-classical model by arguing that there is little in the workings of individual labour markets to suggest that the supply and demand are regulated by wages-as-prices. By focusing on the issue of skill formation, he suggests, instead, that something like ILMs are the norm because of the burdens of training. For the alternative, *occupational labour markets* to operate, there has to be some co-ordinated provision of training in general skills, so that workers may move freely between employers. Because either all employers or the state have to take responsibility for this training, says Marsden, the resultant supply of skills represents a kind of 'public good'. Marsden ends by concluding that 'the scope for competitive pressures within the labour market is greatly reduced' and 'product markets' ability to bring the relative pay of a particular occupation into line . . . will be greatly blunted' (Marsden 1986: 231–2). In times of economic instability occupational labour markets are likely to erode as employers fall back on internal arrangements by which they can control their own skill requirements.

Thus occupational labour markets come closest to the neo-classical paradigm in the sense that they operate with free movement of qualified workers between firms, potentially on the basis of price (wage) competition. Yet the initial supply, through training and apprenticeships, is not called forth through market mechanisms. Moreover the usual social barriers to entry identified by segmentation theory will apply. It was indeed such arrangements for skilled occupations that led Clark Kerr to analogise the resulting 'balkan' complexes as 'private governments' of exclusive occupational 'citizens' – in contrast to the supposedly 'open' labour markets operating through price/wage competition (Kerr 1954).

This trend of analysis has progressively eroded the applicability of the economists' notion of a market to the field of employment. The ultimate question is whether there is any remaining utility in the concept of a market? If, most of the time, only a minority of employment processes correspond to the neo-classical concept of a market, should the term 'market' be abandoned? There are arguments for doing just that. Maurice and his colleagues have proposed that the contingency-laden, imperfectly competitive, labour market that survives the preceding criticisms is best replaced. In its stead they propose 'labour domains' which are given coherence not by the immediate exchange relationships but by the unity of various social and societal institutions which reproduce particular sets of employment relations (Maurice *et al.* 1986). This idea may or may not be productive. It does not appear to have been elaborated, either in the subsequent work of the Aix group or more generally. An alternative approach is to re-examine markets as social institutions, i.e. before neo-classicism simplified them into complexes of exchange transactions.

Although neo-classical economics often parades 'the market' as its central idea it has no systematic concept of what a market is. Indeed the level of abstraction at which most economists work means that the notion of a pricing system functions equally well (Arrow 1974: 15–29). When economists attempt serious definitions of the market they invariably have to incorporate social institutions of contract, property rights, information transmission, and trust, as central elements (Hodgson 1988: 173–9; Etzioni 1988). Indeed the eponymous place markets of the Middle Ages were distinctive for the detailed civic and social regulation which sought to maximise public access and limit exclusive dealings (Braudel 1982). Ironically the expansion of commercial exchanges which ushered in modern capitalism was primarily based on attempts to evade these markets (Thompson 1971). Economics' abstraction of the mediation of supply and demand by price enters the language as a definition of 'market' only during this transition at the end of the seventeenth century (OED).

During this period food markets were subject to intense political conflict over the maintenance of social regulations. Riot, civic interventions and popular take-overs of sales and distribution were common and quasi-legitimate occurrences. Significantly, at the beginning of the nineteenth century, the focus of popular agitation switched to the expanding industrial labour markets (Thompson 1971). The outcome of these struggles, of course, has been the various forms of trade union action to regulate the supply, reward and retention of labour skills. In its essentials union regulation takes two forms. Either it sets general standards for wages, recruitment, and terms of employment – acting as a representative agency. Alternatively, or additionally, it provides resources for individual trade unionists to seek and secure work; as in the hiring halls of some US unions, the 'tramping' facilities of nineteenth-century British unions (Piore and Sabel 1984: 116, 122; Steiger 1993; Hobsbawm 1964).

When, in the mass manufacturing period, union bargaining rights within workplaces became generalised, another channel of recruitment and regulation extended outwards from the firm into the 'external' labour market, to such an extent that 50 per cent of new recruits would be friends or relatives of existing employees in unionised firms (Windolf and Wood 1988: 130). It is hard to imagine a more decisive contradiction of the classical sociological dichotomy between community and association. More importantly, perhaps, union and collectively-bargained rules linked the primary and secondary stages of the exchange of labour. The length of the hiring period was no longer for fixed periods determined by the employers' needs (Webb and Webb 1897: 431–2); where not codified by statute it became negotiable by unions. The content of tasks could be more tightly specified on hiring because it could be continuously monitored and policed by union representatives, or, in the USA, blended into the 'job ladder' and work rules provisions of ILMs.

Historically then, markets for commodities have been organised on the basis of social and political regulation of access, unilateralism, and opportunity. The development of labour markets has followed similar lines. To the market economist, however, the absorption of labour market processes by the evolution of these collective social controls – or indeed other institutions such as professional associations (Marsden 1986: 251)

– might be dismissed as unnecessary distortions of the elemental functions of markets (see Hanson and Mather 1988). Thus an examination of labour markets where collective controls are absent or negligible, helps to confirm whether markets are more likely to function because price clearing competition is not so impeded. Two labour market areas lacking union or professional regulation are the utilisation of self-employed workers in the construction industry and the employment of graduate engineers in large manufacturing firms. These will be examined to test out this possibility, while the latter case also allows consideration of existing, alternative institutional theories. Before presenting this evidence, however, it is necessary to clarify the concept of social constitutions in labour markets.

LABOUR MARKET PROCESSES: THE ROLE OF SOCIAL CONSTITUTIONS

Studying changing work practices in small and medium-sized German machinery firms, Hildebrand adopted the term 'social constitution' to describe the framework of norms and powers which underlay the formal systems of managerial authority and collective bargaining in these plants (Hildebrand 1990). The idea can be extended to market exchanges in general to express the combination of moral standards and acceptable powers – the residual political framework – which regulate transactions, market entry and participants' freedom of action. Closer elaboration of the metaphor of constitution allows us to posit a variety of market frameworks. These range from a virtual 'anarchy' as in unrestricted competition, through autocratic and paternalist constitutions – corresponding to 'monopolies' in the language of economics – to virtually democratic regimes – in which individual participants have recognised rights of protection – and acountability of the agencies and bodies who regulate and enforce standards (Jones 1994).

The significance of this conception to current debates is that it provides a means of differentiating markets. The problem with neo-classical typologies is that they are mainly conceptualised as so many departures from an assumed essence: the open price-competitive paragon. Even if these other types of closed, monopolistic, oligopolistic, etc., markets were exhaustive they would not, by themselves, describe the vital social forces which lead to these states of imperfect competition. Identifying the institutional elements, or social constitutions, can show that even if there are price competitive markets, which approximate the neo-classical ideal, they are just one special strand amongst a broader range of 'market' forms.

If markets are regarded as political arenas in which power is maintained or redistributed through the exchange of commodities then there must be common recognition of eligibility to participate, powers of regulation, and standards of action. In other words: who can enter the market, who or what arbitrates amongst its participants, and what is the permissible range within which the buyers and sellers can transact. Thus the normative framework, or social constitution, would have three central features: entitlement, authority, and rights.

Entitlement consists of the qualities which define whether an individual is eligible to participate in the domain of labour transactions, and for some or all of attendant rights and responsibilities. Authority is the legitimate designation of powers of regulation over the various elements of the exchange relationships, including not just legal authority but that conferred by custom and practice to the roles of organisations and individuals. Rights, which are as much tacit as legal, define the range of exchange actions deemed permissible and the general scope of rewards and obligations.

These abstract components of a social constitution cover the stages in labour market processes as conventionally defined. These in turn can be summarised as:

- accreditation
- signalling/canvassing
- screening/identification/inclusion
- bargaining/price fixing
- secondary bargaining.

Accreditation suggests formal certification, but it could be a social or even a physical confirmation that the potential worker has preferred qualities: training, strength, language, gender, skin colour, means of production, and so on. Some individuals may lack the bundle of qualities appropriate for a particular category of employment, but still attempt to get acceptance of their general eligibility. However, most will not try to enter the labour market without these.

Accreditation occurs through the completion of apprenticeships, training and educational courses, or simply by recognition of adult status in certain ethnic and occupational communities. It applies to the graduates of engineering courses, as much as to the school-leaving sons of miners in traditional mining districts; to the immigrant who joins the migrant workers' network in an industrial locality, as much as to the mother whose resulting contacts with other parents initiates employment as a child-minder. Accreditation is the acquisition of membership of a labour market.

'Signalling' is the economists' term for employers' notification of job vacancies and requirements, and would-be employees' communication of their availability and qualities to employers or their agents. In everyday practices it will take the form of advertisement and canvassing. Signalling of availability of jobs often takes place within broader multi-functional institutions: kinship or friendship groups, local union bodies; or, in ILMs, the workplace itself. Most research suggests that these 'non-market' channels are used more than apparently more dedicated arrangements such as newspaper advertisements, Job Centres and so on (Blackburn and Mann 1979: 121; Mackay *et al.* 1971: 365; Windolf and Wood 1988). The reasons for this social grounding are three-fold.

First, there is a virtual vacuum between the potential employer and the potential employee. Both tend to make use of their own organisational and social contacts to inform of availability because mere interest in exchange has no corresponding social media for initiating exchange. Second, the notification of a job, or of availability, is often not detached from other relational commitments. The employer may be offering a job, or jobs, in return for some previous favour or contribution by a third party, for example, concessions in wage bargaining by a trade union; or because the intermediary previously supplied recruits. Third, the intermediary can be trusted to corroborate the signals that the employer/employee transmits about the quality of the skills or the job on offer (Brooks and Singh 1979; Manwaring 1988; Granovetter 1974: 12–14).

Screening, identification or inclusion are the processes by which the employee or employer gains recognition that they satisfy the general requirements of the other party. Typical practices here include interviewing, CV examination, inspection of premises, working practices and so on. The terms *screening, identification and inclusion* are used here to refer not only to the technical selection devices posited by labour economists and personnel specialists, but also to the relational processes by which employers 'adopt' the potential recruit, or – more rarely – the job seekers satisfy themselves of their likely rapport with the potential workplace (see Blackburn and Mann 1979: 132–3). As Stephen Wood has argued, this a complex practice. From the employers' side, corroboration of recruits' technical skills is interwoven with identification of their social skills (Wood 1988: 17–25). Empirically there is likely to be a gamut of decisions made by employers; ranging from the exclusively practical – has the recruit the strength, dexterity and experience to execute well defined tasks? – to the predominantly social – capacity for team work, respecting authority and responsiveness to customers.

For a broad core of jobs, however, employers' judgements are highly likely to start from social criteria. Does the prospective employee fit within their definition of the appropriate social category: a 'craftsman', a pliant female, a youth who is a willing learner, and so on? These ascribed identities are important rules of thumb because formal measures of practical skills – certificates, CVs, previous employers – cannot guarantee that the accredited skills will indeed be practised to the required level. Once again supplementation by referrals from existing members of the network/ firm, or interdependent agencies such as union hiring halls can help to corroborate identification (Granovetter 1974; Steiger 1993). One of the world's first Flexible Manufacturing Systems – computer-integrated machining complexes – was staffed initially by cumulative recruitment of machinists from one small batch-machining workshop (Jones 1988: 105–6).

Bargaining/price fixing may be detailed or perfunctory. The wages and other terms of employment may not be negotiable. They may be fixed by prior decisions, collective bargaining or rigid customs. Alternatively there may be some discretion, especially over assignment to a particular point on a salary scale, times of starting or finishing, fringe benefits, etc. From the employees' side they may be able to offer one type of task or responsibility rather than another.

In economists' models of labour markets bargaining or price fixing is the core element, as these transactions fuse the interests of buyers and sellers. Sociological analyses, on the other hand, tend to dismiss them as naive or unrealisable, because institutional forces mean wages cannot be varied to secure individuals' employment (Granovetter 1974: 38–9; Blackburn and Mann 1979: 118–22). However, in the hiring of self-employed workers considerable negotiation, haggling even, may occur. Even in standardised occupational employment there may be some scope for bargaining over non-wage rewards in certain kinds of technical, professional or managerial grades. Fringe benefits may be variable; as will promises of promotion or further training opportunities. In the mid-1980s national or sectoral systems of collective bargaining were the biggest influence on most UK wage scales and terms of employment. They may still be collectively set but now the business itself, or company bargaining unit, is more likely to be the regulator (Millward *et al.* 1992: 351–5).

Secondary bargaining refers to any subsequent negotiations over the secondary stage of the exchange of labour; over pace of work, modification of the set of tasks, changes in hours or working conditions. Such negotiation after employment is perhaps the most important element of the wage–labour transaction. Yet it is strictly not part of the labour market process at all. Whether individually or collectively the effort for a particular job will be frequently varied due to new or unforeseen circumstances. Because new contracts and recruitments are often impractical the employer or managers will negotiate formally or informally with the existing employees. Thus there are a mass of submerged transactions which neo-classical economics rarely investigates (Fallon and Verry 1988: 2). Yet these either substitute for labour market transactions or are connected to them via social links – industrial relations tensions, quits, institutionalised co-operation with workers and their families. Moreover, these often evade commodity relations by utilising reciprocal and gift exchanges (Akerloff 1984; Solow 1990), all of which require subscription to customary or communal norms and codes.

Most of these analytical terms, though sociologically pertinent (see Fevre 1992), are compatible with neo-classical analysis. They are introduced here because each illustrates the involvement of social institutions.[1] They also show that basic labour market processes are not just supplemented by social institutions. At the key points they occur as institutionalised social processes rather than price–commodity transactions. At a higher analytical level these institutions can be seen to cohere into types of social constitutions. Recruitment on purely technical criteria is overlaid with considerations of social eligibility. Such identities are seen as conferring minimal obligations of fair treatment. The exercise of sheer bargaining and ownership powers is constrained by trust relations. Thus in addition to the legal framework covering employment rights there are also normative codes and standards, shared amongst the parties 'in the market', which designate membership – a tacit 'citizenship', rights and authority.

Membership or entitlement to participate in a labour market is conferred by occupational qualifications – often from institutions external to the market (Granovetter 1974: 124), colleges, professional bodies, unions – and broader social identities – ethnicity, gender, kinship and industrial community. Such membership will also entail tacit rights of eligibility and equity. These rights include expectations that other members or agencies will accept, signal or canvass ('put in a word for') job seekers; employers will accept eligibility in preference to other social categories; normative standards of 'fair wages', 'equal treatment', 'Buggin's Turn' will be applied to members. Authority, and not just the exercise of power, is needed.

Labour market members will, perforce, accept the authority of governmental agencies such as UK Job Centres, but trade union branches, or even individuals who act as 'brokers' for ethnic and other social groups (Brooks and Singh 1979), will play legitimised roles. Not least participants will have to accept the authority of the larger firms which is obviously based on their economic power, but whose exercise is modified by countervailing norms and powers in many circumstances. Moreover, the power of multiple employers may be constrained by the greater influence of occupational groups or collectives such as union branches (Steiger 1993).

It is not possible to say whether such socially constituted labour markets predominate in given economies without special empirical studies. Clearly there are situations, such as casual employment, where the social constitution is weak, or undeveloped. Casual work corresponds more closely to the neo-classical paradigm. Yet even here commodity processes may be tempered by social norms (Stymeist 1979). Moreover it can be argued that the power imbalance in favour of the employer simply represents a kind of autocratic social constitution (Jones 1994).

TWO TEST CASES:
SELF-EMPLOYED CONSTRUCTION WORKERS AND
GRADUATE ENGINEERS

Construction work is a significant test case of the existence of social constitutions because of the shift from employment to the use of self-

119

employed since the early 1970s. This change has made this labour market seem largely unregulated; 'freed' from social constraints and governed primarily by cost and price criteria. In the language of labour market segmentation analysis it has taken on the character of a casualised 'external labour market'. Similarly, from the point of view of neo-classical economics, erosion of restrictions on the buying and selling of labour in construction has established a price competitive market. Closer analysis will show that transactions in this labour market are structured by the operation of a social constitution. The employment of graduate engineers conforms even less to a price-clearing, purely economic model. However, closer inspection shows that the alternative categories of labour market segmentation analysis are also inapplicable to this British phenomenon. A social constitution approach provides a more complete explanation of this apparently anomalous case. In both instances the processes of accreditation, signalling, screening, and bargaining are governed by social-constitutional rights, entitlements, and designations of authority.

Neo-liberal, and Conservative de-regulationary, labour market philosophies seem to be vindicated by the growth of self-employment in construction. Although this trend began long before the accession of the Conservative government in 1979 (Winch 1993) its spread has greatly increased employers' freedom over the financial costs of employment and – inasmuch as it has superseded union regulation – over the disposition of labour on site (Evans and Lewis 1989; Evans 1990: 244). A scenario of self-employed construction workers apparently now competing with each other, outside collective bargaining rules, for one-off cost-sensitive contracts, resembles very much the price-clearing, open labour market of the economics textbook. De-unionisation and contracts of self-employment have been advocated as means of achieving such 'free' labour markets (Hanson and Mather 1988).

Prima facie the recruitment of engineers represents a quite different case of skill acquisition by employers. Rather than 'grow their own' engineering skills, through craft and technical apprenticeships, manufacturing employers have recruited increasing numbers of young graduates from college and university degree courses. The significance of this labour market configuration is that it seems to represent a break from the traditional craft-centred model of occupational controls and social networks of the 'extended internal labour market' type. Yet it does not constitute the kind of professional regulation of the market for engineering skill which appears typical of other highly-qualified occupations, and of engineers in other countries.

Marsden's (1986) assessment of the manufacturing employment of engineers in Britain exposes the weaknesses of the internal-social versus external-economic pigeon-holing of labour markets. He establishes that 'occupational' labour markets are the strongest empirical instance of the external-economic form of market. On the other hand, he believes that graduate-level engineers in British industry do not fall into this category. They have the necessary technical skills, Marsden argues, but their labour market lacks the sufficient condition of institutional regulation by professional organisation. However, in his typology any failure of institutional regulation leads not to the revival of price-competitive markets for engineering skills. For free transfer of skills between enterprises depends on collective provision and co-ordination to make them 'public goods'. Marsden infers that, without this element, all occupational markets are prone to break-down and regression towards the opposite pole of firm-specific internal labour markets (Marsden 1986: 212–15, 231). In the labour market for graduate engineers skills are transferable, but they are also both publicly-supplied – through state higher education – and controlled by firms. The clarity of Marsden's scrutiny only exposes the limitations of the categories of segmented labour market analysis. If graduate engineers cannot be members of both ILMs and occupational markets, is a different conception of labour markets more coherent?

Self-employment in construction: casualisation, competitive contracting or constitutional norms?

In several countries firms' search for cost-savings coupled with technical complexity and the fixed duration of projects, have made construction work prone to labour market instability. A common phenomenon is the replacement of regular employees by some form of temporary hire; even if such workers' contracts may continue for some years with the same employer (Moore 1981; Villa 1981). In the UK these workers are termed labour-only sub-contractors (LOSCs). Commentators typically register this trend as the 'casualisation' of employment in the industry (Moore 1981; Austrin 1980; Evans 1990: 244). The implication is that firms' treatment of workers as self-employed takes them out of the statutory and social protection of employee status and national agreements with trade unions. In some interpretations the strengthening of this shift is seen as increasing the potential threat of relative disadvantage for the self-employed (Evans and Lewis 1989: 80, 85), a shift implicit, but not always acknowledged, in models of flexible employment (Winch 1993; Evans and Lewis 1989: 86; Atkinson 1985; Bruhnes 1989). Thus the more 'casualised' construction becomes, in terms of variation in job opportunities and payments, the greater the relevance of the neo-classical, competitive labour market.

Self-employed construction workers move between sites, taking jobs either as individuals, or as informal gangs. It is assumed that the main contractor, or sub-contracting firm responsible for a particular phase or operation of the construction, will hire self-employed workers with the necessary skills at a competitive price. In practice many LOSCs are hired at 'day rates' – calculable in relation to the national and locally agreed rates paid to employed workers – or at composites of day and piece rates (Evans and Lewis 1989: 75). An irony of the decline of official training provision is that workers with full skills training are a diminishing resource, so in times of high demand they have the upper hand in negotiating job prices with contracting-out firms. Self-employed workers can also increase their earnings by completing jobs quickly and moving on to the next contract, or in some instances by working on two or more contracts simultaneously.

Another complication to a simple 'casualisation' picture of self-employed construction workers is that many appear to have chosen, rather than been forced into, self-employed status in preference to a standard employment relationship (Austrin 1980; Moore 1981). Many LOSCs may also be able to supplement their earnings by working directly on other jobs for the final customer – e.g. house repairs and improvements – rather than for a construction firm which contracts out parts of the project to them. Such mobility is often tied into informal associations amongst the self-employed, either between groups of workers or with one or more sub-contracting firms (Bresnen *et al.* 1985). These semi-permanent relationships belie the connotations of insecurity and atomised dependence often associated with the term 'casual' labour. New research on different grades of construction workers in the south and south west of England reveals a more complex picture which problematises both a 'segmentation' perspective on their labour market and, yet again, the functionality of a neo-classical, price-clearing market for a particular skill (Nisbet 1995).

In Nisbet's study, as Austrin (1980) might have predicted, a number of groundworkers, electricians and surveyors were found to have entered self-employment in search of the opportunity for superior financial rewards. A greater number, however, became self-employed *involuntarily*. Yet they subsequently came to prefer self-employment. Their reasons ranged from levels of job satisfaction, and flexibility in time management, to a greater sense of independence than direct employment. Majorities preferred self-employment because it gave opportunities to exercise skills, boost incomes, and exploit taxation provisions. It should be stressed that these perceived advantages were not identical to the notorious practice of evading tax and national insurance contributions which has brought 'lump labour' in the construction sector into disrepute.

Contrary to views (Austrin 1980) that LOSCs have only a different contractual status for unchanged work roles, a majority of Nisbet's self-interviewees claimed that self-employment meant more independence over times and execution of work. This is a partial confirmation that the secondary stage of the exchange of labour, effort bargaining and the like, is more equal when an employer negotiates the terms of a job with a self-employed worker. There is a variation in the exercise of *authority*.

Even more significant was the strength of the *entitlement to participate* in contracting. In the majority view self-employment was not necessarily more disruptive of continuous earnings than being in employment. Both the self-employed and employed workers in the sample thought that it was easier for the former category to get new jobs. Majorities of the self-employed also thought the opportunity to exploit the method of payment was an advantage but this was not always associated primarily with taxation arrangements.

Virtually all of the self-employed respondents had begun their construction careers as employed workers. What emerged from the interviews was the importance of being members of informal but well-defined networks of contractors and other self-employed workers. Information and contacts about jobs were shared between LOSCs. Whether contacts in these networks were strong or occasional, they were the most important method of securing fresh or repeat jobs (see also Bresnen *et al.* 1985; Marsh *et al.* 1981). Significantly the most dissatisfied of the self-employed were those new to that status who were outside networks. As a result these individuals were dependent either on agencies, or on offering their skills unsolicited by 'cold-calling' prospective customer firms – a particular disadvantage during recession.

Contrary to implicit and explicit segmentation theories, or assumptions of the 'flexible firm' model, the sub-contracting of formerly 'in-house' jobs to self-employed workers was not universally favoured by the larger contractors. It was seen as a necessary evil which gave the self-employed considerable autonomy in their dealings with the firms. The benefits of 'financial' or 'numerical' flexibility were offset by managerial difficulties, particularly in times of labour shortage.[2] At such times the self-employed appear to gain the greatest autonomy in their dealings with firms. Yet firms also admitted to recurrent use of the same members of a self-employed network; they justified this practice, *inter alia*, because of the shortages of reliable skills accompanying the decline of regular employment and related apprenticeships.

However, the presence of tacit 'rights' is also perceptible. Employers keep regular lists of 'their' labour-only sub-contractors. In contrast to flexibility theories at least one employer had retained 'his' labour-only sub-contractors during the latest recession, through a mixture of collective loyalties and anticipation of reciprocity during the upturn. Personal recommendation or previous experience of self-employed workers was a better guarantee that they could apply the required skills than was open bidding, advertisements, interviewing, and so on, of unknown candidates. The labour market for self-employed construction workers is not, therefore, directly explicable as 'casualisation' – in ways that corroborate either the segmentation perspectives, or the price-competitive markets models. Most of the self-employed workers in this sector preferred their status because it allows a different set of social and economic relations with their peers and with employers. As independent operators the taxation and contractual arrangements give some skilled LOSCs a semi-autonomous authority and informal status as 'economic citizens' – equal or superior to their employed counterparts. They become eligible for work because the network of co-workers and employers recognises ('accredits') them as skilled workers, and sometimes as independent bargainers.

This snap-shot of the social constitution of the construction labour markct for some skilled workers conforms to Winch's interpretation that workplace labour relations regulation in the industry became 'hollow' in the post-war period. In other words, the decline of site-level union activity and employers' and unions' adherence to centralised and national created a regulatory vacuum in the detail of labour relationships (Winch 1993). From this vacuum a set of semi-spontaneous, informal social relationships has developed in which some sub-contracting workers, at least, derive economic benefits from norms of membership, reliability, skilled auton-omy, and sometimes even mutual obligation. Thus the absence or decline of the institutionalised collective controls of trade unionism do not mean that there is an absence of social regulation. Trade unionism may or may not confer superior material advantages on construction workers, but a specific social constitution provides a broader basis for the resulting 'de-regulated' labour market functions than price mechanisms and casual hiring practices.

The proto-professional market for engineers

The labour market for higher-level engineers provides us with a sharp contrast to that for self-employed construction workers, as another test of the importance of a social constitution. It seems more insulated from the cost-price mechanisms of the formally unregulated market for self-employed construction workers. Yet, as we shall see, it does not confer on graduate engineers a greater influence over their employers. The difference is in the nature of the social constitution, which also explains the heterogenous character of this labour market. It is neither a series of self-contained ILMs, nor a commercially-regulated external labour market.

Increasingly, in the UK, large manufacturing firms have been recruiting young graduates of higher education courses, rather than promoting or training ex-apprentices trained to craft and technician levels. Graduates of mechanical or electrical/electronic engineering courses accept employ-ment on the expectation that the firm will offer them a career; or they expect at least the further training that will provide career opportunities in other fields of expertise, or with other firms. It has become generally accepted that limited pay levels, and shortages of senior engineering posts, will require some of the more ambitious engineers to switch to managerial occupations at some point.

This pattern is not easy to fit into existing quasi-economic typologies of labour markets. It is difficult, as the earlier summary of Marsden (1986) suggests, to classify it as an 'occupational labour market' because of the weak role played by the professional associations. Many employers do not encourage membership of the relevant engineering institute, such as the Institute of Electrical Engineers or the Institute of Mechanical Engineers. These also lack the regulative powers to insist upon such a qualification being a condition of employment. Young engineers look to their employer to provide further training and promotion channels for senior posts, a factor which is consistent with the ILM model.

However, loyalty to firms is weaker than would be expected of an ILM. In times of economic expansion large numbers of engineers use the external labour market to get higher rewards, or more promising positions, in other firms or sectors (Berthoud and Smith 1980; Parsons 1985; Connor 1988; Jones et al. 1993). The Bath University study of Technicians and Engineers' Skills and Training (TEST) found that an ILM model is also problematic for these workers because the 'job ladders' in their areas of expertise are frequently short – one or two grades of practising engineer, a supervisory post, and then senior engineer – with numerous internal competitors. Transfer to a management stream may be difficult and, even with additional training, the engineer will be several steps behind the business school graduate. With engineers' employment, unlike the labour market for self-employed construction workers, employers and employees have fewer shared expectations on the scope of rewards.

The problems stem from the non-commodity character of the relevant skills. Remember that a regulated 'occupational' market, as defined by Marsden, depends upon non-commercial provision of skills, as a 'public good' which may then be traded between buyers and sellers. The initial expertise, that graduate engineers sell to their first employer, derives from the public higher education process. This expertise is a 'public good'. For the skills are applicable to a range of employers and neither employer nor employee have individually met the full cost of their acquisition through the education system. Why, then, are there skills which are public goods but no 'occupational labour market'? Weak professional regulation, as diagnosed by Marsden, is one factor. Another limitation is that the general skills acquired from an electrical, electronics or mechanical engineering degree are normally insufficiently specific, or practical, for the jobs to which the firm allocates its new recruits. Further training, or at least learning on-the-job, is almost always necessary. Because firms also include further training as a career resource, when 'selling' their qualities to prospective graduate employees, training within the firm becomes a contested issue.

Graduate engineers see additional training as a right which will enable them to advance within the engineering or related fields, if necessary by leaving for another employer. The employer, on the other hand, has an interest in providing training only up to the level necessary for the competence in the existing job, or for transfer to a new post within the organisation. In large organisations, it has been found that continuing education and training (CET) represents a contested entitlement between employer and employee. The employees' interest is in the continuous acquisition of competence outside their immediate job – with a view to movement to another firm or department. The employers – and some-times the immediate departments – may have a contrary interest in rationing CET to avoid 'poaching' or quitting (Jones and Causer 1990: 14–16; Jones *et al.* 1993).

A more sophisticated ILM strategy by some firms aims at systematic CET which will groom the most able graduates for senior level positions in both engineering and general management fields. Unfortunately, this approach can, by definition, reward only a small minority. It may result in even tighter rationing for the majority and resentment – and thus reduced job commitment – amongst those who are not included (Jones *et al.* 1993).

One of the peculiarities of the engineers' labour market is therefore that accreditation does not correspond completely with the award of a higher education degree. Full accreditation, in the sense of eligibility to compete on the external labour market, occurs only after two or three years' experience and/or additional training; this point coincides with acceptability for membership of one of the professional institutions. The element of discretion, in the employers' control over the post-degree training and experience phase, thus gives them the informal **authority** over full labour market eligibility.

The initial stage of recruitment has consisted mainly of a semi-open market based on the 'Milk Round' whereby employees and prospective graduate employees meet in interviews on university premises. The signalling, canvassing and screening which takes place at this stage approximates to a price-governed market. However, it is embedded in, and subject to, the institutional procedures of higher education. The TEST study also found that some employers took only graduates of particularly favoured colleges and universities. Others were becoming dissatisfied with the quasi mass-market method of recruitment and were adopting more direct methods of recruitment. There was renewed interest in higher-level training for specific technicians. Moreover, the employment offers, in reality, are sold on the non-wage package of CET and career opportunity. These also provide only interim membership of the labour market. Their primary function is, therefore, largely not to allocate on the basis of wage/price and skills offered. Bargaining and price fixing is largely limited by standardised salary scales and degree qualifications. The employees' main opportunities for bargaining, in the sense of an economic market, arise when subsequent movement to different positions within the firm becomes feasible later on.

Thus in the social constitution of the labour market for graduate engineers' *entitlement* for the engineer after graduation and initial employment is limited. Entitlement through CET is at best contested, and largely controlled by the *authority* which is predominantly ceded to the employer. Partially compensating for this paternalistic regime are the tacit *rights* of career opportunity. Employees are increasingly able to express their grievances in terms of insufficient career development opportunities. Firms offer these as rewards for the early years of confinement to relatively routine tasks, some of which could be done by technicians. In manual work the immediate effort bargain is often the main issue in the secondary exchange of labour. For junior engineers, on the other hand, it is the consummation of the tacit right to CET and career development.

CONCLUSION

Markets, especially labour markets, do not function because of price-regulated individual transactions by multiple participants. Social institutions are needed which will allow such transactions to take place. Moreover, the relevant decisions are frequently taken on the basis of normative criteria embedded in the social institutions, and not on the basis of relative prices and costs. The normative framework which gives particular markets their coherence and their functionality, and tempers the outright exercise of economic power, is best viewed as a form of micro-political regulation, as a social constitution.

When Clark Kerr first tried to classify labour markets outside of a neo-classical economic paradigm, it is surely not accidental that he chose quasi-political metaphors: the 'guild' and 'manorial' labour markets, unions' sovereignty over job territories of 'citizens' of 'private governments' (Kerr 1954). However, Kerr – and the subsequent segmentation tradition – retained the open, competitive model as the benchmark from which to conceptualise these micro-politically regulated forms. Building on the insights of Marsden, and the socio-economics paradigm of economic action, the idea of a social constitution scheme entails a more radical agenda.

In this approach all labour markets are arenas of political action. What differentiates them is the nature of the social conventions by which labour skills are accredited, signalled, defined, and bargained. Where the social constitution is weak, power may be exercised autocratically. The truly casual labour markets, where minimal skills are hired and discharged with minimal rights at the discretion of the employer, is one such example. Although even here there are usually some norms of conduct involved in the exchange. In these types of social constitutions transactions approach

127

the neo-classical ideal, but not because of the symbiosis of wages and individual utilities.

Price-competitive market processes are not an essential standard by which 'internal' or segmented markets should be measured. Rather there is a range of market constitutions which are differentiated according to features such as entitlement – as distinct from Kerr's spatial metaphor of 'ports of entry' – authority and rights. The question for labour markets analysis is not how far they depart from neo-classicism's price-competitive open markets. Rather the problems centre on clarifying the social processes which give rise to varying degrees of openness and competition. What social processes and identities confer entitlement to participate in markets? What authority regulates transactions and on what normative basis? What rights are perceived and how much agreement is there on their extent?

When neo-classical economists call for deregulation of labour markets and the dilution of trade union controls there is an underlying assumption that pristine, price-clearing dynamics are being stifled by these social distortions. Labour markets where regulation is minimal and trade unionism is excluded should, on these assumptions, be governed primarily by the dynamics of prices and costs. Instead, in the case of junior engineers and self-employed construction workers, it appears that immanent social processes are decisive.

Even without union controls, hiring in the latter depends upon membership of social networks. Employers do not recruit on the basis of price alone. Nor do they discharge workers in order to seek out lower cost substitutes. Payments are complex composites of output and time rates – customs, national standards and incentives. Nisbet's (1995) sample of groundworkers, electricians and quantity surveyors suggests that rewards, stability of employment and prospects are believed to be as good, if not better for the self-employed. Reviving Kerr's imagery the social constitution of such labour market areas could be described as a limited form of 'yeoman democracy', although in a much more restricted sense than Piore and Sabel's societal proposal of this term (Piore and Sabel 1984: 303–6). In the absence of unions, the definition and enforcement of rules rests, ultimately, with the residual authority of state agencies. In many cases, the firm and its management exercise a more immediate and often arbitrary authority, but in construction informal intermediate agencies exist in the overlapping networks of contractors, sub-contractors, gangs and individual labour-only sub-contractors. In this sphere authority and rights are largely tacit.[3] The tacit rights cover information and access to job opportunities, target rates of pay, expectations of preferment, or even continuity, in re-hiring, as well as norms of independence in the execution of work tasks. Graduate engineers, on the other hand, encounter a more paternalistic framework dominated by the authority of large firms. Initial membership of this labour market often remains provisional because of the firms' control of the further training necessary to complete the engineer's occupational qualifications. Employees, however, retain tacit rights in this sphere because of shared normative assumptions about the eligibility for careers.

The preceding formulations are tentative and incomplete. Empirical study which tests out the ideas over a wider range of employment situations is indispensable. Nevertheless the theory offers a more comprehensive framework than is currently available, for overcoming some of the limitations of the long tradition of work in the institutionalist and segmentation traditions. It also re-aligns older sociological difficulties with the 'a-social' sphere of market transactions to more recent re-discoveries of the 'moral dimension' of economic action (Etzioni 1988). Above all it provides a method of *delimiting* as well as criticising the plausibility of neo-classical market prescriptions. If 'market' solutions continue to dominate policy-making, the key issue for the future should not be the extension or limitation of markets, because of their inherent efficiency or inequity. The more important question is which social constitutions can and should make different kinds of market possible?

ACKNOWLEDGEMENTS

I would like to thank Peter Nisbet for his advice on the sections dealing with the construction industry. Any errors of interpretation and formulation are, of course, my responsibility. The data on the recruitment and use of graduate engineers derive from a joint ESRC–SERC project: 'A Cross-Sectoral Investigation of the Training and Utilisation of Engineers, 1991–1993'. This project was undertaken in collaboration with Dr B. Bolton, Professor A. Bramley and Dr P. J. Scott.

NOTES

1 A similar but separate sequence of processes applies, of course, to the diminution and termination of employment: working to rule, short-time working, temporary lay-offs, redundancies and quits.
2 'However, not all employers make widespread use of the sub-contracting system. Some prefer to have a full time labour force, even though this will entail greater administrative costs. The advantages were aptly summed up by an owner-controller. . . . "If we don't employ our own staff, there's no way we can stick to schedules. With sub-contractors we would be at some one else's beck and call. . . . if we want something done, we can manipulate our men in different ways towards that end . . . we have the control over where they go, what they do, when they do it, and how they do it"' (Scase and Goffee 1980: 61–2).
3 In their sample of small businesses, largely drawn from the construction sector, Scase and Goffee found some employers who preferred a quasi-egalitarian, consultative relationship, rather than a directive one, with those who worked for them (Scase and Goffee 1980: 58–61).

REFERENCES

Akerlof, G. A. (1984) *An Economic Theorist's Book of Tales*, Cambridge: Cambridge University Press.

Arrow, K. (1974) *The Limits of Organization*, New York: W. W. Norton.

Atkinson, J. (1985) *Flexibility, Uncertainty and Manpower Management*, Report 89, Brighton: Institute of Manpower Studies.

Austrin, T. (1980) 'The "Lump" in the construction industry', in T. Nichols (ed.) *Capital and Labour*, London: Fontana.

Baldamus, W. (1961) *Efficiency and Effort*, London: Tavistock.

Berthoud, R. and Smith, D. J. (1980) *The Education, Training and Careers of Professional Engineers*, London: HMSO.

Blackburn, R. M. and Mann, M. (1979) *The Working Class in the Labour Market*, London: Macmillan.

Braudel, F. (1982) *Civilisation and Capitalism 15th–18th Century, vol. II, The Wheels of Commerce*, London: Collins.

Bresnen, M., Wray, K., Bryman, A., Beardsworth, A. D., Ford, J. R. and Keil, E. T. (1985) 'The formalisation of recruitment in the construction industry: formalisation or re-casualisation?', *Sociology* 19(1): 108–24.

Brooks, D. and Singh, K. (1979) 'Pivots and presents: Asian brokers in British foundries', in S. Wallman (ed.) *Ethnicity at Work*, London: Macmillan.

Bruhnes, B. (1989) 'Labour flexibility in enterprises: a comparison of four European countries', in OECD, *Labour Market Flexibility: Trends in Enterprises*, Paris: OECD.

Burawoy, M. (1979) *Manufacturing Consent*, Chicago, IL: University of Chicago Press.

Connor, H. (1988) *Transfer of Engineering Skills between Sectors*, Report 154, Brighton: Institute of Manpower Studies.

Craig, C., Rubery, J., Tarling, R. and Wilkinson, F. (1985) 'Economic, social and political factors in the operation of the labour market', in B. Roberts *et al.* (eds) *New Approaches to Economic Life*, Manchester: Manchester University Press.

Doeringer, P. B. and Piore, M. J. (1971) *Internal Labour Markets and Manpower Analysis*, Lexington, MA: D. C. Heath.

Etzioni, A. (1988) *The Moral Dimension: Towards a New Economics*, New York: Free Press/Macmillan.

Evans, S. (1990) 'Free labour markets and economic performance: evidence from the construction industry', *Work, Employment and Society* 4(2): 239–52.

Evans, S. and Lewis, R. (1989) 'Destructuring and deregulation in the construction industry', in S. Tailby and C. Whitston (eds) *Manufacturing Change*, Oxford: Basil Blackwell.

Fallon, P. and Verry, D. (1988) *The Economics of Labour Markets*, Hemel Hempstead: Philip Allan.

Fevre, R. (1992) *The Sociology of Labour Markets*, Hemel Hempstead: Harvester Wheatsheaf.

de Gaudemar, J-P. (1987) 'Mobilisation networks and strategies in the labour market', in R. Tarling (ed.) *Flexibility in Labour Markets*, London: Academic.

Gouldner, A. (1964) *Patterns of Industrial Bureaucracy*, New York: Free Press.

Granovetter, M. (1974) *Getting a Job: A Study of Contacts and Careers*, Cambridge, MA: Harvard University Press.

Granovetter, M. (1985) 'Economic action and social structure: the problem of embeddedness', *American Journal of Sociology* 91(3): 481–510.

Green, F. and Ashton, D. (1992) 'Skill shortage and skill deficiency: a critique', *Work, Employment and Society* 6(2): 287–301.

Hanson, C. G. and Mather, G. (1988) *Striking Out Strikes*, London: Institute of Economic Affairs.

Harris, C. C., Lee, R. M. and Morris, L. D. (1985) 'Redundancy in steel: labour market behaviour, local social networks and domestic organisation', in B. Roberts *et al.* (eds) *New Approaches to Economic Life*, Manchester: Manchester University Press.

Hildebrand, E. (1990) 'Social constitution of a company: an under-rated impact on the introduction and design of new production technologies' (Berlin: Wissenschaftzentrum), paper to the XIIth World Congress of Sociology, Madrid, 9–13 July.

Hirst, P. Q. and Zeitlin, J. (eds) (1988) *Reversing Industrial Decline? Industrial Structure and Policy in Britain and her Competitors*; Oxford: Berg.

Hobsbawm, E. (1964) *Labouring Men: Studies in the History of Labour*, London: Weidenfeld & Nicolson.

Hodgson, G. (1988) *Economics and Institutions*, Cambridge: Polity.

Jones, B. (1988) 'Flexible automation and factory politics: the UK in comparative perspective', in P. Q. Hirst and J. Zeitlin (eds) *Reversing Industrial Decline?*, Oxford: Berg.

Jones, B. (1994) *The Social Constitution of Markets: An Outline*, SCAN Working Paper, School of Social Sciences, Bath University.

Jones, B., Scott, P. J., Bolton, B. and Bramley, A. (1993) 'Human resource elite or technical labourers? Professional engineers in transnational businesses', *Human Resource Management Journal* 4(1): 34–46.

Jones, C. L. and Causer, G. A. (1990) 'Human resource management policies and the retention of technical specialists in the electronics industry', paper presented to the 'Employment Relations in the Enterprise Culture' Conference at Cardiff Business School Employment Research Unit, Southampton, University of Southampton New Technology Research Group.

Kerr, C. (1954) 'The Balkanisation of labour markets', in E. W. Bakke, P. M. Hauser, G. Palmer, C. A. Myers, D. Yoder and C. Kerr, *Labor Mobility and Economic Opportunity*, Cambridge, MA: MIT Press.

Mackay, D. I., Boddy, D., Brack, J., Dick, J. A. and Jones, N. (1971) *Labour Markets Under Different Employment Conditions*, London: Allen & Unwin.

Manwaring, T. (1988) 'The extended internal labour market', in P. Windolf and S. Wood (eds) *Recruitment and Selection in the Labour Market*, Aldershot: Avebury.

Marsden, D. (1986) *The End of Economic Man? Custom and Competition in Labour Markets*, Brighton: Wheatsheaf.

Marsh, A., Heady, P. and Matheson, J. (1981) *Labour Mobility in The Construction Industry*, London: HMSO.

Maurice, M., Sellier, F. and Sylvestre, J-J. (1986) *The Social Foundations of Industrial Power*, Cambridge, MA: MIT Press.

Millward, N., Stevens, M., Smart, D. and Hawes, W. R. (1992) *Workplace Industrial Relations in Transition*, Aldershot: Dartmouth.

Moore, R. (1981) 'Aspects of segmentation in the United Kingdom building industry labour market', in F. Wilkinson (ed.) *The Dynamics of Labour Market Segmentation*, London: Academic.

Nichols, T. (ed.) (1980) *Capital and Labour*, London: Fontana.

Nisbet, P. (1995) 'Dualism, flexibility, and self-employment in the UK construction industry', PhD thesis, School of Social Sciences, University of Bath.

OED (1968) *Shorter Oxford English Dictionary*, London: Oxford University Press.

Parsons, D. (1985) *Graduate Recruitment and Retention*, Brighton: Institute of Manpower Studies.

Piore, M. and Sabel, C. (1984) *The Second Industrial Divide: Possibilities for Prosperity*, New York: Basic Books.

Roberts, B., Finnegan, R. and Gallie, D. (eds) (1985) *New Approaches to Economic Life*, Manchester: Manchester University Press.

Scase, R. and Goffee, R. (1980) *The Real World of the Small Business Owner*, London: Croom Helm.

Solow, R. (1990) *The Labour Market as a Social Institution*, Oxford: Basil Blackwell.

Steiger, T. L. (1993) 'Construction skill and skill construction', *Work, Employment and Society* 7(4): 535–60.

Stymeist, D. (1979) 'Controlling the job: levels of organisation in casual work', in S. Wallman (ed.) *Ethnicity at Work*, London: Macmillan.

Tailby, S. and Whitston, C. (eds) (1989) *Manufacturing Change*, Oxford: Basil Blackwell.

Tarling, R. (ed.) (1987) *Flexibility in Labour Markets*, London: Academic.

Thompson, E. P. (1971) 'The moral economy of the English crowd in the eighteenth century', *Past and Present* 50: 76–136.

Villa, P. (1981) 'Labour market segmentation and the construction industry in Italy', in F. Wilkinson (ed.) *The Dynamics of Labour Market Segmentation*, London: Academic.

Wallman, S. (ed.) (1979) *Ethnicity at Work*, London: Macmillan.

Webb, B. and Webb, S. (1897) *Industrial Democracy*, vol. I, London: Longmans, Green.

Wilkinson, F. (ed.) (1981) *The Dynamics of Labour Market Segmentation*, London: Academic.

Winch, G. M. (1993) 'Self-employment and industrial relations: the example of construction', mimeo, London: Bartlett Graduate School, University College.

Windolf, P. and Wood, S. (eds) (1988) *Recruitment and Selection in the Labour Market*, Aldershot: Avebury.

Wood, S. (1988) 'Personnel management and recruitment', in P. Windolf and S. Wood (eds) *Recruitment and Selection in the Labour Market*, Aldershot: Avebury.

7

SKILL, GENDER AND THE QUALITY OF EMPLOYMENT

Duncan Gallie

How have the processes of economic restructuring in Britain since the 1980s affected the skill levels and the experience of the work task of those in employment? In contrast to the pessimistic expectations of labour process theory, the most comprehensive studies on skill trends in the mid-1980s (Daniel 1987; Gallie 1991; Penn *et al.* 1994) concluded that by far the strongest general tendency was for a marked rise in the skill requirements of jobs. However, there were grounds for thinking that the later 1980s might have witnessed a rather different pattern. Whereas in the early 1980s, employers were restructuring the work process in the context of still powerful workplace trade unionism, there was a marked retreat of the unions' organisational power in the second half of the decade (Millward *et al.* 1992; Millward 1994). At the same time, the public sector which had provided particularly strong institutional safeguards for employees was being whittled down by successive waves of privatisation. Employers in the later 1980s, then, had much greater freedom of action to implement the types of policies that they preferred. If there was an inner logic to capitalist relations of production that encouraged employers to deskill, then it could be expected to manifest itself much more clearly in the second half of the decade than in the first.

Even if there had not been a shift in employer skill policies towards the workforce in general, it was possible that there had been a move towards strategies that involved an increased differentiation or polarisation of employee experiences. It was a period of growing public discussion of the notion of the flexible firm, with its distinction between a core of relatively skilled and secure employees and a periphery of low-skilled workers that could be easily dispensed with in times of recession (Atkinson 1985, 1986; Atkinson and Meager 1986). One sector of the supposed flexible workforce – that of female part-timers – had been expanding rapidly through the 1980s (Hakim 1987). Research in the mid-1980s had confirmed that part-time employees were, indeed, particularly disadvantaged in skill terms, although the evidence with respect to job insecurity was rather less

133

convincing (Gallie 1991; Gallie and White 1994). With their particularly low levels of unionisation and weak employment protection, it was conceivable that employers had moved increasingly in the later 1980s to a core/periphery model of employment, with female part-timers experiencing a sharp deterioration in their relative position.

Given the pace of change, it is clearly important to re-assess the underlying trends with respect to skill. At the same time, earlier research had cast little light on what skill change, whether negative or positive, implied for the everday experience of work. The general theoretical assumption was that there were very close links between skill level, the discretion that employees could exercise in the work task and the intrinsic quality of work. Thus those who advocated a tendency towards the long-term upskilling of the workforce also suggested that employers would increasingly decentralise decision-making to employees and that many of the traditional disadvantages of manual work would disappear (Kerr *et al.* 1960; Blauner 1964). On the other hand, the theorists of deskilling underlined the way in which employees would lose control over the work process and be subjected to forms of work that would be increasingly routine, monotonous and meaningless (Braverman 1974; Crompton and Jones 1984). While some results from social–psychological studies supported the view that skill levels were a major determinant of other job characteristics (for an overview, see Warr 1987), these were mainly based on relatively small-scale studies.

Evidence from the early 1990s not only puts us in a position to study the development of skill trends from the mid-1980s, but also provides a far better basis for assessing their implications for the experience of work. In 1992 a nationally representative survey – the Employment in Britain survey – was carried out, providing a sample of 3,477 employees aged 20 to 60 (Gallie and White 1993). The survey was designed to include a number of indicators that would allow for comparison with two surveys that had been carried out in the mid-1980s. The first of these was the Class in Modern Britain survey (see Marshall *et al.* 1988). This was a national survey, carried out in 1984, with a total sample of 1,770. The original survey included a wider age range (16–64 for men; 16–59 for women), as well as non-active people. To ensure comparability, our analyses are based on the 945 employed people aged 20 to 60. The second survey used was that of the Social Change and Economic Life Initiative (SCELI) in 1986 (Gallie 1991). This involved a sample of 6,111 people drawn from six localities – Aberdeen, Coventry, Kirkcaldy, Northampton, Rochdale and Swindon. The analyses presented here are again based on the subsample of 3,877 employees aged 20 to 60. Although the SCELI surveys were based on localities rather than a representative national sample, the class composition of the aggregate sample turns out to be virtually identical to national estimates for 1986.

We begin by examining the general pattern of change in skill, taking a number of different measures, and its implications for the quality of work experience. We shall then turn to examine gender differences in skill experiences and the extent to which these can be related to part-time work. Finally, we shall consider the argument that employers' response to the spread of computer technologies may be an important factor underlying patterns of skill change.

THE RISING DEMAND FOR SKILLS AND QUALIFICATIONS

The general trend from the mid-1980s to the early 1990s was towards an expansion of higher level jobs, in particular those in management and the professions. It could be argued, however, that this may give a misleading picture of real skill change. Shifts in the occupational structure might reflect in good part changes in the use of titles for describing jobs. Further, it is difficult to evaluate the significance of a growth of higher level occupational positions without knowing about the trends in skills *within* occupational categories. It might be the case that jobs in the expanding occupational classes were at the same time undergoing a process of deskilling, resulting in little change in the overall distribution of skills.

An evaluation of the different theories of skill change is made more complex by the fact that there is little consensus about the way in which skill should be assessed and, indeed, different perspectives tend to base their arguments upon rather different conceptions of skill (Gallie 1991; Spenner 1990; Vallas 1990; Attewell 1990). Arguments about upskilling have been linked to the view that there has been a long-term shift in the nature of skill, particularly in the manual occupations. The nature of technical change has led to the replacement of traditional craft skills by new forms of conceptual and decision-making skills that primarily require much higher levels of general education. In this respect, the most important measure of skill change is change in the level of educational qualifications that are required to carry out a job. Theorists of deskilling, on the other hand, have continued to view skill primarily in 'craft' terms and have tended to take as an indicator of skill development the duration of the vocational training that people have received.

The approach adopted here has been to take multiple indicators of skill development. We begin by examining the qualifications required for jobs. We then consider trends in the frequency and duration of training and on-the-job experience. Finally, we turn to people's own perceptions of whether or not skills have increased since the late 1980s, leaving them free to define skill in the way that is most relevant to them.

135

Qualifications required, training and on-the-job experience

Our measure of the qualifications required for jobs focuses on employers' demands with respect to new recruits. We asked 'If they were applying today, what qualifications, if any, would someone need to get the type of job you have now?' The emphasis on current requirements rather than on personal qualifications was designed to take account of the fact that people's own qualifications might have been acquired many years ago, when the skill requirements of the work were quite different. One advantage of the question is that it can be directly compared with survey results for 1986, drawn from the Social Change and Economic Life Initiative's comparative study of local labour markets.

There was a clear increase over the period in the overall level of qualifications required for jobs. Between 1986 and 1992, jobs requiring no or low level qualifications declined (Figure 7.1), whereas those requiring higher level qualifications increased. The proportion of jobs where no qualifications were required was 6 percentage points lower in 1992, whereas jobs requiring A Level or more had increased by the same amount.

A very similar pattern emerges with respect to training and on-the-job experience (Figure 7.1). Whereas, in 1986, 52 per cent of employees had received no training for the type of work that they were doing, by 1992 this was the case for only 42 per cent. The requirement for on-the-job experience was measured with a question asking how long it had taken after the employee first started the type of work to do the job well. In 1986, 27 per cent had said that it had required less than a month, whereas by 1992 this was the case for only 22 per cent.

This pattern of change in skill levels over time can be seen within each occupational class, although it was more marked for some classes than for others. The change in qualification requirements was particularly strong among lower non-manual employees. Whereas, in 1986, 25 per cent of lower non-manual employees reported that their job required A Levels or a higher qualification, by 1992 this was the case for 35 per cent. The increase in training was also particularly clear among lower non-manual employees, together with technical and supervisory employees. In contrast, the increase in the proportion needing more than a month's on-the-job experience to be able to do the work well was greatest among semi- and non-skilled manual workers.

The experience of changing skill demands

This increase in the skill demands of work is confirmed by people's own accounts of changes in the skills required by their jobs. A majority of employees (63 per cent) reported that the level of skill they used in their job had increased over the previous five years (Table 7.1). In contrast, only 9 per cent said that the skills they used at work had decreased.

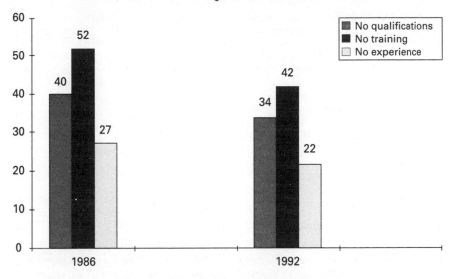

Figure 7.1 Changes in qualifications, training and on-the-job experience
requirements 1986–92

A majority of employees at all job levels experienced an increase in their skills, with the exception of semi- and non-skilled manual workers. The increase was particularly marked among professional and managerial workers (74 per cent), technicians and supervisors (73 per cent) and lower non-manual workers (70 per cent). But it was also the case that 64 per cent of skilled manual workers thought that the skills involved in their work had increased. Moreover, even semi- and non-skilled manual workers were much more likely to have experienced an increase than a decrease in their skills (45 per cent compared with 15 per cent). These changes in skill level were regarded by most people as substantial. Of those that had experienced an increase in the skills they used at work, 85 per cent said that they had increased either a great deal or quite a lot.

How far did such upskilling represent a change in job requirements? Skills may have increased because of changes in the demands of the job or because, with time, people have learned to do their jobs better. While both factors were important, it was changes in the demands of the job that were more commonly cited. Whereas 84 per cent said that their skills had increased because the job required a higher level of skill than before, 64 per cent said they had increased because they had learned to do the same job better.

The view that the experience of upskilling reflects important changes in the content of jobs is reinforced when changes over time are examined (Table 7.1). Compared to the mid-1980s, the process of upskilling appears to have extended to a substantially wider sector of the workforce. Survey data for 1986 also showed a general tendency for skills to have increased at

Table 7.1 Skill change in the job in previous five years
(percentage experiencing an increase in skill)

	1986	1992
Professional/managerial	67	74
Lower non-manual	55	70
Technician/supervisory	56	73
Skilled manual	50	64
Semi- and non-skilled manual	33	45
All employees	52	63

all job levels. But the overall proportion that experienced an increase in their skills has gone up from 52 per cent in 1986 to 63 per cent in 1992. This increase had been particularly sharp among technicians and supervisors (+17 percentage points), lower non-manual workers (+15 points) and skilled manual workers (+14 points). The proportion that had experienced a decrease in their skills was unchanged at 9 per cent.

While there is good reason to think that reported changes in skill levels reflect to a considerable degree changes in the requirements of jobs, this could still be accounted for in rather different ways. Since respondents had been asked to compare their current work with what they were doing five years before, skill levels might have risen either because a person had been upwardly mobile into a higher level job or because the existing job had been restructured in a way that increased its skill content. The apparent skill increase within social classes might then be artefactual, reflecting primarily upward mobility.

A number of analyses has been carried out to assess the extent to which changes in skill levels reflect such mobility processes rather than changes occurring within specific jobs. These focus on those categories which had seen little or no mobility, by using the detailed work history data that were collected to compare the jobs that people were in at the time of interview with their jobs five years earlier. The striking feature of the results, however, is that, even among those who had experienced little or no job mobility, a majority had still experienced an increase in their skills. Overall, 62 per cent of those who were in the same type of occupation as five years earlier and 56 per cent of those in exactly the same job said that their skills had increased, while the proportions that had experienced deskilling were only 5 per cent and 4 per cent respectively.

The overall picture is a clear one. The dominant trend was towards an increase of skills. This was the case not only for those who had been upwardly mobile, but also for those who had remained in the same job over the five years. This strongly suggests that a major factor behind the rise in skill levels was the restructuring of existing work tasks.

SKILL CHANGE AND THE QUALITY OF THE WORK TASK

The growth of task discretion

Writers who have emphasised the trend towards rising skill levels have also tended to argue that this will be accompanied by a significant process of decentralisation of responsibility in work (Blauner 1964; Littek and Heisig 1991; De Tersac 1992). Whereas traditional forms of detailed specification of duties were compatible with the relatively simple tasks associated with a high developed division of labour, they became, it was suggested, altogether inappropriate with the emergence of more complex tasks requiring more highly skilled personnel. Increasingly, the nature of the work involves anticipating difficulties, and handling unexpected problems in conditions of environmental uncertainty. The detailed regulation of tasks is inherently unsuitable for guiding decisions in situations of uncertainty; rather decision-making power has to be confided to the people closest to the task.

Three approaches have been adopted to assess the argument of increased devolution of task discretion in work. To begin with, an index of task discretion was constructed using a number of items that had been shown to scale well and that formed a common factor.[1] The items were: 'I have a lot of say over what happens in my job', 'My job allows me to take part in making decisions that affect my work', 'How much influence do you personally have on deciding what tasks you have to do?' and 'How much influence do you personally have in deciding how you are to do the task?'

There is strong support for the view that greater job complexity is accompanied by higher levels of task discretion. The index of task discretion varies from 0.21 among those who have increased their skills to –0.29 among those who have seen no change and to –0.55 among those whose skills decreased over the period. This was not simply a reflection of the fact that skill increases were more marked in higher occupational classes. There was a strong relationship between skill change and task discretion *within* each occupational class. Nor could the association be explained away in terms of some association between age and the responsibility given to employees. An increase in skill was related to higher levels of task discretion within each age category. Overall, it seems likely that the increase in skill levels was integrally linked to the increase in responsibility in the job. As tasks become more complex, employers are increasingly obliged to rely on the judgement of individual employees.

A second approach was to ask people directly whether or not the responsibility involved in their job had increased, decreased or stayed much the same over the previous five years. A substantial majority of employees (65 per cent) had experienced an increase in responsibility, while only 26 per cent reported that the responsibility involved in the work had stayed much the same and 8 per cent that it had decreased. There were considerable variations by class (Table 7.2). Increased responsibility in the job had been most marked among professional and managerial and among technical/supervisory employees, where it was the case for three-quarters of employees. It was least common among semi- and unskilled manual workers, but, even among these, 50 per cent reported that they had more responsibility than before and only 11 per cent felt that their responsibility had been reduced.

Since increasing responsibility is also likely to be affected by life-cycle factors, it is again important to compare with a similar indicator at an earlier period of time. Data are available for 1986 from the Social Change and Economic Life Initiative. As can be seen in Table 7.2, the tendency for responsibilities to increase had become more marked over time. In the mid-1980s, 60 per cent of people had seen the responsibilities involved in their job increase over the previous five years, compared with 65 per cent in 1992. The most marked changes compared with 1986 were with respect to employees in lower non-manual jobs and and in semi and non-skilled manual work.

The evidence (see Figure 7.2) is highly consistent with the view that the increase in skill requirements may have been a major factor underlying the growth of responsibility in work: 82 per cent of those who had experienced a skill increase felt that the responsibilities of the job had grown greater, compared with 38 per cent of those whose skills had stayed the same. This relationship was evident within all job levels, although it was particularly strong for lower non-manual workers and weakest for skilled manual workers.

Finally, to provide a stronger assessment of changes in the level of task discretion over time, we introduced two indicators of task discretion that had been used in an earlier national survey carried out in 1984: the Class in Modern Britain survey (Marshall *et al.* 1988). These were asked of a random half of the sample: 'Do you decide the specific tasks that you carry out from day to day or does someone else?' and 'Can you decide on your

Table 7.2 Change in the responsibility involved in the job in previous five years (percentage experiencing increased responsibility)

	1986	1992
Professional/managerial	72	79
Lower non-manual	60	66
Technician/supervisory	75	78
Skilled manual	59	62
Semi- and non-skilled manual	42	50
All employees	60	65

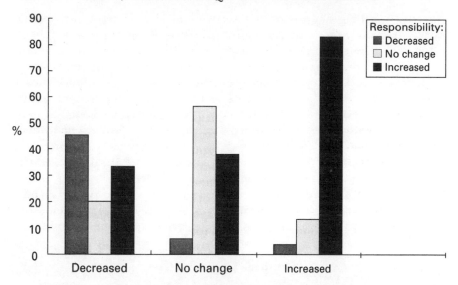

Figure 7.2 Changes in responsibility in work in previous five years by experience of skill change

own to introduce a new task or work assignment that you will do on your job?' In practice these were highly correlated with the main measure of task discretion (0.56 and 0.50 respectively) and when introduced into a factor analysis with the task discretion measure were shown to be part of a single underlying factor.

As can be seen in Table 7.3, both indicators show a clear increase in task discretion over the years. Whereas 48 per cent of employees had discretion over normal daily tasks in 1984, this was the case for 55 per cent in 1992. Similarly, the proportion of employees with discretion to introduce new tasks increased from 48 per cent to 54 per cent.

For both years there were strong class differences in task discretion, with professional and managerial workers distinctly higher than any other

Table 7.3 Task discretion 1984–92

	Decides normal daily tasks		Initiates new tasks	
	1984	1992	1984	1992
Professional/managerial	81	75	74	75
Lower non-manual	48	56	48	47
Technician/supervisory	54	69	54	59
Skilled manual	20	33	27	45
Semi- and non-skilled manual	26	37	29	38
All employees	48	55	48	54

141

category in their degree of self-determination in work, and manual workers relatively rarely having control over their job tasks. However, with respect to change over time, the most marked increases in task discretion are among manual workers and technicians/supervisors. Manual workers were distinctive in that they increased their discretion substantially over both normal and new tasks, whereas technicians and supervisors mainly increased discretion over normal tasks. It is notable that this contrasted with the pattern among professionals and managers who appear to have seen increased constraints on their ability to take everyday decisions.

Overall, the pattern suggests that the second half of the 1980s and the early 1990s saw a marked decentralisation of decision-making within organisations. This is consistent with the view that it was a period characterised by significant de-layering in which employers were reducing the numbers of middle level managers, and devolving responsibilities.

Intrinsic job interest

Both of the major theories of skill trends posit a close relationship between skill change and the intrinsic interest of the work task. The more pessimistic scenarios of the evolution of work argued that, with deskilling, the ever-increasing division of labour and tightening systems of management control, a sharp deterioration was occurring in the quality of work. As tasks became simpler and more fragmented, work became more repetitive, routine and monotonous. Further, since the central process of change involved the removal from ordinary employees of the more conceptual and creative parts of the work process, they were increasingly in job tasks where they were unable to utilise the skills they had developed earlier in their careers and they were involved in a type of work that offered few possibilities for self-development through the work itself. In contrast, those who have emphasised the tendency for skills to become more complex and for skill levels to rise have suggested that work will become more varied and intrinsically more interesting. The relationship of skill change to the intrinsic quality of the work task was explored with respect to three key dimensions: the variety of the work, the extent to which people feel that they can utilise their skills and the opportunities the job provides for self-development.

There were two main measures in the survey relating to the repetitiveness or variety of work. The first asked people whether the variety of their work has increased, stayed the same or decreased over the previous five years. The second asked to what extent the work involved short repetitive tasks, with responses recoded into four categories: three-quarters of the time or more, half the time, a quarter of the time, almost never.

The general relationship between skill change and the variety of work is clearly confirmed. Those who had experienced upskilling were much more likely to have seen the variety in their work increase over the previous five years. While 84 per cent of those in jobs where skills had increased had also experienced an increase in the variety of the work, this was the case for only 39 per cent of those in jobs where the skill level had remained unchanged and for 28 per cent of those whose skills had decreased. This strong relationship between skill increase and variety was evident within each job level. Similarly, there was a highly significant relationship between skill change and the extent to which people were carrying out work that involved short repetitive tasks. Where people were in jobs where skill levels had increased, only 20 per cent of employees were involved in such work for three-quarters or more of their time, whereas among those whose work had been deskilled the proportion rose to 38 per cent.

Upskilling also appeared to be associated with a better match between people's skills and the job. People were asked: 'How much of your past experience, skill and abilities can you make use of in your present job?' Of those who had increased their skills, 44 per cent felt that they could use almost all their previous experience and skills, while this was the case for 34 per cent of those who were in jobs where the skills had remained unchanged and 20 per cent of those in jobs where skills had decreased. Conversely, only 11 per cent of those who had experienced upskilling, compared with 40 per cent who had been deskilled, felt that they could use very little of their previous skills and experience.

Another major aspect of job quality is whether or not the the task is one that encourages self-development through the challenges that it provides for new learning. The question used to assess this asked people how strongly they agreed or disagreed with the view that 'My job requires that I keep learning new things'. An increase in skills was strongly associated with the likelihood that people would be in a job that allowed self-development. Overall 33 per cent of those whose skills had increased agreed strongly that they were in a job where they could keep on learning new things, compared with only 13 per cent of those whose skills were unchanged.

Finally, if skill change is genuinely improving the quality of the job task, this should be reflected in the level of involvement that employees feel in the work they are doing. The survey included three measures of job involvement that sought to tap the amount of discretionary effort that people were prepared to put in, the extent to which the work was experienced as boring and the level of job interest. The items asked how much effort people put into their job beyond what was required, how often time seemed to drag on the job and how often they thought about their job when they were doing something else. Again, upskilling was strongly related to each of these.

An overall measure of intrinsic job interest was created from the seven items discussed above.[2] A more detailed measure of upskilling was also

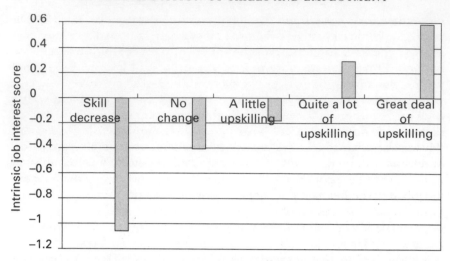

Figure 7.3 Intrinsic job interest and skill change

used for the analysis, taking account not only of the direction of skill change but also of people's report of the extent to which their skills had changed. It includes five categories: skill decrease, no change, a little upskilling, quite a lot of upskilling and a great deal of upskilling. As can be seen in Figure 7.3, there was a strong linear relationship between skill change experience and the overall score of intrinsic job interest.

A range of other factors was also associated with these aspects of the quality of employment – such as people's age and the occupational class of their job (although not their sex). Yet, the striking fact is that, even allowing for the influence of these, the association between skill change experience and the intrinsic interest of the work still emerges very clearly. Further, a more detailed examination shows that skill change has a consistent and powerful effect within each occupational class.

SKILL CHANGE, RESPONSIBILITY AND THE INTENSIFICATION OF WORK

For the pessimistic theorists of skill change, the evolution of work involved not only the increased prevalence of repetitive and uninteresting work, but at the same time the intensification of work effort. Indeed, one of the essential reasons behind the supposed desire of employers to simplify work tasks was that it would facilitate greater managerial control and thereby make it easier to enforce higher levels of work effort. In contrast, the theorists who emphasised tendencies for skills to increase had remarkably little to say about the likely implications of such developments for work effort. It has, however, been suggested that upskilling is linked with a tendency to break down the rigidity of traditional skill lines, in particular through a growth of multi-skilling or polyvalence. Such a requirement to provide greater flexibility in work could be seen to represent a potentially important source of increased work demand.

There were a number of questions in the survey that provide information about the level of work pressure. Two were designed to tap the general level of work pressure, taking account of both physical and mental pressures. People were asked how strongly they agreed or disagreed that 'My work requires that I work very hard' and that 'I work under a great deal of tension'. There were a further two items on the time pressures in work: whether or not people felt they had enough time to get everything done on the job and whether they often had 'to work extra time, over and above the formal hours of the job, to get through the work or to help out'. There was a question asking people whether they were expected to be more flexible in the way they carried out their work than two years earlier. Finally, to get an overall indication of whether or not people felt that there had been a change in the level of effort, they were asked whether, over the previous five years, 'the effort you have to put into your job' had increased, stayed the same or decreased.

It is clear from the results for each of these items that, while the rise in skill levels was associated with an improvement in the quality of work task, it led at the same time to a marked increase in the effort involved in work. A summary picture of the relationship between skill change and work pressure can be obtained by creating an overall index of work pressure.[3] The pattern of the results can be seen in Figure 7.4. Work pressure is least among those who have been deskilled, followed by those who have

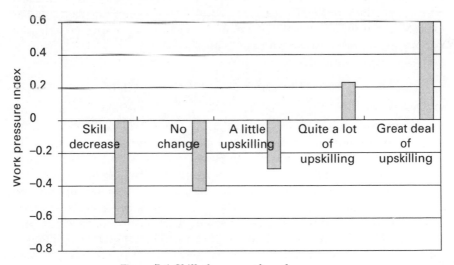

Figure 7.4 Skill change and work pressure

145

experienced no change in their skill level. Those whose jobs have been upskilled a little report greater pressure than those with no change, but the difference is a modest one. It is above all those that have experienced either quite a lot or a great deal of upskilling who report much higher levels of work pressure.

It is possible that this apparently strong relationship between experiences of skill change and work pressure reflects primarily the influence of other factors. For instance, higher class positions may be both more demanding in terms of work load and more affected by processes of upskilling. A fuller test of the significance of upskilling has been carried out introducing controls for class, age and sex. Yet even when these factors had been taken into account the influence of skill change is still highly significant. Indeed, its effect appears to be even more pronounced once these factors had been controlled for.

GENDER, SKILL CHANGE AND RESPONSIBILITY

There can be little doubt that the overall trend has been towards a raising of skill levels, although the implications of this for the quality of work must be judged ambivalent. Yet have such developments affected men and women in broadly similar ways or have the processes been gender specific? Those who have argued for a high degree of segmentation in the labour market and for a degree of polarisation of skill experiences through the division between core and peripheral sectors of the labour market have also tended to regard the privileged core as more heavily masculine and the secondary or peripheral labour market as more heavily femine. If this is the case, there should have been very marked differences in skill experiences by sex. Further, if the direction of change has been towards greater polarisation of skill experiences, it could be expected that the gender gap would have widened over time.

The gender gap in skill and responsibility

A comparison of the measures for skill and responsibility for men and women showed that there was a significant gender gap in the early 1990s. Women were more likely to be in jobs where no qualifications were required (39 per cent compared with 30 per cent) and they were less likely to be in jobs requiring at least A Level qualifications (32 per cent compared with 41 per cent). They were also less likely to have experienced an increase in their skills over the previous five years (Table 7.4). Whereas 66 per cent of men reported that the skills they used in their work had increased, this was the case for 60 per cent of women. There are similar gender differences with respect to task discretion and responsibility. On the measure of task discretion, women had a score of −0.04, whereas men had a score of 0.04 (a

146

Table 7.4 Change in skill and responsibility by sex

	% increase in skill		% increase in responsibility		Task discretion score	
	Men	*Women*	*Men*	*Women*	*Men*	*Women*
Professional/managerial	72	77	80	77	0.44	0.40
Lower non-manual	75	68	77	62	0.13	−0.11
Technician/supervisory	78	56	81	66	0.34	0.10
Skilled manual	65	55	62	58	−0.19	−0.33
Semi- and non-skilled manual	50	41	55	46	−0.52	−0.35
All employees	66	60	70	61	0.04	−0.04

difference statistically significant at the $p < 0.05$ level). Similarly, women had benefited less from the the growth of responsibility in work, with 61 per cent of women, compared with 70 per cent of men, saying that the responsibility involved in their job had increased.

Women's disadvantage in skill development was evident in all occupational classes other than that of professionals and managers, where they were somewhat more likely to have experienced an increase in skills. The gender gap was particularly marked among technicians/supervisors, manual workers and lower non-manual employees. Women were also less likely to have seen the responsibility in their job increase in all classes, although the difference between sexes was very slight among those in professional/managerial positions and in skilled manual work. In contrast, there was a 15 percentage point difference among those in technical/ supervisory grades, a 14 point difference among lower non-manual workers and a 9 point difference among those in semi- and non-skilled manual work. In general men have higher levels of task discretion than women even within specific occupational classes; the only class in which women have higher levels of task discretion than men is that of semi- and non-skilled manual workers.

Change over time in gender differences

While these differences in the experiences of men and women are marked and very consistent, what has been the trend over time? Have the differences between men and women been decreasing or increasing? The evidence suggests that there was a significant decline over the decade in gender disadvantage with respect to skill but not with respect to task discretion.

To begin with, while there was a rise in the qualifications required for jobs for both sexes, the shift was particularly marked for women (Figure 7.5). As a result the differential between the proportions of men and

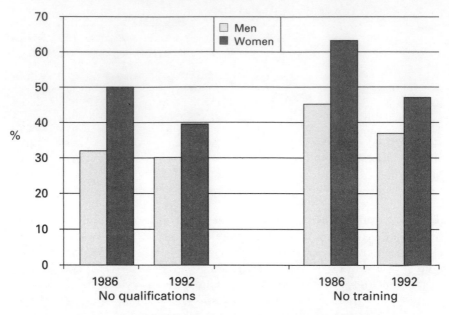

Figure 7.5 Qualifications and training by sex 1986–92

women in work without qualification requirements declined from 17 percentage points in 1986 to 9 points in 1992, while the gender gap for jobs
requiring degree level qualifications declined from 7 to 4 percentage
points.[4]

Further support for the view that there has been a major change in the
relative level of qualifications required for men's and women's jobs is the
age pattern. The differential between men and women decreases strongly
with age, with the pattern inversed in the youngest age group. The proportion of women in jobs not requiring qualifications is 18 percentage
points higher than that for men among those aged 55 or more, 14 points
higher for those 45–54, 11 points for those 35–44 and 10 points for those
25 to 34. Among those aged 20 to 25, however, not only does the differential disappear, but also it is men who are more likely to be in jobs not
requiring qualifications (+7 points). At the other end of the spectrum, the
differential between men and women for those in work requiring A Level
or more reaches a peak of 16 percentage points among those aged 45 to
54. Among those aged 20 to 25, however, it is women who are more likely
to be in work requiring this qualification level (+2 points).

The trends in the gender gap for training and for on-the-job experience
follow a similar pattern (Figures 7.5 and 7.6). The difference in 1986 in
the proportions of men and women who said that they had no training for
their type of work was one of 18 percentage points, whereas by 1992 it had

148

Figure 7.6 On-the-job experience and skill increase by sex 1986–92

been reduced to 10 points. There was a corresponding reduction in the gender differential from 18 to 12 percentage points in the proportions with a year or more training. With respect to on-the-job experience, the gender differential declined from 20 to 13 percentage points in the proportions needing less than a month to be able to do the job well, and from 26 to 19 percentage points in those needing a year or more.[5]

As with the evidence for qualifications, training and on-the-job experience, the data on subjective experiences of skill change indicate that the gender gap is narrowing.[6] In 1986, there was a gap of 11 percentage points in the proportions of men and women who had experienced a skill increase; by 1992, this had diminished to 6 points. The gender gap closed most strikingly at the top and the bottom of the occupational hierarchy: in professional/managerial jobs on the one hand and in semi- and non-skilled manual jobs on the other. Indeed, while, in 1986, women professionals and managers were less likely to have experienced a skill increase than their male equivalents, in 1992 they were more likely to report upskilling. However, in sharp contrast, in lower non-manual work the relative advantage of men with respect to upskilling had grown greater.

A striking feature of the data is that, while there are clear signs of a decline in the gender gap with respect to the various criteria of skill, there is no similar overall pattern for task discretion (Figure 7.7). There was very

149

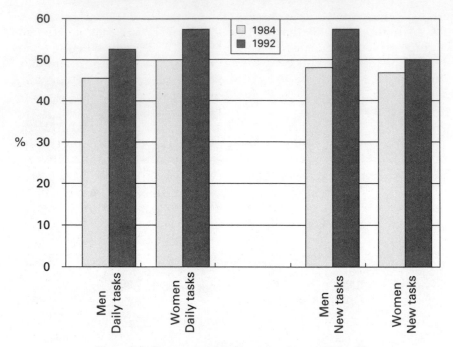

Figure 7.7 Change in task discretion by sex 1984–92

little change between 1984 and 1992 in the gender gap with respect to control over usual daily tasks. In both years women were slightly more likely than men to have this type of discretion. However, men appear to have benefited more than women from the general trend towards higher levels of discretion over the introduction of new tasks. The proportion of men exercising this type of control increased from 48 per cent in 1984 to 58 per cent in 1992, compared with an increase from 47 per cent to 50 per cent for women.

These overall figures conceal quite substantial variations between different occupational classes. Among professional and managerial workers, there is a consistent narrowing of the gap between men and women with respect to discretion both over normal tasks and over the introduction of new tasks. In contrast, among lower non-manual employees, the gender gap widened, especially with respect to control over the introduction of new tasks.

The implications of part-time work

An earlier analysis for the mid-1980s of trends in skill (Gallie 1991) showed that most of the difference between men's and women's experiences was related to the particularly disadvantageous position of women in part-time work. Women in full-time work were closer to the pattern for male employees than they were to that of female part-timers. As has mentioned, arguments that have focused on the emergence of the flexible firm have often depicted part-time workers as a core component of the growing flexible workforce. Could it be that skill experiences were polarizing not along the lines of gender *per se*, but along the line of part-time/full-time work?

Taking first the level of qualifications required for the job, there remained in 1992 a sharp distinction between part-time and full-time workers (Figure 7.8). Among female part-timers, 56 per cent reported that no qualifications were required of people currently being recruited for their type of work, whereas this was the case for only 27 per cent of female full-timers and 29 per cent of men in full-time work. On the other hand, only 37 per cent of female part-timers said that O Levels were needed, compared with 67 per cent of female full-timers and 63 per cent of male full-timers. As can be seen in Table 7.5, women in full-time work were also closer to men than to women in part-time work on the training and on-the-job experience criteria of skill. It is clear that the main division on all of the skill criteria lies not along gender lines, but between women in full-time and women in part-time work.

However, while the distinction between part-time and full-time work still remains a fundamental one for skill levels, the trend over time has been for the disadvantage of part-time workers to diminish rather than to grow

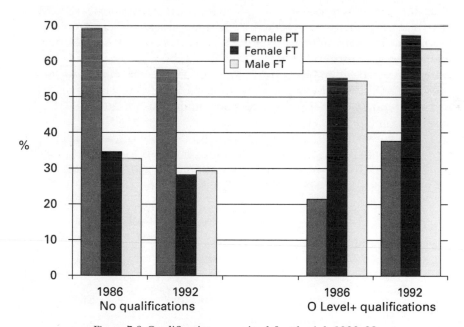

Figure 7.8 Qualifications required for the job 1986–92

151

greater. In terms of qualification change, the period saw rather modest changes for men, rather more substantial changes for women in full-time work, but above all quite major changes for women in part-time work (Figure 7.8). For instance, taking those who reported that no qualifications were required, the proportions dropped by 3 percentage points for men, by 7 percentage points for women in full-time work, and by 14 percentage points for women in part-time work. On the other hand, the increases in the proportions saying O Level equivalent or higher was required were respectively 9, 12 and 15 percentage points.

A similar pattern emerges with respect to training and the on-the-job experience required to do the job well (Table 7.5). The proportion of female part-timers who had received no training fell by 19 percentage points between 1986 and 1992, whereas the decrease among women in full-time work was 13 points and among men 8 points. Similarly, the proportion of female part-timers who reported that they needed less than a month of on-the-job experience to do their job well declined by 17 percentage points, whereas that for female full-timers fell by only 2 points and for male full-timers by only one. It should be recognised, however, that the improvement in the position of female part-timers was primarily in the intermediate categories of training and on-the-job experience. They improved their position only very slightly in the category of those who had had a year or more training or required a year or more on-the-job experience.

Finally, if subjective reports of skill increase are considered, it is again clear that the position of female part-time workers has improved relative to that of full-time workers since the mid-1980s. It can be seen from Figure 7.9 that while both full-timers and part-timers were more likely to have experienced an increase in their skills in 1992 compared with 1986, the change was considerably greater among part-timers. The proportion reporting a skill increase was 12 percentage points higher among male full-timers, 11 points higher among female full-timers, but 20 points higher among female part-timers.

Table 7.5 Comparison of women in full-time and part-time work training and on-the-job experience 1986–92

	% no training		% one year training or more		% less than one month experience needed		% one year + experience needed	
	1986	1992	1986	1992	1986	1992	1986	1992
Women in PT	78	59	9	14	58	41	10	13
Women in FT	51	38	24	26	23	21	27	28
Men in FT	44	36	35	33	17	16	45	42

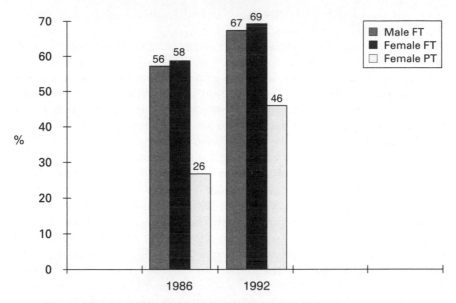

Figure 7.9 Experience of skill increase among full-time and part-time
employees 1986–92

ADVANCED TECHNOLOGY AND TRENDS IN SKILL AND RESPONSIBILITY

In the literature, the issue of skill trends has been closely linked with arguments about the implications of new technologies of work, in particular the spread of diverse forms of automation. The development of large-scale continuous-process technologies in manufacturing industry in the 1950s and 1960s led to an extended debate about the reconstruction or degradation of skills (for an overview, see Gallie 1978). However, the assumption at the time that advanced automation would spread rapidly across industry proved premature and it was not until the 1980s, with the spread of microprocessor technologies, that there was a marked renewal of interest in the implications of automation for skill.

Our evidence certainly underlines the very rapid change that occurred in work technologies in the second half of the 1980s. Whereas the SCELI comparative local labour market study showed that, in 1986, 39 per cent of employees were working with computerised or automated equipment, by 1992 the figure had risen to over half of the workforce (56 per cent). Its use was most prevalent in the white-collar sectors, affecting the work of 76 per cent of professionals and managers, 80 per cent of lower non-manual employees and 54 per cent of technicians and supervisors. But even among blue-collar workers, a substantial minority were using technologically

153

advanced equipment (33 per cent of skilled manual workers and 29 per cent of semi-skilled and non-skilled).

Men were more likely than women to be using such equipment in all occupational classes other than lower non-manual work; however, the extent of change since 1986 has been even more marked among women than among men. For men the proportion using advanced technology rose from 46 per cent to 59 per cent, while for women it rose from 33 per cent to 53 per cent. Thus a gender differential of 13 percentage points in the mid-1980s was reduced to one of 6 percentage points by the early 1990s.

What have been the implications of the rapid spread of advanced technologies for skill and responsibility in work? Those who used advanced technology in their work showed markedly higher skill levels than those that did not on all of the measures. For instance, only 19 per cent of those using advanced technology had no qualifications, compared with 55 per cent of those not using it. Conversely, the percentages for those with O Level or higher qualifications were 75 per cent and 36 per cent respectively. Those working with advanced equipment were much less likely to be without training (31 per cent compared with 56 per cent) or to have required less than a month's on-the-job experience to do the job well (15 per cent compared with 33 per cent). Finally, as can be seen in Table 7.6, the use of advanced technology was strongly associated with having experienced an increase in skill requirements in the previous five years (73 per cent compared with 49 per cent). The association of the use of advanced technology with higher skill levels is evident within all occupational classes.

Turning to task discretion, it is again clear that the overall tendency is for the use of advanced technology to be associated with greater responsibility in the job. The index of task discretion was 0.12 for those using computerised or automated equipment, but only −0.16 among those that did not use it. It was also strongly related to recent experiences of increased responsibility (Table 7.6). Whereas 73 per cent of those using advanced

Table 7.6 Advanced technology and changes in skill and responsibility

	Using advanced technology		Not using advanced technology	
	% experiencing increases in		% experiencing increases in	
	Skill	Responsibility	Skill	Responsibility
Professional/managerial	78	81	63	72
Lower non-manual	72	67	61	60
Technical/supervisory	84	82	60	72
Skilled manual	71	69	61	58
Semi- and non-skilled manual	60	58	38	46
All employees	73	73	49	55

technology had seen the responsibility in their work increase in the previous five years, this was the case for only 55 per cent of other employees.

However, there is now a substantial literature which shows that employers can respond in very different ways to broadly similar technological developments and that patterns of work organisation are best understood as resulting from the interplay of employer organisational strategies, employee organisation and technical constraints (Gallie 1978; Kalleberg and Leicht 1986; Wall *et al.* 1987; Jurgens *et al.* 1993). An area of considerable speculative contention has been whether, as the result of cultural beliefs or relative power resources, employers tend to adopt rather different patterns of work organisation depending upon the sex of their employees (see for instance, Steinberg 1990; Wajcman 1991).

To assess this, the analyses were re-run introducing an interaction term, which indicated whether or not men benefited significantly more than women in terms of skill and responsibility (Table 7.7). With respect to skill, this showed that the effects of advanced technology were as significant for women as for men. There was no difference between men and women in its effects on the qualifications required for the job, the on-the-job experience needed and the experience of skill development over the previous five years. The exception was training: men were more likely to have received training.

The picture with respect to task discretion is very different. Whether one takes the level of task discretion or recent experiences of change in the responsibility involved in the job, there is a clear gender divide. In both cases, the interaction term shows that men benefited significantly more than women. It might be the case that advanced technology still provided women with more responsibility in the job, albeit to a lesser extent than for men. However, separate analyses for men and women showed that, while it was strongly associated with higher levels of task discretion and increased responsibility for men, there was no such relationship for women.

Table 7.7   Advanced technology, skill and responsibility

	Model 1 Without sex interaction	Model 2 With sex interaction	
	Advanced tech.	*Advanced tech.*	*Advanced tech. (Male)*
Qualifications required	0.44 ***	0.40 ***	0.08
Training	0.22 ***	0.10	0.25 **
On-the-job experience	0.18 **	0.25 **	−0.14
Skill increase	0.36 ***	0.39 ***	−0.06
Task discretion	0.03	−0.08	0.23 ***
Responsibility increase	0.08 **	0.03	0.11 **

Note: *** denotes p = < 0.001; ** p = < 0.01; * p = < 0.05

155

Overall, it is clear that the development of computerised technology has been powerfully linked with the general movement towards increased skill in work. This has been true for all occupational classes and it has been the case for both men and women. It also has been associated with higher levels of task discretion and increased responsibility in work for men, but this was not the case for women. This suggests that employers have responded to the demands of technical change with rather different organisational policies depending upon the gender characteristics of the workforce, and that such policies play an important role in mediating the relationship between skill and responsibility.

CONCLUSIONS

Our evidence indicates that skill developments in the late 1980s and early 1990s continued the pattern of the previous decade, but in accentuated form. Employers responded to increasingly rapid technological change and to more intense market competition primarily by raising skill levels and by job enrichment rather than by the degradation of work. The most striking feature of our data is the very extensive upskilling of the workforce. At the same time, there has been a significant devolution of responsibilities for more immediate decisions about the work task. The most prevalent employer policy with regard to work organisation has been a move towards 'responsible autonomy'.

This process of upskilling and increasing responsibility, however, has had highly ambivalent implications for employees' experience of the quality of work. In some respects, it was associated with marked improvements. This was particularly the case for the variety of the work, the ability of employees to feel that they were making full use of their skills and the opportunities for self-development through the everyday work process. But, at the same time, there was clearly a significant negative side to these developments. Upskilling was associated with a substantial intensification of work effort.

Further, the extent of the process of upskilling varied substantially by occupational class. There has been a particularly marked increase over time in the opportunities for skill improvement of skilled manual workers, technicians and supervisors and lower professionals and managers. However, semi- and non-skilled manual workers continued to have much lower chances of skill development and did not share the relative improvement in position that characterised other occupational classes. This points to a process of growing polarisation in skill experiences between lower manual workers and other employees.

Our evidence also confirmed the marked differences that remain between men's and women's experiences of opportunities for skill development and self-determination at work. However, an important finding was that the trend over time has been for gender differences in skill to diminish. This was not simply the case for women in full-time work. There also has been a clear tendency for the disadvantages of part-time workers to decline relative to those of full-timers. The rapid spread of computer-based technologies in the second half of the 1980s was a factor strongly associated with rising skill levels for both men and women.

However, in sharp contrast to the pattern for skills, there was no evidence of any improvement over time in gender differentials with respect to responsibility over work decisions. The analysis of the effects of working with new technologies gives some insight into why this was the case. While the use of computerised or automated equipment was linked to greater task discretion for men, this was not the case for women. Employers appear to have adopted gender specific organisational policies. It is clear that there is no direct translation of changes in skill requirements into changes in wider work roles. Rather this is mediated by employers' organisational philosophies and their culturally-derived assumptions about the capacities of different categories of employee.

ACKNOWLEDGEMENTS

This chapter draws on a programme of research conducted with Michael White of the Policy Studies Institute. It has benefited greatly from continuous discussions with him on the analysis of the survey.

NOTES

1 Each item had a four point response set. The items scaled with a Cronbach's alpha of 0.80. Factor analyses, including a range of other variables, confirmed that these four items constituted a distinct dimension. A reduced factor analysis, restricted to four items, gave one underlying factor, accounting for 63 per cent of the variance and with an eigenvalue of 2.52. The factor score has been taken as the measure of task discretion, with positive scores indicating higher levels of discretion.

2 The measure represented a statistically satisfactory scale, with a Cronbach's alpha of 0.64. A principal components analysis showed that the seven items formed a single factor, with an eigenvalue of 2.24, accounting for 32 per cent of the variance. The factor scores have been taken as the measure of intrinsic job interest.

3 The six items discussed above form an acceptable scale with a Cronbach's alpha of 0.70. A principal components analysis revealed a single factor, with an eigenvalue of 2.41, accounting for 40% of the variance. The factor scores have been taken as the values for the index of work pressure. An anova test of the bivariate relationship between the overall work pressure index and the measure of skill change shows these are associated at a high level of statistical significance (p < 0.000).

4 The overall gamma correlation between sex and qualifications required for the job fell from 0.25 (t-value 10.23) in 1986 to 0.16 (t-value 5.94) in 1992.

5 The gamma coefficient for the overall relationship between sex and length of training fell from 0.34 (t-value 13.69) in 1986 to 0.20 (t-value 8.05) in 1992,

while that for on-the-job experience fell from 0.43 (t-value 19.55) to 0.32 (t-value 13.61).
6 The overall gamma correlation between sex and skill change decreased from 0.16 (t-value 5.11) in 1986 to 0.09 (t-value 2.88) in 1992.

REFERENCES

Atkinson, J. (1985) *Flexibility, Uncertainty and Manpower Management*, Report 89, Brighton: Institute of Manpower Studies.
Atkinson, J. (1986) *Changing Work Patterns: How Companies Achieve Flexibility to Meet New Needs*, London: NEDO.
Atkinson, J. and Meager, N. (1986) *Changing Work Patterns*, London: NEDO.
Attewell, P. (1990) 'What is Skill?', *Work and Occupations* 17(4): 422–88.
Blauner, R. (1964) *Alienation and Freedom*, Chicago, IL: University of Chicago Press.
Braverman, H. (1974) *Labor and Monopoly Capital*, New York: Monthly Review Press.
Crompton, R. and Jones, G. (1984) *White-Collar Proletariat*, London: Macmillan.
Daniel, W.W. (1987) *Workplace Industrial Relations and Technological Change*, London: Frances Pinter.
De Tersac, G. (1992) *Autonomie dans le travail*, Paris: Presses Universitaires de France.
Gallie, D. (1978) *In Search of the New Working Class*, Cambridge: Cambridge University Press.
Gallie, D. (1991) 'Patterns of skill change: upskilling, deskilling or the polarization of skills?', *Work, Employment and Society* 5(3): 319–51.
Gallie, D. and White, M. (1993) *Employee Commitment and the Skills Revolution*, London: Policy Studies Institute.
Gallie, D. and White, M. (1994) 'Employer policies, employee contracts and labour market stucture', in J. Rubery and F. Wilkinson (eds) *Employer Strategy and the Labour Market*, Oxford: Oxford University Press.
Hakim, C. (1987) 'Trends in the flexible workforce', *Employment Gazette* (November): 549–60.
Jurgens, U., Malsch, T. and Dohse, K. (1993) *Breaking from Taylorism: Changing Forms of Work in the Automobile Industry*, Cambridge: Cambridge University Press.
Kalleberg, A. and Leicht, K.T. (1986) 'Jobs and skills: a multivariate structural approach', *Social Science Research* 15: 269–96.
Kerr, C., Dunlop, J.T., Harbison, F. and Myers, C.A. (1960) *Industrialism and Industrial Man*, Cambridge, MA: Harvard University Press.
Littek, W. and Heisig, U. (1991) 'Competence, control and work design', *Work and Occupations* 18(1): 4–28.
Marshall, G., Newby, H., Rose, D. and Vogler, C. (1988) *Social Class in Modern Britain*, London: Hutchinson.
Millward, N. (1994) *The New Industrial Relations*, London: Policy Studies Institute.
Millward, N., Stevens, M., Smart, D. and Hawes, W.R. (1992) *Workplace Industrial Relations in Transition*, Aldershot: Dartmouth.
Penn, R., Rose, M. and Rubery, J. (1994) *Skill and Occupational Change*, Oxford: Oxford University Press.
Spenner, K. (1990) 'Meanings, methods and measures', *Work and Occupations* 17(4): 399–421.
Steinberg, R.J. (1990) 'Social construction of skill: gender, power and comparable worth', *Work and Occupations* 17(4): 449–82.

Vallas, S.P. (1990) 'The concept of skill', *Work and Occupations* 17(4): 379–98.
Wajcman, J. (1991) 'Patriarchy, technology and conceptions of skill', *Work and Occupations* 18(1): 29–45.
Wall, T.D., Clegg, C.W., Davies, R.T., Kemp, N.J. and Mueller, W.S. (1987) 'Advanced manufacturing technology and work simplification: an empirical study', *Journal of Occupational Behaviour* 8: 233–50.
Warr, P. (1987) *Work, Unemployment and Mental Health*, Oxford: Clarendon Press.

8

SEGMENTATION AND INEQUALITY IN THE NURSING WORKFORCE
Re-evaluating the evaluation of skills

Carole Thornley

This chapter develops an alternative theoretical perspective on the acquisition, recognition and valuation of skills, paying full attention to the role of competing representative organisations and employer strategy in underpinning historic and hierarchical divisions within the workforce.[1] It draws for illustration on the case study of nursing, where the most important factors differentiating the workforce, now and in the past, have been based around issues of 'skills' and 'qualifications'.

Nursing has been characterised historically by attempts by the upper echelons of the nursing hierarchy at 'controlling the profession' by tightly delineating 'nursing work' and hence those 'fitted' to 'qualify' as nurses. This has given rise to competing forms of representation divided on the basic issue of skills recognition. Hence a recent drive to 'reprofile' the nursing workforce exposes the Achilles' heel of nursing, namely the historic conflict over the acquisition, recognition and valuation of skills, the relationships to tasks actually performed and their translation into grades, and the shape which an 'ideal' nursing workforce should actually take.

At the same time successive historic attempts by employers at restraining labour costs by capitalising on these divisions have been limited by the effects of a growth in trade unionism when strategies of pay restraint and grade dilution have been followed; in this way employers have been pincered by the threat of trade unionism on the one hand, and the effects on the paybill when nursing skills are fully acknowledged for the workforce as a whole on the other. By focusing on the ways in which skills are defined and made subject to ownership by the dynamic interaction of employer and labour strategy, a richer framework can be developed by which to grasp the intricacies of the changing profile of the nursing workforce and patterns of segmentation and inequalities.

SKILLS AND SEGMENTATION

Studies of the relationship between skills and segmentation have been hampered by a tacit adherence in much social science literature to the idea that skills are measurable, linked directly to technological requirements or education and training, and reflected in pay grades. This kind of linkage gives rise to data on social stratification by skills, for example the manual/non-manual distinction, which is far from unproblematic (see Gallie 1991: 325 for a discussion of problems with occupational classifications). At a rather different level, literatures around the concepts of 'human capital', 'flexibility' and 'deskilling' are rooted in the idea that skills are objectively quantifiable.

Nonetheless, a richer literature exists which is more critical of this purported linkage. This chapter builds on three distinct strands. First, there is a strand of enquiry which looks at women's particular experiences of skill. In the early 1990s it has been suggested that these are strongly influenced by the degree of occupational and workplace gender segregation, because of the associated prevalence of part-time working and its effect on skills acquisition (see for example Gallie 1991: 345–9). At a most fundamental level, the notion of 'skill' itself is highly problematic where 'skill definitions are saturated with sexual bias', and an associated 'undervaluation of women's skills' occurs more generally (Phillips and Taylor 1980: 79).

A second strand of literature pertains to the models of internal hierarchies (Gintis 1987) and labour market segmentation within capitalist economies (Reich 1981; Gordon *et al.* 1982; see also Edwards *et al.* 1975). Here it is argued that employers actively foster and exploit divisions in the labour force to counter worker solidarity and class identity, and to reduce labour costs. It is thus suggested that 'artificial' hierarchies may be formed and 'skills' or productive qualities may not be easily correlated with grades or rewards – not least because employers seek to exploit along ascriptive characteristics (Gintis 1987: 84). However, there is an evident interest in exploring Rubery's proposition that 'it is the limitations on capitalists rather than their ability to control that becomes the interesting question' (1978: 23).

A third strand of theoretical enquiry therefore concerns the response of labour to both patriarchal and capitalist exploitation. The ways in which workers strive to improve their own terms and conditions, and the diversity of means employed, is explored in early work on strategies of 'closed' and 'open' unions. As Turner (1962) notes, labour supply restrictions might be a more important factor in the delineation of 'skills' than the inherent nature of an occupation; skill is thus highly contingent upon workers' own struggles. The theoretical and empirical development of this line of enquiry is pursued by, for example, Wilkinson (1975, 1977, 1988) in the context of segmented labour markets, closure strategies and differentials.

Gordon *et al.* (1982) themselves distinguish between the strategies of craft and general unions. Here, worker self-identification is seen historically as an active development, with endogenous as well as exogenous (managerial) elements in acts of denial and division.

THE NURSING CASE STUDY

These strands of enquiry are pursued in the present case study of nursing. Numbered at around half a million workers, nurses form the largest single occupational group in the National Health Service (NHS), itself one of the largest sources of employment in Western Europe. Policy towards the nursing paybill and workforce therefore assumes a major significance.[2]

Nursing employment holds particular theoretical interest. Around 90 per cent of nurses are female and the workforce has long been regarded as 'the most extreme example of the influence of gender on occupational choice; the classic case of "women's work"' with distinct patterns of horizontal and vertical gender segregation (Thornley and Winchester 1994; see also Institute of Manpower Studies 1985; Skevington and Dawkes 1988). This carries implications for the 'undervaluation of women's skills' not only for the workforce as a whole but also for internal differentiation and grading in terms of the types of skills that nurses seek to claim at different levels in the hierarchy.

At the same time, active employer strategies have been pursued, predicated upon the nebulous and gendered nature of skill in nursing, and tending to foster and exploit divisions within the nursing workforce. Most recently, an important aspect of corporate restructuring in the NHS has revolved around the concepts of 'labour flexibility' and 'reprofiling' with nurses forming a particular target for changes. Here Atkinson's model of the 'flexible firm', which asserts a 'new' polarisation between a 'core' and 'peripheral' workforce based on skill and labour market attachment has proved attractive (see Atkinson 1984, 1985; for a general critique, see Pollert 1987, 1988; for nursing and the civil service, see Mailly 1988 and Fairbrother 1991 respectively). The model has been implicitly incorporated into a succession of recent policy initiatives, purporting to address the issue of 'skillmix', and widely interpreted as 'deskilling'.

Differing labour strategies have also been pursued by nurses themselves, largely along class lines and again predicated on the shifting character of skill. These strategies have split between the ambitions of 'professional closure' (or 'professional unions' – see Burchill 1994) and of what may be typified by contrast as an evolving form of more open or general 'trade unionism', drawing strength from size and diversity of memberships (for example, Salvage 1985: 115), with a more militant style and broader labour movement affiliations, and recruiting from the lower end of the nursing hierarchy upwards.

The case study provides a possibility to explore the dynamics of employer and labour strategy in tandem, over time, and in the context of broader social and economic inequalities. It thus allows the exploration of the relationship between skills and segmentation in more depth and casts fresh light on concepts such as 'flexibility' and 'deskilling'. This argument is pursued first through an historical analysis, and then brought up to date to focus on current employer and labour strategies and conceptualisation around the 'ideal' shape of the nursing workforce.

ASSOCIATIONS AND UNIONS

The twentieth century has seen a secular growth in nurses' membership of representative organisations but the forms these organisations have taken have differed in important respects, predicated initially on a class-based provision of healthcare and healthcare division of labour, and subsequently upon diverging strategies pursued both by the labour organisations themselves and by successive governments.

Nursing as a whole was early distinguished as a gender-segregated occupation (Stacey 1988: 59), but internal divisions also reflected the class-based provision of healthcare. Early healthcare built on a Victorian system of Poor Law workhouses and asylums, where working-class people were treated, and voluntary hospitals, where the middle classes were treated alongside some of the 'better-off' working-class; the wealthy were treated privately.[3] Workhouse facilities and asylums were staffed mainly and respectively by working-class women and men, whilst the voluntary sector offered more opportunity for middle-class women to enter nursing, supported by a greater number of untrained working-class women.

In the latter part of the nineteenth century expansion of the voluntary sector and further development of the great teaching hospitals were accompanied by attempts on the part of upper- and middle-class women to 'redefine' nursing into a respectable occupation for themselves and for the 'better type' of working-class woman. This was achieved through connections in the male public and political domains, but the model of nursing which emerged was deeply patriarchal, hierarchial and class conscious (Abel-Smith 1960). Influenced by Victorian ideologies and by the religious and military roots that formed parts of the nursing reformist strand, the ethos was one which stressed 'vocation, selflessness and dedication' (Stacey 1988: 109).

By the early 1900s a wide variety of nurse associations had arisen, located mainly in the upper echelons of the voluntary sector and sharing a common goal of 'closure' for the nursing profession, to be achieved by national standards of training and examination which would 'draw a firm line between those who were fitted to practice as nurses and those who were not' (Abel-Smith 1960: 61): Mrs Bedford Fenwick, a 'very blue Tory' and accomplished organiser, saw her association as a 'union of nurses for professional objects' which would represent only the 'elite' (ibid.:131, 69).

The College of Nursing, later the Royal College of Nursing (RCN), was founded in 1916 and emerged as the dominant nursing association following formal registration of nurses in 1919 by Act of Parliament. Founded by matrons and doctors, against striking and backed by peers, the college exhibited all of the hallmarks of exclusion apparent in earlier attempts to build professional associations. Thus student nurses were not admitted prior to 1926 (Carpenter 1988: 178), nor male nurses until 1960 (Salvage 1985: 113), while unqualified nurses were excluded by definition.

The main competition to the early associations was the trade union movement, spurred by the 'New Unionism' of the late nineteenth century: in reaction to the conservatism and exclusive nature of the professional associations, trade unions were formed for Poor Law Workers (PLWTU) and National Asylum Workers (NAWU) that would provide an alternative route for nurses to improve upon their own conditions (for accounts, see Carpenter 1988; Dix and Williams 1987; Fryer and Williams 1994). Because the associations were more immediately concerned with the aims of 'professional closure', nurses' pay and conditions remained generally poor, so that through the 1920s and 1930s increasingly militant qualified nurses opted to join trade unions that would win 'status' by campaigning for material benefits (Carpenter 1988; Abel-Smith 1960). These recruits accompanied working-class nurses who formed the majority of healthcare workers yet had been largely excluded from the process of registration and membership of the healthcare associations.

EMPLOYER STRATEGY

At the outset professional associations were viewed by the state as a bulwark against the 'greater evils' of trade unionism and by the then major political parties as a hedge against the wider labour movement. This was an important consideration evident at the time of the 1919 Act, when parliamentary debate swung in favour of registration after the First World War had exposed the first of many nursing shortages:

> If you force nurses [by opposing registration] to form trade unions in order to secure that which they regard, and rightly regard, as a measure of justice and a right to them, you will simply throw them into the arms of the Labour Party.
>
> (Lord Ampthill, cited Abel-Smith 1960: 93)

Thereafter, particular use was made by successive governments of the fact that the associations generally held more conservative views on pay than the trades unions.

Thus, when the NHS was established by the 1946 Act, the associations were given preference in the accompanying national Whitley system of collective bargaining for the determination of nurses' pay.

The need for some system of national pay determination had been previously identified in the 1939 report of the Athlone Committee, which was appointed two years earlier to identify the causes of the endemic nursing shortages that characterised the inter-war years (at this time national bargaining machinery existed for only a minority of nurses, while most fell outside the scope of any form of collective bargaining, national or otherwise) (Thornley 1994b). With the advent of the Second World War change became inevitable and in 1941 the Rushcliffe Committee was established and a system of standard rates imposed by the government. Despite a 'long-standing opposition to state involvement in nurses' pay negotiations' the RCN was allocated 'more seats on the staff side than any other individual organisation', a precedent then carried forward in the new Whitley system for the NHS (Dingwall et al. 1988: 104–5). The resulting bias was compounded by the fact that the membership claimed by the college included many non-active nurses so that staff-side representation bore little relation to the proportions of active nurses attached to the different organisations involved (Abel-Smith 1960: 103).

However, if the first major strand of the state's policy with respect to the employment of healthcare workers had been to promote nurses' professional associations as a bulwark against their trade unions, the second was to resist demands for closure in order to maintain and take advantage of a pool of 'cheaper' labour at the bottom end of the resulting grade hierarchy.

The associations had failed to achieve closure with the 1919 Act (Witz 1992), and many 'unqualified' people continued to engage in duties that could be defined as nursing and many nurses in duties that could be defined as ancillary or auxiliary. But it was clear from the details of the registration process that the delineation and ownership of 'skills' was a contested terrain in which class-based advantage played a leading role. Many who were qualified to register never did so, and people without formal training or certification were admitted at the outset but three years' training was needed thereafter for admission (Abel-Smith 1960). From this point untrained nurses or nurses with incomplete training were completely excluded from the future of the profession.

With the early failure to achieve professional closure, the line which was drawn between nursing and non-nursing duties tended to be fluid over time. In particular, the role of experience versus formal training remained a point of contention and the 'intellectual' requirements of nursing an unresolved issue. Thus the state was able to play on the nebulous character of 'skill' in nursing, and by redefining grades and grade boundaries was able to substitute cheaper labour for the more expensive grades, a process which can be described succinctly as 'grade dilution'.

For example, the Nurses' Act of 1943 introduced a new grade of nurse called the 'Enrolled Nurse' (EN). This gave statutory recognition to assistant nurses and was based on absorption of existing staff with subsequent examination and admission of new staff to a 'Roll' of the General Nursing Council contingent on two years' training (reduced to one year in 1947). The RCN had originally opposed this development on the grounds that promotion of the assistant nurse constituted a *de facto* policy of labour substitution but was finally moved to accept enrolment to gain some 'control' of the new grade. However, the outcome of the Act was a new category of qualified nurse with a shorter period of training and limited career advancement.

The subsequent expansion of this grade illustrates both the substitutability of experience for training and the problem of shortages associated with training requirements. The vast majority of those originally assimilated to the new grade did so through the experience mechanism. However, as these nurses retired the number of new 'trainees' failed to keep pace because the limited pay and prospects of enrolled nursing were not particularly attractive to prospective recruits. The state dealt with this impasse by vigorously recruiting from ex-colonial and British commonwealth countries in the 1950s,[4] and encouraging married women and part-timers to enter nursing (for government's 'Codes of Working Conditions', see Carpenter 1988: 254). This had the indirect effect of reinforcing and accentuating existing patterns of segmentation by race and gender. By the end of the 1970s enrolled nurses had grown to account for around one-third of qualified nurses.

Further grade dilution was also achieved through the formal recognition of the 'Nursing Auxiliary' (NA) role in 1955 and expansion of this grade throughout the post-war years. By 1958 alone there were more untrained staff working in hospitals than had been the case before the war (Dingwall *et al.* 1988: 116). This new grade was disproportionately occupied by ethnic minorities and women working part-time. Together, enrolled nurses and nursing auxiliaries were to account for much of the spectacular rise in the proportion of part-timers in the workforce: from 15 per cent in 1949 to nearly 40 per cent in 1977 (calculated from Gray and Smail 1982: 6).

Thus employer strategy had been characterised by an institutionalised attempt to skew pay determination mechanisms in favour of the more conservative associations and an historical imperative towards grade dilution.

CONTRADICTIONS OF THE SYSTEM

The particular dynamics of the interaction of labour and employer strategies in the decades following the establishment of the NHS meant that the system was to evolve in a paradoxical way.

As governments obtained a measure of success in restraining pay, the material conditions were simultaneously created for the further growth of trade unions, particularly as these latter grew more adept at claiming their own 'victories' rather than letting these accrue to the associations, as had tended to be the case previously (for example, Carpenter 1988: 273; Abel-Smith 1960: 208); where nurses instead 'voted with their feet', public pressures to improve wages and conditions to resolve recurrent shortages in the post-Second World War era became critical electoral factors.

Moreover, grade dilution itself had a perverse effect in as much as the compositional changes it occasioned favoured trade union recruitment. Nursing auxiliaries who were excluded from RCN membership were an automatic recruiting ground for the unions, while many enrolled nurses also chose to join the TUC-affiliates because of the lower pay and status attached to enrolment, the reluctant attitude of the RCN itself, and sustained trade union efforts to attract them.

The net result was a secular growth in trade union membership and by 1980 the combined nurse membership of the Confederation of Health Service Employees (COHSE, the lineal descendant of PLWTU and NAWU) and the National Union of Public Employees (NUPE, both now UNISON) stood at some 200,000 (with 120,000 and 80,000 members respectively), compared with a total RCN membership of just 177,000. However, despite a review of the Whitley system by Lord McCarthy in 1976, the professional associations remained dominant on staff-side representation, with the collective voice of the traditional unions still largely unheard through official wage determination procedures. Conflict thereby emerged outside the process of formal wage machinery, culminating in a challenge to government policies of wage restraint when a dispute erupted in the NHS in 1981. The subsequent industrial unrest lasted through most of 1982 and accounted for the loss of some 3 million working days (*Hansard* 18 January 1983).

Over this period, the position and status of the old professional associations was itself brought into question by the gathering strength of the TUC-affiliates. Under pressure for membership, the RCN was finally pushed to adopt trade union status in 1977, both to gain access to bargaining rights which had been secured for trade unions in the 1970s by new legislation, and to resist encroachments by the union COHSE into areas previously considered a 'professional' domain. While this was a purely tactical response which eschewed affiliation either to the TUC or to the Labour Party, the RCN was nevertheless forced to some extent to adopt a new role by nurse militancy. With the outbreak of industrial action in the early 1980s RCN members were among the general nurses who for the first time protested, picketed, worked to rule and even withdrew their labour (Carpenter 1988).

The immediate crisis of the state was at the same time compounded by the fact that the secular growth in employment of nursing auxiliaries and enrolled nurses had been accompanied by a concomitant decline in the number of trainees for registration. By the 1980s this in itself was becoming a problem because at the same time as the number of learners of all types was declining (students, pupils and post-registration), both proportionately and absolutely, sources of cheap labour were also starting to dry up. Unsurprisingly for a grade referred to as 'one of the health service's biggest confidence tricks' (Clay 1987: 105), the supply of foreign recruits for the EN grade declined from the 1970s, with trainees falling from over 20,000 in 1982 to 6,000 in 1986 (with only 347 new entrants by 1991) (Health Departments 1992; Department of Health, 1992/93 and selected years).

By the late 1980s the gap between numbers of nurses completing nurse training and net losses of qualified staff narrowed to the extent that few managers in interview were confident of keeping up their 'professional' workforce. Shortages were noted throughout the 1980s (Pay Review Body Reports, various years) and almost universally acknowledged to be a growing problem in the light of demographic trends and increasing opportunities for alternative employment for women. On one account, nursing would need to recruit almost half of all girls with five O Levels or two A Levels by 1995 in competition with other sources of employment, a deeply implausible proposition (Dingwall *et al.* 1988:224).

CURRENT POLICY RESPONSES

If past policy contradictions appeared to culminate in new problems, the policy reactions were historically predictable. These were based on a combination of pay restraint and an attempt to redefine the boundaries of nursing to capture cheaper labour at the bottom end of the wage hierarchy.

First, a 'new' pay determination mechanism was sought which would give weight to the 'professionalising' elements in nursing representation. This was in the form of the new Pay Review Body for Nurses and Midwives (PRB), which turned out to be the 'government's trump card' (Salvage 1985: 141–2). After the RCN accepted a third offer with the promise of a PRB, and nurses were effectively split from other health service workers, the dispute 'limped to an end' (ibid.).

The establishment of the PRB was to a large degree considered something of a 'fillip' to the RCN. The RCN at first wanted to restrict its operation to qualified staff, arguing that it feared that it might be difficult to hold unqualified staff to a no-strike commitment for which it regarded the review body as a sort of quid pro quo. It revealed continuing ambitions for professional closure when it informed the prime minister, Mrs Thatcher, that it wanted to see the NHS moving towards the provision of a 'wholly qualified nursing service' and suggested that 'to include nursing auxiliaries within the PRB would give them a credibility as nurses that would not service this objective' (*Glasgow Herald* 30 June 1983).

However, despite an announcement by Mrs Thatcher in the House of Commons that the government would 'reserve the right to exclude . . . any groups that do resort to industrial action' (*Hansard* 28 July 1983), unqualified staff were in the end included in the remit of the PRB. This was a tacit acknowledgement of the pragmatic strength of the points made by COHSE and the other TUC-unions to the effect that:

> For nursing assistants and auxiliaries to be excluded would . . . cut right across the reality and continuing need for a strong and unified nursing team in the hospitals. Nursing assistants and auxiliaries work is nursing work; their duties, nursing duties. . . . There is considerable evidence showing that without unqualified staff the vast majority of psychiatric, geriatric, and mental handicap hospitals simply would not function.
>
> (COHSE 1983: 3–4)

This demonstrated a limit to policy concessions to 'professionalism' in pay mechanisms (see Salvage 1985: 114), but did not mark the end of the RCN's ambitions. The 'fillip' to the 'professionalisers' represented by the PRB, combined with nurse shortages, gave rise to a fresh impulse for professional closure that re-awakened debates from the turn of the century. The government then turned to re-address the second policy strand of grademix.

In the mid-1980s, proposals arose for nursing education to be more closely associated with the rest of the higher education system in the UK, with a final report submitted to the government in 1987. These proposals became known as Project 2000. The project was heavily influenced in its content both by the RCN and by the United Kingdom Central Council for Nursing, Midwifery and Health Visitors (UKCC) and English National Board (ENB) which had been established earlier by the government as 'stalling operations' in response to demands for training initiatives (Dingwall *et al.* 1988: ch. 10).

Project 2000 ostensibly represented a remarkable achievement by the professionalisers, and was initially greeted by professionalisers as 'the biggest change in nursing since the days of Florence Nightingale' (Clay 1988). It proposed that student status should be protected and student nurses not used as a significant part of the labour force. A common foundation programme was suggested, after which students could specialise. A new single level 'registered practitioner' was to replace the current two-tier system of registered and enrolled nurses and the *de facto* reduction in EN pupils was thus incorporated. It was generally assumed that auxiliary labour would fill the gaps.

However, a 'warm welcome for such an expensive venture seemed unlikely' (Gould 1988). There appeared to be little in Project 2000 to re-assure the policy makers on either demographic or cost grounds. Far from widening the entry gate, Project 2000 looked set to raise the standards and slam the gate shut to achieve a degree of professional closure. The immediate cost and staffing implications included the reduction of student labour input on wards, extra educational investment, and the loss of ENs. Potential cost benefits were supposed to be grants rather than a competitive wage, reduction of wastage during training and of ward staff teaching time. However, the cost-benefit estimates of the RCN and UKCC proposals that suggested moderate or no additional expenditure (Dingwall *et al.* 1988: 225–6) failed to be very convincing.

The first signs that the aims of professional closure were not to be obtained swiftly followed. The government attempted to impose restrictions on the terms of Project 2000; for giving nurses in training true student status, the profession would have to be generous and flexible in formulating entry requirements so more school leavers and mature students could qualify for admission, with credit being given for 'experience', and 'aides' being able to earn a place in training schools.

In addition, and almost concurrently with Project 2000 and the idea of 'aides' or 'support workers', government-led proposals for National Council for Vocational Qualifications (NCVQ) certificates for Health Care Assistants (HCAs) arose. These undoubtedly added to the speculation over grade dilution. NVQs are intended to be acquired mainly on-the-job with maximum horizontal and vertical flexibility for both worker and employer through a system of module and performance-assessed credits. A Care Sector Consortium was established to examine all work below the 'professional' level with different 'levels' envisaged (NHS Training Authority 1988).

This scheme was linked with the idea of Project 2000 and Support Workers in an NHS Training Authority report, which Dingwall *et al.* (1988: 226) note 'ceased to be available shortly after its publication in March 1987'. The report put forward a view of support workers differing 'radically' from that of the nursing professionalisers. Here support workers were seen as having clear and direct responsibility for patient care, with specific training forming part of a modular pattern of education across the service. Entry might come from unqualified school leavers on a Youth Training Scheme (YTS: see also Department of Health and Social Security (DHSS) *et al.* 1987) or mature men and women with limited past educational opportunities. The scheme raised a great deal of speculation about 'levels' and 'entry' points. A third level was planned which could be an entry point to registered nurse training (*Nursing Times* June 1988: 13), and further levels were envisaged as 'professional' levels. These proposals could threaten the 'educational' qualification basis of entry to Project 2000 training and the basis for traditional nurse training.

Thus, to this extent the historical phenomenon of grade dilution was already apparent in what had ostensibly appeared to be a step forward for professional closure.

These training changes have subsequently been driven forward by a series of initiatives. Whilst they purport to relate to 'skillmix', most in fact relate to grademix and potential grade dilution.[5] A National Audit Office (NAO 1985) report found large variations in nurse staffing levels. This was followed by *Mix and Match*, a report from the then DHSS which found wide variations in skillmix and staffing levels which, it was claimed, appeared unrelated to dependency levels and standards of care (DHSS 1986). Studies by Robinson *et al.* (1989) and Ball *et al.* (1989) suggested that some degree of 'non-nursing' duty reallocation to support staff was possible. The issue has since been driven along by the Department of Health (DoH), whose 'Value for Money Unit' has toured the country 'recommending reductions in the level of qualified staff' (Staff Side Evidence 1992: 14–15). The NHS Management Executive Personnel Unit has also provided workshops for NHS managers on changes to labour utilisation. This drive has been supported by specially commissioned academic studies on 'reprofiling' (e.g. Dyson 1991), drawing implicitly on Atkinson's work (1984, 1985).

Not surprisingly, these initiatives have been resisted by representative organisations drawing on a number of academic studies, mainly suggesting that registered nurses actually provide a cost-effective method of delivering patient care because they can perform the widest range of tasks and spot potential problems earlier (see Buchan and Ball 1991; also Carr-Hill *et al.* 1992). Staff Side have attacked the drive for 'reprofiling' on two main grounds. First, the drive is seen as 'deskilling' in its implications for the contraction of registered staff. Second, and crucially, the impetus towards employing 'non-nursing generic care assistant' posts is being resisted as in no way comparable to existing NA posts and the skills acquired through experience (Staff Side Evidence 1992:14–15).

These policies, which most have interpreted as being *de facto* exercises in grade dilution, are precisely predicated upon the nebulous character of skill and divisions in the workforce. Their exact effects on the future shape of the workforce, implications for representation and, therefore, cost implications remain, however, less clear.

IDEAL MODELS OF THE NURSING WORKFORCE: SKILLS AND STRATEGY

The models in Table 8.1 illustrate the main ideal type models of the nursing workforce which emerged from fieldwork and documentary research. Though there were variants on these models, they demonstrate logical extremes (for an alternative typology see White 1985). The models crystallise the historic tensions around skill in a way which captures the competing perspectives and strategies of different parties to the struggle over the ownership and valuation of skills, and begins to clarify the cost and strategic implications.

171

Table 8.1 Ideal type models of the nursing workforce

Main features	Professional	Traditional	Radical
Academic entry/training for 'professional' status	Yes	Yes	No
On-the-job learning/experience stressed	No	No	Yes
Employment ratio in favour of 'professional' staff	Yes	No	Depends on definitions
Curative role stressed	Yes	Yes	No
Prior caring experience valued and recognised	No	No	Yes
Task-based rather than practitioner-based ethos	No	Implicit	Explicit
Mobile promotion structure	No	No	Yes
Flexible task borderline with doctors	Only if incorporated	Unacknowledged	Possibly
Flexible task borderline with ancillary staff	No	Unacknowledged	Yes
Higher ratio qualified (registered) viewed as cost effective	Yes	No	Unclear

The professional model embodies the ideal type and closure ambitions of the 'professionalisers'; the traditional model embodies the workforce profile which traditionally emerges as a result of the usual policy response of grade dilution. These two models underlie much writing on nurse employment:

> The professionalizers appear to favour moves to strengthen the competitive position of nursing by increasing the attractiveness of its training, working conditions, and salaries. The managers seem to prefer the idea of dilution, looking for nursing tasks that could be performed by less expensive and more readily available labour.
>
> (Dingwall *et al.* 1988: 220–30)

Moreover, it is also possible to identify a third model, the radical model, which has become increasingly important in the 1980s and early 1990s (see also brief mention by Dingwall *et al.* 1988: 227). This emerged as an important, though minority, strand in interviews with managers and trade unionists and accords with much of government rhetoric on 'flexibility' of both labour utilisation and pay.

Each of the models incorporates the main training changes of the 1980s; thus, ENs are removed as 'red-circled' and supernumerary students under Project 2000 also largely come out and the focus is placed on the registered/unregistered split and mode of qualification.

The professional model

The professional model is grounded in the search for professional closure. As can be seen from Table 8.1, the model favours academic entry restrictions and stresses 'curing' (technical) above 'caring' (communicative) aspects. The model attempts to define nursing as a profession, clearly distinguished from doctors and ancillary workers. A more extreme version of 'successful' professionalisation could lead to an 'all-qualified' workforce. However, it is generally assumed that there is some need for a second tier of workers. It is axiomatic to proponents of this model that skills can be fairly clearly aligned with qualifications, grades and valuation.

The traditional model

The traditional model encapsulates the historical development of nursing and is associated with government or employer cost-curtailment strategy through the means of grade dilution. Its two main distinguishing features are that 'less-qualified' or 'unqualified' staff balance out or even surpass 'registered' or 'professional' nurses, and flexible task borderlines exist but are unacknowledged. The model does not address the barrier to the profession – this remains intact and NAs/aides/support workers/health care assistants (and ENs whilst they remain) are still clearly subordinate. It is axiomatic that skill and valuation issues are not explicitly addressed.

The radical model

The main features of the radical model are a much more complex, possibly flatter, hierarchy and blurring of traditional grade boundaries. The workforce profile here consists of a number of 'levels' with greater flexibility and mobility and less likelihood of professional barriers. 'Caring' aspects and experience are acknowledged. The model seeks to deal much more explicitly with tasks, skills and valuation.

STRATEGY

The philosophy of the professional model is founded upon a certain, hierarchical, view of socio-economic structures and behaviour and the 'intellectual' skills required for professionalism. It usually draws on the more technical field of acute care to argue that nursing requires 'a certain level of intelligence, skill and knowledge' and can no longer be compared to nursing of the past (Clay 1987: 80–105). Skills are clearly seen as stemming from academic training. The problems involved in educational disadvantage as a barrier to gaining professional qualification are sometimes acknowledged, but it is generally felt that the solution should rest upon the 'self-motivation' of individuals and improvements in the wider educational system (ibid.).

Despite a clear attachment to the concept of an 'all-qualified workforce' (ibid.), limited pragmatism emerges to the extent that short-term cost implications are acknowledged in a need for a secondary tier. However, in an attempt to forestall the inevitable policy reaction by management which could leave the profession dominated by a periphery of 'non-registered' workers (e.g. Dyson 1991), professionalisers suggest appropriate ratios; for example, a split of 70:30 between practitioners and aides (UKCC 1986: 43).

Both elements of the model become evident in suggestions that the role of helpers working alongside ever-more specialised nurse practitioners should be carefully delineated. It is argued that instruction for helpers should be 'limited' and 'suited to the setting' in which they work. They should be advised that 'all the normal entry requirements' to professional practice will apply. Work as a helper 'will serve to give an appropriate character reference', but 'cannot operate either as an entry gate or as a credit towards professional preparation'. The helper's title is seen to be extremely important. The title 'Aide' (later to become Support Worker) was suggested in 1986 as it appeared 'simple' conveying 'the notion of being a helper and not a practitioner . . . there is even a chance that, being short, it may actually pass into everyday use and put an end to the indiscriminate use of the term "nurse"' (ibid.: 43). A wide variety of titles are now in use, including 'health care assistant'.

The flaws in the professional model are evident not only in an historical failure to actually achieve professional closure, but also in a failure to establish the premise of intellectual closure against the light of practical experience.

The strength of the traditionalists' hand is evident in the weakness of the professionalisers, and it plays upon contradictions in the latter. The 'preference' for professional unions in pay determination is limited by the subsequent pressure for expensive training changes and richer grademix. By leaving the 'ethics' of the nursing hierarchy well alone and exploiting the variation between learning actually acquired and tasks actually performed and current valuation systems, the scope for grade dilution for a given grade structure is provided and ostensibly consistent with a cost-curtailment strategy.

However, since pay levels at each point in a structure are not immutable but susceptible to upward pressure from trade unions, there is always a natural limit to the extent to which this can be sustained. 'Simple' grade dilution does not resolve the central conflict over valuation and material outcomes, and the grade dilution itself has union membership implications which then impact on pay and labour cost.

The roots of the radical model lie in the struggle over the delineation of skills and its application neatly exposes the contradictory nature of this struggle. Proponents come from both the radical right and the radical left, and its emergence is a natural development in terms of both the search for cost curtailment and, paradoxically, the search for 'fairer' valuation.

The main philosophy is grounded in the idea that the skills required for nursing are not fixed or immutable or agreed upon. Thus, whilst the view acknowledges the need for a range of 'intellectual' capital (body of specialist knowledge), the extent of this range and the way in which it is to be acquired (for example, through full-time academic study or on-the-job tuition or by simple experience and self-tuition) is deeply disputed, and has different significance in different branches of nursing (acute, psychiatric, geriatric). It is further felt that 'caring' skills (practical or communications) are undervalued because of wider social valuation. This reflects the fact that healthcare and associated skills are defined in 'male', technical terms rather than emphasising 'psychic' elements in a more holistic view of care. Caring skills are also seen to be 'undermined' by their association with ancillary and domestic activity (through broader undervaluation of 'housework', and the role of 7 million carers at home).

Finally, the approach also focuses on utilisation and tasks actually performed by different grades of staff. It is felt that there is a general mismatch for many grades and individuals between their grade, tasks actually performed and skill recognition (see for example, Keyser 1992: 115). Many interviewees made the same point; there is a relative inter-changeability of roles between registered and non-registered staff, particularly for care-giving activities and the case of night duty.

For managers who resent the lack of meritocratic appraisal in the existing hierarchical structures there is often a coincidence of personal experience with the main tenets of the radical model. These radical managerialists view closer job evaluation as a way of escaping the professional hierarchy. While academic qualifications as well as experience and on-the-job training would be recognised, skills would be defined against the tasks to be performed and a 'meritocracy' established as people acquire skills by whatever means possible. However, the formal recognition of skills would remain firmly management's prerogative, and the resulting meritocracy would be a strange mixture of managerial control and flexibility combined with some recognition that the current system is not 'fair'.

Whereas managers tend to stress a form of individual meritocracy a minority of trade unionists and educationalists identify possibilities for a more egalitarian and collective system within the rubric of the radical model. On these grounds some welcome the debate occasioned by the grading and training reforms and note that experienced auxiliaries and enrolled nurses have been 'losers' throughout the history of nursing despite regularly exceeding job specifications in practice, and sometimes substituting for registered nurses to the extent of taking charge of wards.

In turn, a low 'valuation' of care work in contrast to the more technically-defined aspects of nursing means that such work is typically delegated to these lower grades of staff. Thus registered nurses are progressively trapped in a 'medical role', which is distanced from a rounded view of nursing encompassing a variety of tasks and requiring a range of skills acquired both through the job and life experience. The general elasticity of the system can then be seen in the use of registered nurses to substitute for doctors in the performance of their tasks, and of ancillary and auxiliary staff to substitute for registered nurses.

The limits to the radical managerialist model are the historical constraints which have helped define and support the existing hierarchies. There is little agreement over the pay and cost implications of the model but most acknowledge that one outcome might be a spiral in pay so that limits on upwards mobility would still be required. At this point the model veers towards a more extreme version of the traditionalist. For example, managers are particularly uncertain about the role of care assistants and auxiliaries, whether vocational qualifications will supplement or challenge the existing hierarchy, what kinds of people will take these jobs, what the training and funding implications are, and how these will affect representational forms and pay rates (see also findings in Buchan 1992: 17–27). On some versions, these staff are simply seen as 'cheaper' and the emerging workforce profile under normal resource constraints conforms to traditional boundaries and ratios.

However, if management is limited by the resource implications of the radical model, trade unionists are equally concerned not to undermine past successes. This involves some difficult strategic considerations. The success of radical trade unionists in pushing for improved recognition, upward mobility and pay for staff lower in the hierarchy has to be carefully differentiated from management objectives, and balanced with a support for professional training and appropriate validation of NVQs. To date, they have been remarkably successful in this, even to the extent of now using the substitution of the term 'non-registered' for the previous term 'unqualified' as a bargaining push in PRB evidence.

THE FUTURE?

Proponents of the different models all hold a high degree of scepticism about the government's apparent support for a 'meritocracy'. All those interviewed felt that the traditional grade dilution model was bound to re-emerge in full force. However, this view has to be qualified by the findings in this chapter. The workforce 'profile' emerges as a historical progression through the interplay of government, managers, professional associations, trade unions and nurses themselves, with divergent views within these groups. Moreover, the extent to which 'deskilling' takes place is very contingent on the view of skill adopted and the background and length of service of staff. The process is thus complex and liable to produce uncertain outcomes.

For the employers this means that, although the early evidence suggests the cost-driven nature (see Seifert 1992) of initiatives will reinforce the tendency to grade dilution, the ultimate cost implications and shape that the future nursing workforce will take will depend upon a number of factors upon which governments have more or less control. Initial grade dilution is uncertain in its detail and will only be the first step in a sequence of complex feedbacks. This situation is both reflected in, and reinforced by, current policy changes towards local pay determination (see Thornley 1994a, 1994b).

With respect to the unions, a strategic response to the *de facto* occurrence of this model undoubtedly causes more problems for the RCN than it does for UNISON. The RCN retains a coherent identity and membership base if it follows an overt policy of 'professional closure'; however, lack of success leaves it open to grade dilution and to membership disenchantment over pay.[6] It is no surprise that the RCN has considered taking lower parts of the hierarchy into membership – particularly as NVQs could provide a measure of justification for this. However, this would involve a major reformulation of the union's goals, particularly on its prior justification for the intellectual and material component of skills that enabled it to argue for professionalisation.

Conversely, UNISON has a much more disparate membership and seeks to organise across grades, competing most directly with the RCN for 'qualified' staff. As such, it cannot support a simple grade dilution model, even if this has historically and objectively benefited it – and improved the lot periodically and substantially of both lower-paid and registered nurses through 'ratcheting'. It is, however, in a very strong position to support a re-assessment of the ways in which qualifications are gained, the way in which prior experience is recognised and rewarded, and the way in which 'skills' are defined and impact on a holistic version of 'healthcare'.

CONCLUSIONS

It has been argued in this chapter that the concept of skill suggested by simplistic forms of analysis such as 'core–periphery' analysis is flawed. The nursing case study has illustrated that skills become defined, acquired, recognised and valued by the dynamic and complex interplay between employer strategy and the strategy of differentiated representative organisations, professional or trade union, set in the wider context of relatively 'rigid' socio-economic and valuation systems (Wootton 1955). Segmented labour markets and inequalities are both formed, re-formed, and ultimately challenged, in this way. The current drive to 'reprofile' the nursing workforce needs to be understood in this context, and a review of historical parallels and the arguments revealed in the wider debate over these proposals also shows that this is both driven, and limited, by the continuing importance of the deep underlying conflict over 'skills' which has been so important throughout the history of nursing. The study signals the need for a wider re-evaluation of 'skills' to take full account of the above 'fluidity' and strategies in giving rise to segmentation and inequalities.[7]

ACKNOWLEDGEMENTS

My thanks to Duncan Gallie and Dan Coffey for many helpful comments.

NOTES

1 This chapter builds on fieldwork and documentary research conducted in the course of completing an ESRC-funded doctorate (supervised by David Winchester and awarded 1993) and preparing a commissioned research report for the ILO (Thornley and Winchester 1994).

2 The sheer magnitude of the overall nursing paybill places both the determination of nurses' pay and strategy pertaining to the compositional effects of the nursing workforce on the paybill at the forefront of NHS and public sector policy. For the accounting year 1992–3 the paybill for nurses and midwives stood at just under £8 billion ('Estimate for Great Britain', Review Body Report, 1994: 23), the largest single element in NHS expenditures, accounting for nearly 40 per cent of all Hospital and Community Health Services (HCHS) revenue expenditures and almost one half of HCHS salaries and wages – where the HCHS sector accounts for almost 70 per cent of all NHS spending (Department of Health 1992/93).

3 See Abel-Smith 1960; Dingwall *et al.* 1988; Doyal and Pennell 1979; Clegg and Chester 1957.

4 Immigrants were disproportionately channelled into EN training, unpopular specialities, and less likely to be employed and have visas renewed after training. A number of studies have recorded both the significant presence of black and ethnic minorities in the 1980s (Salvage 1985: 38; Pearson 1987; COHSE 1990: 2), with substantial evidence of continuing racial inequalities (King Edward's Hospital Fund for London 1990).

5 See review in Buchan and Ball (1991: 28); for prescriptive literature purporting to advise managers on skillmix review see, for example, Nessling (1990). An overwhelming number of managers in interview interpreted these initiatives as grade dilution.

6 This may already be reflected in the RCN's current moves to change its 'nostrike' rule. Despite membership gains in the 1980s, fieldwork suggests it is coming under increasing pressure from UNISON again for membership; see also Owens and Glennerster (1990: 24), who argued that 'a more open divide' was emerging between the RCN and other unions during the period of their study as a result of NHS policy.

7 Since writing this chapter, two new books have appeared as welcome additions to the attempt to analyse nursing. Walby and Greenwell (1994) in particular offer an interesting discussion on the boundaries between doctors and nurses and the issue of professionalism; Davies (1995) argues for the importance of gender analysis in the policy development of nursing.

REFERENCES

Abel-Smith, B. (1960) *A History of the Nursing Profession*, London: Heinemann.

Athlone Committee (1939) *Inter-Departmental Committee on Nursing Services, Interim Report*, Ministry of Health Board of Education, London: HMSO.

Atkinson, J. (1984) 'Manpower strategies for flexible organisations', *Personnel Management* August: 28–32.

—— (1985) *Flexibility, Uncertainty and Manpower Management*, Report 89, Brighton: Institute of Manpower Studies.

Ball J., Hurst, K., Booth, M. and Franklin, R. (1989) *'Who will make the Beds?'*, Mersey RHA/Nuffield Institute for Health Service Studies.

Buchan, J. (1992) *Flexibility or Fragmentation? Trends and Prospects in Nurses' Pay*, London: King's Fund Institute.

Buchan, J. and Ball, J. (1991) *Caring Costs: Nursing Costs and Benefits*, Brighton: Institute of Manpower Studies.

Burchill, F. (1994) *Professional Unions in the National Health Service: Membership Trends and Issues*, University of Keele.

Carpenter, M. (1988) *Working for Health: The History of COHSE*, London: Lawrence & Wishart.

Carr-Hill, R., Dixon, P., Gibbs, I., Griffiths, M., Higgins, M., McCaughan, D. and Wright, K. (1992) *Skill Mix and the Effectiveness of Nursing Care*, York: Centre for Health Economics, University of York.

Clay, T. (1987) *Nurses, Power and Politics*, London: Heinemann.

—— (1988) Quoted in 'NAHA demands full funding for Project 2000', *Health Service Journal* 26 May: 575.

Clegg, H. and Chester, T. (1957) *Wage Policy and the Health Service*, Oxford: Basil Blackwell.

COHSE (1983) *Response to the Government Consultation Document on the Review Body for Nursing and Midwifery Staff and PAMs*, Banstead: COHSE.

—— (1990) *Membership Survey*, Banstead: COHSE.

Davies, C. (1995) *Gender and the Professional Predicament in Nursing*, Buckingham: Open University Press.

Department of Health (1992/93 and selected years) *Health and Personal Social Services Statistics for England*, London: HMSO.

Department of Health and Social Security (1986) *Mix and Match: A Review of Nursing Skill Mix*, London: HMSO.

Department of Health and Social Security, MSC, NHSTA and UKCC (1987) *Commissioned Study 'Feasibility Study into YTS in Health and Social Care Programmes'*, November, London: HMSO.

Dingwall, R., Rafferty, A. and Webster, C. (1988) *An Introduction to the Social History of Nursing*, London: Routledge.

Dix, B. and Williams, S. (1987) *Serving the Public, Building the Union: The History of NUPE*, London: Lawrence & Wishart.

Doyal, L. and Pennell, I. (1979) *The Political Economy of Health*, London: Pluto.

Dyson, R. (1991) *Changing Labour Utilisation in NHS Trusts: The Re-Profiling Paper*, Centre for Health Planning and Management, University of Keele.

Edwards, R., Reich, M. and Gordon, D. (eds) (1975) *Labor Market Segmentation*, Lexington, MA: D. C. Heath.

Fairbrother, P. (1991) 'In a state of change: flexibility in the Civil Service', in A. Pollert (ed.) *Farewell to Flexibility*, Oxford: Basil Blackwell.

Fryer, B. and Williams, S. (1994) *A Century of Service: An Illustrated History of NUPE 1889–1993*, London: Lawrence & Wishart.

Gallie, D. (1991) 'Patterns of skill change: upskilling, deskilling or the polarization of skills?', *Work, Employment and Society* 6(3): 319–51.

179

Gintis, H. (1976/87) 'The nature of labor exchange and the theory of capitalist production', in R. Albelda, C. Gunn and W. Waller (eds) *Alternatives to Economic Orthodoxy*, New York: ME Sharpe.

Gordon, D., Reich, M. and Edwards, R. (1982) *Segmented Work, Divided Workers*, Cambridge: Cambridge University Press.

Gould, D. (1988) *Nurses: The Inside Story of the Nursing Profession*, London: Unwin Hyman.

Gray, A. and Smail, R. (1982) *Why has the Nursing Paybill Increased?*, Discussion Paper 01/82, Health Economics Research Unit, University of Aberdeen.

Health Departments (1992) *Written [Management Side] Evidence to the Review Body for Nursing Staff, Midwives and Health Visitors*, London: Department of Health.

Institute of Manpower Studies (1985) in citation in *Staff Side Evidence to the Review Body for Nursing Staff, Midwives and Health Visitors, 1991*, Brighton: IMS.

Keyser, D. (1992) 'Nursing policy, the supply and demand for nurses: towards a clinical career structure for nurses', in J. Robinson, A. Gray and R. Elkan (eds) *Policy Issues in Nursing*, Milton Keynes: Open University Press.

King Edward's Hospital Fund for London (1990) *Racial Equality: The Nursing Profession*, Equal Opportunities Task Force Occasional Paper 6, London: King Edward's Hospital Fund for London.

Mailly, R. (1988) 'An insight into the magic circle', *Health Manpower Management* 14(3): 18–20.

National Audit Office (1985) *Control of Nursing Manpower*, London: HMSO.

Nessling, R. (1990) *Skillmix a Practical Approach for Health Professionals*, London: Manpower Monograph 2, DoH/MPAG.

NHS Training Authority (1988) *The Role, Selection and Training of Support Workers/Helpers in the NHS: The Way Forward*, London: NHSTA.

Owens, P. and Glennerster, H. (1990) *Nursing in Conflict*, Basingstoke: Macmillan Education.

Pearson, M. (1987) 'Racism', *Nursing Times*, 17 June.

Phillips, A. and Taylor, B. (1980) 'Sex and skill: notes towards a feminist economics', *Feminist Review* 6: 79–98.

Pollert, A. (1987) *The 'Flexible Firm': A Model in Search of Reality (or a Policy in Search of a Practice)?*, Warwick Papers in Industrial Relations 19, Coventry: University of Warwick, Industrial Relations Research Unit.

—— (1988) 'The "Flexible Firm": Fixation or Fact?', *Work, Employment and Society* 2 (3): 281–316.

—— (ed.) (1991) *Farewell to Flexibility?*, Oxford: Basil Blackwell.

Reich, M. (1981) *Racial Inequality: A Political–Economic Analysis*, New Brunswick, NJ: Princeton University Press.

Review Body for Nursing Staff, Midwives, Health Visitors and Professions Allied to Medicine (1984–94), *Reports 1–11*, London: HMSO.

Robinson, J., Stilwell, J., Hawley, D. and Hempstead, N. (1989) *The Role of the Support Worker in the Ward Health Care Team*, Nursing Policy Studies Centre and Health Services Research Unit, University of Warwick.

Rubery, J. (1978) 'Structured labour markets, worker organisation and low pay', *Cambridge Journal of Economics* 2: 17–36.

Salvage, J. (1985) *The Politics of Nursing*, London: Heinemann Nursing.

Seifert, R. (1992) *Industrial Relations in the NHS*, London: Chapman and Hall.

Skevington, S. and Dawkes, D. (1988) 'Fred Nightingale', *Nursing Times* 25 May: 49–51.

Stacey, M. (1988) *The Sociology of Health and Healing*, London: Unwin Hyman.

Staff Side Evidence (various dates) *Evidence to the Review Body for Nursing Staff,*

Midwives and Health Visitors, London: Nursing and Midwifery Staffs Negotiating Council Staff Side.

Thornley, C. (1994a) 'Nursing pay policy: chaos in context', paper presented to Cardiff Business School Employment Research Unit Annual Conference, September.

—— (1994b) *Back to the Future: Learning the Lessons from 1930s Local Pay Determination for Nurses*, London: UNISON.

Thornley, C. and Winchester, D. (1994) 'The remuneration of nursing personnel in the United Kingdom', in D. Marsden (ed.) *The Remuneration of Nursing Personnel*, Geneva: International Labour Office.

Turner, H.A. (1962) *Trade Union Growth, Structure and Policy*, London: Allen & Unwin.

United Kingdom Central Council for Nursing, Midwifery and Health Visitors (1986) *Project 2000*, London: UKCC.

Walby, S. and Greenwell, J. with Mackay, L. and Soothill, K. (1994) *Medicine and Nursing: Professions in a Changing Health Service*, London: Sage.

White, R. (1985) 'Political regulators in British nursing', in R. White (ed.) *Political Issues in Nursing Past, Present and Future* vol. 1, Chichester: Wiley.

Wilkinson, F. (1975) *Demarcation in Shipbuilding*, mimeo, Cambridge: Department of Applied Economics.

—— (1977) 'Collective bargaining in the steel industry in the 1920's', in J. Saville (ed.) *Essays in Labour History 1918–39*, London: Croom Helm.

—— (1988) 'Where do we go from here? 2. Real wages, effective demand and economic devclopment', *Cambridge Journal of Economics*, 12: 179–91.

Witz, A. (1992) *Professions and Patriarchy*, London: Routledge.

Wootton, B. (1955) *The Social Foundations of Wage Policy*, London: Allen & Unwin.

9

WORK ORGANISATION, SKILLS DEVELOPMENT AND UTILISATION OF ENGINEERS

A British–Japanese comparison

Alice Lam

Skill requirements have been widely discussed in terms of numbers of people trained and the types of training and formal qualifications they receive. It is often assumed that the nature and quality of skills in industry are determined by a country's vocational training and qualification systems. Such a conception of the skill development process ignores skills utilisation patterns in the workplace and neglects work organisation and its role in shaping the real skill content of jobs and opportunities for skill development. This chapter takes up an increasingly important yet much neglected theme, namely the way firms utilise qualified labour and how work organisation shapes skill development in the workplace.

The chapter argues that skills cannot be separated from the work context and that on-the-job learning is a critical element in skill formation. It illustrates how work organisation shapes workers' skills and role competence through a detailed comparison of the actual work roles and skills development experience of a similar occupational group in two different societal settings. It considers the case of one specific category of qualified labour, namely engineers, in the British and Japanese electronics industries.

The study on which this chapter is based shows that work organisation influences the patterns of division of labour in many ways. It shapes the pattern of coordination and communication between different functional groups, the location and ownership of information and knowledge and determines the structure of authority and control. In their classic comparative study, Maurice *et al.* (1980) demonstrate how the actual skill content and task responsibilities of different occupational groups vary significantly between different societies, reflecting the different national patterns of structuring and organising work. Although one finds a variety of organisational patterns in different societies, international comparisons show that 'societally significant organisational types' exist (Maurice *et al.* 1980; Sorge and Warner 1986; Sorge 1991). For example, various studies have illustrated that the British pattern of organisation tends to be characterised by 'mechanistic features' such as functional segmentation between production, engineering and management, and a high degree of specialisation of work roles (Maurice *et al.* 1980; Child *et al.* 1983). In sharp contrast, the Japanese style of organising is generally characterised by blurred functional boundaries, standardisation of careers across functional units and products, leading to the formation of generalists and the prevalence of team-based job structures. These 'organic' features appear to be common 'country patterns' cutting across product markets, industries and firms in Japan (Westney 1993). A comparison of the different work roles and skills of engineers between these two contrasting organisational forms will serve as a good test of how far skills and actual task contents of similar occupational positions are moulded by organisational structures and day-to-day work.

The study seeks to demonstrate that even for a category of the workforce with high level formal quaifications, such as engineers, on-the-job learning plays a key role in their skill development. Their formal training and education provide them mainly with general conceptual knowledge and skills. Many of the practical skills which are increasingly needed for effective product development in a rapidly changing technological and market environment, for example capacity for flexibility, contextual skills and general capacities for coordination and information processing, can be acquired in the workplace only through on-the-job learning. Work organisation shapes the task responsibilities of engineers and thus the range and type of skills acquired in their day-to-day work. The way work is organised determines the nature of role relationships, patterns of information and knowledge sharing and the extent to which there are opportunities for engineers to acquire a wide range of non-technical and contextual skills.

Work organisation is thus a critical factor shaping the structure and opportunities for skill development in the workplace. It can also affect workers' sense of task involvement and motivation for learning. All these factors could have significant implications for the competitive performance of firms.

In Britain, since the mid-1970s, there has been a great deal of debate about the deficiencies of engineering skills formation and its impact on the poor performance of British manufacturing industries (Finniston 1980; Blears and Bonwitt 1988; Cassels 1987; NEDO 1988). The debate, however, has focused primarily on shortages of qualified personnel, issues of low professional status and the need to raise formal qualifications and training requirements. The discussion has persistently neglected the important issue of effective utilisation in the workplace and how this might affect skills development, the motivation of engineers and their role competence in product development and innovation.

The study presented in this chapter is an attempt to bring a new perspective to the debate by focusing on work organisation issues. Based on a comparison of British and Japanese firms in the electronics industries – one of the most strategic sectors of manufacturing – the study examines how the organisation of technical work affects the skills and patterns of utilisation of engineers in product development. Evidence is drawn from a detailed investigation of the work roles, careers and on-the-job training experience of some 60 Japanese and 55 British R&D engineers in large electronics firms. The analysis focuses on the management and organisation of product development activities and explores the extent to which the work roles of engineers enable full utilisation of their capacity and provide opportunities to exploit the potential for skill development.

Japan is chosen as a comparator because it provides a fresh approach and gives a different framework for judgement. Much of the literature on engineers in Britain has drawn comparison with continental European countries such as Germany or France (Sorge 1979; Sorge and Warner 1986; Hutton and Lawrence 1981). These comparative studies often take for granted many of the existing assumptions and organisational arrangements underlying the European concept of 'professionalism'. This chapter seeks to break out of this 'European bias' by drawing comparison with a non-European, yet equally successful advanced industrial economy.

Japanese firms have achieved a superior level of performance in electronics engineering and yet engineers do not have a high degree of professional control, unlike their counterparts in many continental European countries. The Japanese model of engineering formation is essentially organisation-based and enterprise-driven. Unlike in Britain where firms seek 'ready-made' engineers from the labour market, Japanese companies accept full responsibility for providing firm-specific training and continuous development for their engineers (Lam 1993). The key focus is on effective development in the workplace through systematic on-the-job training and strategic job rotation (Ito 1993; Werskey 1987; Wakasugi 1989). The Japanese enterprise-based approach is based on a training philosophy and skill development practices which are distinctively different from the British craft/professional model (Meiksins and Smith 1993). It is characterised by the absence of external professional labour markets. It provides an alternative model of engineering skills formation and directs our attention to the importance of work organisation and utilisation issues at the enterprise level.

This study adopts a comparative research strategy which allows a detailed examination of the individual role behaviour of engineers over a period of time in the context of their work organisation. The Japanese sample was drawn from eight electronics firms including four R&D centres and the British from six electronics firms including two R&D centres (see Tables

9.1 and 9.2). The Japanese firms were all large diversified companies covering a full variety of electronics products and technology areas such as communication and information systems, computers, industrial electronics systems, electronics devices and consumer electronics goods. The British firms covered a much narrower range of product areas and a high proportion of the sample were engaged in telecommunications equipment, and communication and information systems. These differences mainly reflected the patterns of the electronics industries in the two countries. However, a considerable number of the Japanese engineers were engaged in similar product and technology areas to those of the British sample. Data were collected by a background career questionnaire, tape-recorded in-depth individual interviews, and a critical incidents self-reporting system over six months which focused on the engineers' on-the-job training experience. Details of the research methods and the characteristics of the sample are described in the Appendix to this chapter (pp. 200–1).

WORK ORGANISATION AND THE ROLE OF ENGINEERS IN PRODUCT DEVELOPMENT IN BRITISH AND JAPANESE FIRMS

Evidence from the study shows that there are marked differences in the level of task specialisation and the patterns of horizontal coordination in the product development cycle between the British and Japanese firms.

Table 9.1 Companies and number of engineers participating in the study in Japan

Company code	Product/ activity	Critical incidents study	Individual interviews
A	Industrial equipment, communication and information systems, electronic devices, transport, space, home electronics	21	12
B	Engineering and machinery, equipment	15	9
C	Communication, computers and electronic devices	—	8
D	Electronic devices and equipment	—	3
E	Electronic devices, communication and information systems (R&D)	9	9
F	Electronic devices, communication and information systems (R&D)	—	5
G	Electronic devices (R&D)	—	7
H	Materials, devices and systems in electronics and related fields (R&D)	—	8
Total		45	61 (51 usable transcriptions)

Table 9.2 Companies and number of engineers participating in the study in Britain

Company code	Product/ activity	Critical incidents study	Indvidual interviews
I	(three sites) Communication systems and telecommunication equipment	26	25
J	Electronics and communication systems	6	3
K	Information systems	3	3
L	Military electronics	7	9
M	Communications, electronic devices and industrial applications (R&D)	4	4
N	Communications, electronic devices, industrial applications and military electronics (R&D)	—	9
Total		46	53

It is clear from the interviews that most of the British firms studied operated a functional form of organisation with separate departments for design, development and production. These departments in turn were separated from marketing and sales. Tasks to be accomplished in each stage were clearly delineated and defined and operated within a centralised hierarchical control. The product development process observed in most of the British firms was predominantly sequential, that is, the different phases of product development were relatively independent and distinct from each other. In all the British firms studied, the development laboratories were geographically separated from the manufacturing sites.

One project manager commented on the difficulties and barriers created by the segmented structure:

> Instead of all working together, the marketing, the programme people, the test and development people and the manufacturing are all in different buildings and that makes communication difficult and creates misunderstanding. . . . You have a manufacturing director, development director and you have a test director and quality director, and they each have their own part hierarchy and things move with different levels. Like the equipment will be traded from one department to another as it goes through its cycle of being developed, manufactured and tested, out to sales, installed finally. Things move through in a very watertight way, but you cannot do that, with the type of equipment we work on.

In the British firms, project teams were highly specialised and tended to be made up of staff from the same functional area. Although terminological differences make it difficult to compare the precise composition of project teams between the two countries, our interviews showed that task assignments among the British engineers were much narrower both in the range of functions and product components. Most of the British engineers reported working on their own on individualised tasks ('projects'); whereas the majority of the Japanese engineers reported working in groups of five or six people. Very few of the British engineers interviewed reported job rotation beyond their functional boundaries. Complaints about isolation and the problem of compartmentalisation of R&D from manufacturing were frequently encountered in the interviews:

> Ever since I have been here I have worked on five or six projects and I have never been to the production facility. Although I have designed new equipment, I have never gone to another site of the company. So when I am designing, I don't know.

One design engineer who previously worked in a small firm was critical of how the segmentation between design and manufacture prevented engineers from having a whole view of the product:

> It's done on paper. They don't lay out PCBs [printed-circuit boards] or anything like that which is something I used to do with my old company, so I had a view of how the electronics went together at every stage.

In parallel with the problem of segmentation between R&D and manufacturing is the poor linkage of engineering activities with marketing. In both countries, the majority of the engineers felt that it was important for them to have market and customer information. However, Japanese engineers reported more frequent direct contacts with customers and staff in marketing. Over a third of the British engineers reported that they have never had any contact with the marketing function or customers in their day-to-day work activities. In the British firms, communication and information flow appears to concentrate on a small number of key project managers. Many of the British engineers were highly critical of the lack of direct engineering input into marketing and vice versa. Many felt that engineers could have achieved a lot more. The following remark is illustrative:

> We seem to be marketing led rather than engineering led. So that marketing will come up with the ideas but they won't tell us and ask whether it's feasible. . . . Customer specifications are agreed between marketing and the customer. They could have consulted us earlier. On some of the projects we've had, we got into an almighty row because we don't know exactly what we're doing.

The lack of coordination between the laboratory, the production site and the marketing function often leads to project abortion. The following complaints were common among engineers working in the research laboratories:

There were the immediate sort of requirements to start with and so we kicked the thing off quickly. We were then left to get on with it and after a while we suspected that there was something, you know, they weren't quite as keen on it as before. In the end, it turned out that they had decided for market reasons or production reasons that they weren't really out to take this up . . . it was eventually terminated. I was starting to get disillusioned now, in that this has happened repeatedly.

As a consequence of the functional segmentation and frequent project abortions, many of the British engineers expressed lack of understanding of 'the whole project' and having difficulties in building up a technical identity and full product knowledge.

You find yourself wondering when you come to design things, what the best way to do it is, and you don't know how the whole thing fits together.

We are not told anything so things get screwed up because we don't know what's going on after the [circuit] board leaves us. For example, for manufacture, for buying components and things like that. We don't get to hear anything about it. It's full of time delay and time wasting because we don't know what's going on.

In sharp contrast to the segmented approach found in the British firms, we observed a much greater degree of horizontal coordination across functional boundaries and different phases of the product cycle in the Japanese firms. Cross-functional project teams are frequently used for new product development. The Japanese term 'project' is often used to refer to relatively large-scale R&D activities involving engineers from different departments and functions (Imai *et al.* 1985; Nonaka 1989). It is also a common practice for the R&D engineers to follow the product design and development right through to the stage of manufacture. A development engineer in a central R&D laboratory, soon expected to be transferred to production with his team, explained his position:

As the development project is more or less finished, it will be passed on to the factory and we are following it. . . . Our job is to follow it through to the stage of production. We don't have to in the case of basic research projects, but this one is for a product. It's not going to work if we just pass it on and leave it. The people have got to go at the same time.

The Japanese approach to product development is commonly described as 'overlapping' or 'simultaneous' (Imai *et al.* 1985). The overlap of activities can occur at the interface of adjacent phases or sometimes extends across several phases. Engineers involved in the project are expected to interact on a continuous basis, share information and responsibility. The overlapping approach makes narrow division of labour ineffective. The fluidity and ambiguity of job boundaries mean that R&D engineers are sometimes expected to play a technical support role in production or to be a market researcher if necessary. All project members are expected to reach out across boundaries, to engage in intensive information transfer and to acquire a breadth of knowledge and skills. This is especially evident when engineers are engaged in new product development:

> Our manager asked if the two of us could come up with some ideas for a new product. It's about applying this entirely new technology. We had to carry out market research, and product planning to arrive at the product concept. As we are a central lab here, we had to go the labs in Kyoto where they had the technology and talked to those people. We read the literature, we went out to the field to talk to the market experts to find out what the customers want. . . . We eventually came up with the product specification. That's how we did it, it was a bit like playing around. We hunted around for ideas and information.

Japanese firms put especially strong emphasis on forging a close link between R&D and production. The linkage is supported by a job rotation and career path strategy for the engineers. Most of the Japanese R&D engineers interviewed have had some experience in production – many of them had been assigned to work temporarily on the production site for a period of time as part of their training and career development. The importance of developing the *Genba* (on-site) experience of their engineers, especially at the early stages of their career, is often emphasised.

One manager at a central research laboratory explained how the company used the mobility of engineers as a strategy for integration and coordination:

> It is our policy to transfer our young engineers in the third year of their service to work temporarily on the production site. The secondment could last from a few months to over a year. It is carried out for the purpose of human resource development as well as for information exchange. Once these young engineers get to know the key people on the production site, it helps to smooth our future operation.

Thus, job rotation is used not only for broadening the skills and knowledge base of the engineers, but also as an important mechanism for facilitating information flow across different functions. Job rotation reduces the social distance between different categories of staff, in particular those engaged in upstream scientific activities ('episteme') and those in downstream production activities ('techne'). It creates a human-based network and thus facilitates horizontal coordination and information sharing (Ito 1988).

The evidence presented above illustrates two contrasting forms of work organisation and approaches to the management of R&D. The British approach is based on the principle of individual task and functional specialisation, and the product development cycle is managed on a sequential basis. The job boundaries of the British engineers are much more narrowly defined within their specialist arenas and their role in cross-functional coordination is limited. The Japanese approach is based on the principle of undifferentiated job demarcation and decentralised horizontal coordination: the product developing process is overlapping. Japanese engineers are expected to engage in direct cross-functional liaisons and in scanning market information. Within this model, the coordination function becomes partly embedded in the role of engineers. In the Japanese firms, the ability to coordinate, to process and share information is regarded as an important part of an engineer's skills and role competence.

The two different forms of work organisation define the relationship between technical and managerial work and shapes the location and ownership of different types of knowledge and information in product development.

CONTRASTED RELATIONSHIP BETWEEN TECHNICAL AND MANAGERIAL WORK

Successful product development requires effective integration across different engineering activities and functional groups. Managing communication and information flow across different functions and active linkages between technical work and commercial objectives are key elements in achieving total product integration. The product development process is a total information system (Clark and Fujimoto 1991). As technology becomes more complex and competition in the product market intensifies, organisations come under pressure to increase their coordination and information processing capacity. The more uncertain the market environment, the greater the need for efficient communication, and elaboration of knowledge and information across the product development cycle.

Organisations operating on the principle of functional specialisation create a heavy demand for an administrative hierarchy specialising in co-ordination and integration. The more sub-divided the organisation into individual tasks and functional disciplines, the greater the need for coordinators to act as focal points of communication and information flow. In the British firms, this specialist coordinating role is carried out predominantly by project managers. In our interviews, all the British project managers emphasised the importance of their coordinating function. The following examples of how these people described their 'typical day's work' are illustrative:

As deputy engineering manager on the systems my prime task is liaison among engineering groups in three different divisions of the company. So I spend a lot of time on the phone, at meetings, reading papers generated by engineers in their groups, because the systems function is to really make sure that all the different engineers working in the company on this project are tied into the contract. . . . It's a technical liaison job and you have to trace people for information, go to meetings, help engineering meeting and project meeting. . . . It's basically liaison and coordinating. I am not designing any equipment.

I headed up a team of five, and they did the technical work of producing the workbenches and specs and things, and I had to make sure it all held together . . . I spend quite a lot of time on the phone. . . . If I have an overriding function it's that of coordination. So, yes, I do lots and lots of coordination. I actually produce very little.

Most of the British engineers promoted to project leader positions often become preoccupied with their coordinating role and find themselves having to disengage from their design and development role very early on in their supervisory roles. The separation between managerial and technical work is distinct in the British firms.

In the Japanese firms, the relationship between technical and managerial work is quite different. Although Japanese project managers also have an important coordinating role, they are not 'specialist coordinators' like their British counterparts. The overlapping nature of the Japanese approach to product development means that a great deal of the coordinating functions are carried out by engineers at the working level. Information necessary for the coordinated adjustments in the product cycle tends to flow laterally across the functions through direct communication among the project team members rather than necessarily passing up and down the hierarchy via the project manager. In the Japanese firms, the product development cycle is coordinated by a decentralised network structure of communication and information sharing rather than a centralised hierarchical information system. As a result, Japanese project managers tend to devote more time and effort to product planning and strategic decision-making rather than specialising in operating coordination. They emphasise their technical leadership role and act as product champions in integrating technical development with corporate objectives. A project manager (*Kacho*) at an R&D laboratory described his key role as follows:

In my case, there is of course, the overall policy of the company. The primary concern is to follow the policy, and then deciding how to translate it into concrete details. The top management only provides very broad guidelines and it is really up to the project managers

191

(Kacho) and team leaders (*kakaricho*) to come up with concrete strategies, for example, how we can double the sales figure next year. In order to achieve the objective, I have to carry out detailed analysis in a wide range of areas, including marketing, costing and then consider how to incorporate the technical aspects in order to achieve the overall objective. On the technical side, we know what level of technical performance we want to achieve but it is important to work out how to translate it into actual development work. I have to ensure that my subordinates understand all these.

In the Japanese firms, a project manager effectively functions as a general manager of a product. Their role is 'strategic' in that they are responsible for product planning and concept development; it also contains a strong technical dimension in the sense that they are ultimately responsible for translating the product concept into technical details.

While most of the British engineers promoted to project managers often find themselves having to disengage from their technical work very early on in their supervisory roles, Japanese project managers often remain technically involved – many of them described themselves as 'player managers'. There are two main reasons why Japanese project managers tend to maintain a closer involvement in technical work. First, unlike their British counterparts whose role is to liaise with local representatives from different functions within a vertical administrative hierarchy, Japanese project managers often directly lead a project execution team – members who leave their functions and report directly to the project manager. They have direct contact and stronger influence over the working level engineers. They are responsible not just for coordination but also for product planning and translating product concepts into detailed technical work. It is a technical leadership role and thus knowing the technical details of their subordinates' work and providing on-the-job training is all part of the job. Second, it is important for Japanese project managers to remain technically competent in order to justify their authority and control within the project team. Unlike their British counterparts, they are not specialist coordinators and they do not have monopoly access to organisational information. Japanese project teams have a high degree of integrative autonomy and lateral information processing capacity. The coordinating role of a manager can easily be made redundant and bypassed. Thus, remaining technically active and involved is a good way of ensuring authority and gaining 'competence trust' among the engineers.

SHARING OF KNOWLEDGE AND INFORMATION IN PRODUCT DEVELOPMENT

On the whole, there is a greater degree of vertical interpenetration and sharing of knowledge and information between engineers and managers in the Japanese firms. In the British firms, the separation between managerial and technical expertise is more distinct and the degree of information sharing is lower. The extent of information sharing has important implications for the level of trust between engineers and managers.

The development of a total product requires the effective combination of three types of knowledge and information: specialised technological expertise for development and design; organisational knowledge for cross-functional coordination; and market information to link technical work to commercial objectives of the firm. The product development process is a total information system (Clark and Fujimoto 1991).

In the Japanese firms, knowledge about the technical, organisational and commercial nature of the product is neither clearly delineated nor owned exclusively by specific individuals or groups. There is a high degree of 'shared division of labour', not only horizontally across functions but also vertically between engineers and management. Japanese project managers often remain technically involved and they 'intrude' into engineers' detailed technical work. Clark and Fujimoto described these managers as 'heavy weight project managers' who 'engage the bench level designer on the substance of the detailed design' (Clark and Fujimoto 1991: 260). They are also 'multilingual translators' fluent in the languages of engineers, designers, marketers and customers (ibid.: 259). Nevertheless, Japanese project managers do not have monopoly access to organisational and product market information: working level engineers are often encouraged to step outside their technical boundary to acquire these information. Evidence from the interviews shows that the Japanese engineers spend at least a third of their daily working time on information exchange activities such as discussions and meetings. In addition, searching for market information is also frequently mentioned as part of their daily activities. Organisational knowledge and commercial information does not lie exclusively in the managerial hierarchy; it can be located anywhere in the coordination network.

Nonaka (1989) uses the term 'information redundancy' to describe the Japanese situation in which individuals or groups embrace some kind of extra information in addition to their necessary specific information through 'mutual intrusion of territories'. This duplication of tasks and information appears to be 'wasteful' from the viewpoint of economic efficiency. It also puts excessive demands on the individuals to engage in intensive human interaction and long hours of work. Many of the Japanese engineers complained about fatigue, having too many 'miscellaneous duties' and finding it difficult at times to concentrate on development work. However, Nonaka points out that the duplication of tasks and redundancy of information have positive outcomes in Japanese organisations – it increases the chance of establishing a relationship based on trust and generates a dynamic cooperative relationship (Nonaka 1989: 265).

In contrast, in the British firms, the separation between technical and managerial work is more distinct. The distinction between the two is not only between tasks but also between levels of control and information. Engineers are technical experts in their specialist areas who are often left alone to get on with their own work. Managers specialise in organisational linkages and they are the main source of organisational and commercial information. Engineers are dependent on their project managers to filter down relevant information who, in turn, are reliant on senior management above them for wider knowledge and information. Integration of the total product occurs via a vertical information structure which enables managers to be informed of all problems and decisions. Knowledge and information for coordination of the total product become concentrated within the managerial hierarchy. The division of labour between engineers and managers is clear cut and the location of the type of knowledge and information is highly specific to particular tasks performed. This appears to be economical and efficient as it avoids duplication of human effort and information. However, the clear delineation of job boundaries between engineers and managers and the lack of information sharing between the two groups often generates low trust and further reinforces the split between technical and managerial expertise in the British firms.

To the extent that engineers possess information specific only to their own technical task, there is little scope to exercise discretion and they may lack knowledge and information to cope with emergent problems or any tasks outside their immediate boundaries. Managers may not perceive the need to filter down 'extra' information not immediately relevant to engineers' specific tasks. One engineer pointed out that the amount of information she got was based on a 'need to know' basis:

> I think the 'need to know' business is going too far. They've got to trust their engineers at some point, or else, it doesn't work. It's never going to work if they don't trust their engineers.

In our interviews, complaints about poor communication and lack of company information were frequently encountered.

> Well you don't always know what deadlines you are working to. You don't always know what management is doing here. It would be nice if we knew meetings and things the project manager is going to, because that helps to keep us informed of what's going on. . . . O.K. They are trying to expand the market but you just don't know.

> They don't really tell you what's going on. Perhaps for reasons of their own they just want to keep it to themselves. So you know you don't feel . . . the sort of belonging.

194

Other engineers felt that the withholding of information from engineers is almost a company policy. Many felt they were 'being kept in the dark'.

I don't think we are very well informed. I think there's almost a direct policy of not informing the engineers of what's happening. . . . It's very difficult, most engineers go on as if they're kept in the dark – they're not worthy of knowing. I think they [management] have got to get over that aspect of it.

About the company, I think the amount of information available is abysmal. Size of company, trading position, business orders . . . I mean it really is shocking, you are kept in the dark. I think it's absolutely shocking.

The isolation of engineers from the 'broad picture' may well be an inevitable outcome of the separation of technical and managerial work. The situation, however, could be aggravated by suspicion and the lack of trust between the two parties. To the extent that managers have to abdicate technical skills and knowledge to the engineers, their competence and authority may be questioned and challenged. The disengagement from technical work may put managers in a vulnerable situation, it becomes necessary to legitimise their authority and control by their monopoly access to organisational and commercial information. Information may become an instrument to demonstrate superior worth and defending status. Managers may deliberately withhold information to reinforce their higher rank and control. The polarisation of technical and managerial roles in British firms thus generates low trust and further inhibits vertical information sharing.

ON-THE-JOB TRAINING, SKILLS AND ROLE COMPETENCE OF ENGINEERS

Different forms of work organisation create different role expectations and skills development opportunities for engineers which in turn affect the extent of their full utilisation in product development.

In the British firms, the narrow specialisation of engineers' tasks, the segmentation of the product cycle and the isolation of engineers from the product market restrict the range of skills and knowledge they can acquire and inhibit the exploitation of their full potential for product development. The British form of work organisation tends to produce single-skilled technical specialists. In contrast, the Japanese form of work organisation fosters a high degree of shared division of labour and collective learning; it facilitates the development of 'generalist engineers' with hybrid skills.

The contrasting patterns of skills development are clearly illustrated by our 'critical incidents study' of the on-the-job training (OJT) experience of the engineers over a six-month period. The term OJT is defined here in a broad sense referring to learning which takes place during day-to-day work activities, but excluding formal training courses. A detailed content analysis of the self-recorded reports provided by the engineers shows some striking contrasts in the form of on-the-job training and the type of knowledge/skills acquired. The Japanese engineers reported learning in groups, both for formal and informal OJT; the British, that they learn individually by self-study (Table 9.3). The role of project leaders as key persons in the learning process was frequently mentioned in the Japanese reports but rarely in the British ones. This striking contrast between the group and individual approach to learning is very important as it affects the speed of diffusion of knowledge within organisations – a critical factor determining the speed of product development. Further, the type and range of knowledge acquired by the engineers through their OJT experience also differ. The British engineers reported learning technically-specific skills for solving the immediate problem, whereas the Japanese engineers reported learning more technically-general skills and a broader range of knowledge (Table 9.4).

More importantly, Japanese work organisation encourages their engineers to develop a wide range of non-technical or organisational skills. Aoki (1988: 50) describes these as contextual skills – general capacities for coordination and information processing. Contextual skills enable engineers to cope with emergent tasks and unusual problems in the product development process. They enhance engineers' capacity for flexibility and facilitate cross-functional adjustments. Such skills are increasingly important in a fast changing technological and product market environment where the ability of firms to reduce product development lead time and respond rapidly to changing customer demands is vital for competitiveness (Campbell and Warner 1992: 54–5). The way technical work is organised in the British firms does not allow engineers to develop their contextual skills which severely limits their role in product development. Many British engineers interviewed were persistently frustrated by the lack of full product knowledge and under-utilisation of their skills potential.

On-the-job learning plays a significant part in determining the skills and role competence of engineers. British engineers' limited on-the-job learning experience restricts their opportunities in acquiring a wide range of technical and organisational problem solving skills. As a result, British engineers come to be seen as narrow technical specialists unsuited for promotion to senior management. In contrast, the nature of engineers' roles in Japanese firms encourages engineers to acquire a broad range of skills and knowledge, enabling them eventually to become highly competent technical as well as organisational problem solvers.

Table 9.3 Types of knowledge and skills acquired through on-the-job training
(critical incident analysis; % of incidents)

	Japan	Britain
Technical – specific	24	78
Technical – general	49	6
Non-technical/organisational skills	25	13
Managerial	1	3
Others	1	–
(N = no. of incidents)	(83)	(67)

Table 9.4 Patterns of on-the-job training
(critical incidents analysis; % of incidents)

	Japan	Britain
Spontaneous		
Individual	21	79
Pair	15	9
Group	22	7
Formal		
Individual	–	–
Pair	3	2
Group	39	3
(N – no. of incidents)	(80)	(67)

WORK ORGANISATION, ENGINEERS' SKILLS AND INNOVATIVE PERFORMANCE OF FIRMS

Since the mid-1970s, discussion of the decline in the competitive performance of British engineering industries has focused on the problem of
shortages of qualified personnel and the failure of industry to attract the
best technical talent. Thus far, the main policy solutions proposed have
been to boost the professional status of engineers and to reform the formal education and qualification systems in order to stimulate skills supply.
However, there is little evidence that reforming the qualification systems
and increasing the number of engineers supplied will, on their own, lead
to better performance. It is the argument of this chapter that the debate
about engineering skills formation in Britain has been far too concerned

with the formal education and qualification systems and neglected the important issues of utilisation and skills development in the workplace.

Evidence presented in this chapter has demonstrated the influence of work organisation on skills development and utilisation. The striking contrasts in the way technical work is organised between the British and Japanese firms have significant implications for the roles and skills of engineers, which in turn have important consequences on the motivation of engineers and the innovative performance of firms.

In the British firms, the narrow specialisation of engineers' tasks, the segmentation of the product cycle and the isolation of engineers from the product market restrict the range of skills and knowledge they acquire and inhibit the exploitation of their full potential for product innovation. The mechanistically structured organisation in the British firms has led to a vertical polarisation between technical and managerial roles which generates low trust, and hinders information and knowledge sharing in the product development process. Our interviews show that these organisational factors contribute to the poor motivation of the British engineers and their disillusionment with the technical role early in their careers. Many young British engineers opt to move out of their technical roles as early as possible and aspire to a management position (Lam 1989). This is not because they are frustrated with their low professional status, as is often assumed, but more because they are interested in positions which allow greater involvement in the whole product innovation process. The failure of British firms fully to utilise and develop the capacities of engineers could have long-term detrimental effect on their competitive performance.

In the Japanese firms, the skills formation of engineers is closely embedded in the work process. The Japanese form of work organisation fosters a high degree of shared division of labour and collective learning. The tight linkages between the different phases of the product cycle facilitate horizontal communication and information flow, and engineers are encouraged to develop a broad range of non-technical skills and information processing capacities. The close integration between technical and managerial roles encourages knowledge sharing and the formation of a shared technical culture within Japanese firms. The Japanese patterns of work organisation enable firms fully to exploit and utilise both the technical and integrative problem solving capacities of their engineers. The roles, skills and attitudes of engineers and the ability of firms to foster organisational learning are critical factors behind the innovative performance of Japanese firms in electronics engineering (Imai *et al.* 1985; Nonaka 1988; Clark and Fujimoto 1991).

If inappropriate work organisation and the lack of effective skills development in the workplace is at the heart of the problem in Britain, then policies for bringing about change will need to tackle these issues directly.

The growing pace of technological change and the need for greater product market responsiveness increasingly requires engineers to develop a broader range of non-technical and integrative problem solving skills (Campbell and Warner 1992). These skills can be effectively developed in the workplace only through cross-functional work experience and reciprocal information exchange and knowledge sharing between individuals and functional groups. Organisations can be differentially structured so as to inhibit, facilitate and shape skill development and patterns of knowledge sharing. Any attempt to raise the level of education and qualification for engineers will pay off only if firms organise the work process in a way that encourages continuous skills development and organisational learning. The Japanese case underlines the importance of on-the-job learning and how organisational structure and day-to-day work process determine the effectiveness of such learning.

CONCLUSIONS

The common assumption that skills and knowledge are provided by the formal education and qualification systems is based on a partial and incomplete view of the nature of skills formation. The analysis presented in this chapter has illustrated that a more complete conceptualisation and understanding of the skill formation process must take into account the role of on-the-job learning and the design of organisation.

The study has shown that even for a highly qualified category of the workforce such as engineers who acquire their general conceptual knowledge through the formal training system, a substantial part of the skills and knowledge, e.g. organisational knowledge, contextual skills and capacity for information processing, which are essential for effective product development, can be transmitted only through learning in the workplace. Inoki (1987: 42–4), following Polanyi (1958), points out that human knowledge can be distinguished into two types. The first is conceptualised, general knowledge and the second can be called particular knowledge, knowledge concerned with particular conditions of time and place; it is also characterised by being difficult to conceptualise and codify. Inoki argues that the essence of most skills in the workplace is based on the second type of undefinable knowledge and hence a large part of the skills and knowledge in the workplace are of a type that can probably be transmitted only through the workplace. These latter skills are shaped by the workplace organisation, task responsibilities and role relationships. A full analysis of skills cannot neglect the work context.

This chapter has also illustrated that the actual work roles and task responsibilities of similar occupations can vary substantially in different organisational settings. The degree of role flexibility, level of task discretion and patterns of authority and control not only influences workers'

199

perception of skills development opportunities and motivation for learning, but also determines the patterns of information sharing and diffusion of knowledge within organisations. Management's choice of different organisational models has a significant impact on the effectiveness of the skill formation process.

APPENDIX

Tables 9.1 and 9.2 (pp. 185–6) showed the sample companies and the number of engineers participating. At the initial stage, 90 Japanese and 65 British engineers agreed to take part in the study. All of them completed a background questionnaire and about half of the Japanese engineers and two-thirds of the British engineers engaged in the 'critical incidents' monthly reporting exercise over a period of six months. The critical incident approach was adopted because the main aim was to find out how much actual learning takes place in engineers' day-to-day work activities, and the methods and processes by which it is being facilitated. It is necessary to record the actual details of learning opportunities as they happen; questionnaires are unlikely to yield the kind of information needed. The monthly report was designed to allow engineers to record the most important learning opportunities in a systematic way over a period of six months.

Following the completion of the monthly reports, individual interviews were carried out with 53 British and 61 Japanese engineers. The interviews examined in great detail the actual work roles, job rotation and organisational contexts as experienced by the engineers. Each interview lasted for an average of 75 minutes. All of the British interviews and 51 of the Japanese interviews were subsequently transcribed and analysed.

As the study required a considerable level of collaboration from the individual engineers, a system of 'feedback' meetings was organised, both in the middle and at the end of the data collection period, to discuss the data with groups of engineers and interested personnel staff. Thurley (1988) described this kind of 'feedback' method as 'process analysis' – a specific form of action research in which participants in the research project are involved in the discussion of results and of policy implications. This method proved to be valuable in correcting the researchers' bias in interpretation and for taking into account the views of the individuals involved in the study.

All the engineers who took part in the study were from large firms. The sample consisted of volunteers, and therefore cannot be claimed to be a random sample. The general profile of the interview sample is shown in Table 9.5. They were selected from research laboratories and development factories. The distribution of the interview sample by job functions as shown in Table 9.5 is based on the engineers' own classification in the

Table 9.5 A profile of the interview sample

	Britain	Japan
Age		
25 or under	14	2
26–30	22	17
31–35	10	19
36+	7	13
Education		
Bachelor's degree	36	19
Master's degree	8	28
Doctorate	6	4
Others	3	–
Service with present company		
3 years or less	18	8
4–6 years	17	14
7–9	9	13
10+ years	9	16
Job function		
Research	9	18
Development	20	17
Design	12	7
Technical management	7	8
Others	5	1
Total in sample	53	51

questionnaires. The initial number of Japanese development engineers taking part in the questionnaire survey was higher but some of them were not available for the interviews due to the pressure of work. As a result, we have a higher proportion of research engineers in the Japanese interview sample. However, this did not necessarily bias the study as the majority of the Japanese research engineers were engaged in applied research and development work. Also in Japanese firms, it is difficult to make a clear distinction between the research and development roles of engineers because of the practice of job rotation and flow of staff between research centres and development factories at different stages of the product development cycle.

The engineers were mostly in their twenties and thirties. The Japanese sample was slightly older and on the whole more highly educated. The difference in age composition is partly due to differing recruitment ages in the two countries. It has become increasingly common for large Japanese firms to recruit engineering graduates with a two-year Master's degree. The lower proportion of older engineers in the British sample is probably due to high labour turnover and many engineers moving into non-technical roles in their thirties.

ACKNOWLEDGEMENTS

This chapter is based on a research project started by the author with the late Professor Keith Thurley during 1989–91. Additional fieldwork and interviews were carried out in 1994. The financial support of STICERD, London School of Economics, and the Social Science Research Committee, University of Kent, is gratefully acknowledged. The author would also like to thank Denki Rengo for their support in Japan.

REFERENCES

Aoki, M. (1988) *Information, Incentives and Bargaining in the Japanese Economy*, Cambridge: Cambridge University Press.

Blears, J. and Bonwitt, B.J. (1988) *A Comparison of the Statistics of Engineering Education: Japan and the United Kingdom*, May, London: Engineering Council.

Campbell, A. and Warner, M. (1992) *New Technology, Skills and Management: Human Resources in the Market Economy*, London: Routledge.

Cassels, J.S. (1987) 'Success in electronics: shortening the odds on Britain', Mountbatten Memorial Lecture, 24 November.

Child, J., Fores, M., Glover, I. and Lawrence, P. (1983) 'A price to pay? Professionalism and work organisation in Britain and West Germany', *Sociology* 17(1): 63–78.

Clark, K.B. and Fujimoto, T. (1991) *Product Development Performance*, Boston, MA: Harvard Business School.

Finniston, M. (1980) *Engineering Our Future*, Report of the Committee of Inquiry into the Engineering Profession (Sir Montague Finniston, Chairman), London: HMSO.

Hutton, S. and Lawrence, P. (1981) *German Engineers: The Anatomy of a Profession*, Oxford: Clarendon Press.

Imai, K., Nonaka, I. and Takeuchi, H. (1985) 'Managing the new product development process: how the Japanese companies learn and unlearn', in K.B. Clark, R.H. Hayes and C. Lorenz (eds) *The Uneasy Alliance*, Boston, MA: Harvard Business School.

Imano, K. (1986) 'Gijutsu-sha no jinzai keisei' (Skills formation of engineers), in K. Koike (ed.) *Gendai no Jinzai Keisei* (Contemporary Skill Formation), Kyoto: Minerubiya.

Inoki, T. (1987) 'Skill transfer and economic organization', in K. Koike and T. Inoki (eds) *Skill Formation in Japan and Southeast Asia*, Tokyo: University of Tokyo Press.

Ito, M. (1988) *Gijutsu Kakushin to hyuman nettouwaki gata soshiki* (Technological innovation and human network organisation), Tokyo: Japan Institute of Labour.

Ito, M. (1993) 'Kenkyu kaihatsu gijutsu-sha no kigyo-nai ikusei no genjo' (Development of corporate R&D personnel), *Nihon Rodo Kenkyu Zasashi* (Monthly Journal of the Japan Institute of Labour) 35(6): 22–8.

Lam, A. (1989) *Why do your Graduate Engineers Leave?*, mimeo, STICERD, London School of Economics.

Lam, A. (1993) 'Training and innovation: the Japanese way', *Engineering Management Journal* December: 263–8.

Maurice, M., Sorge, A. and Warner, M. (1980) 'Societal differences in organising manufacturing units', *Organization Studies* 1: 63–91.

Meiksins, P. and Smith, C. (1993) 'Organizing engineering work: a comparative analysis', *Work and Occupations* 20(2): 123–46.

NEDO (1988) *Performance and Competitive Success: Comparative Education and Training Strategies* (Electronics Industry Sector Group), London: National Economic Development Office.

Nonaka, I. (1988) 'Creating organisational order out of chaos: self-renewal in Japanese firms', *California Management Review* 30(3): 57–73.

Nonaka, I. (1989) 'Seihin kaihatsu to inobeshun' (Product development and innovation', in K. Imai and R. Komiya (eds) *Nihon No Kigyo* (The Japanese Enterprise), Tokyo: University of Tokyo.

Polanyi, M. (1958) *Personal Knowledge: Towards a Post-Critical Philosophy*, Chicago: University of Chicago Press.

Sorge, A. (1979) 'Engineers in management: a study of the British, French and German traditions', *Journal of General Management* 5: 46–57.

Sorge, A. (1991) 'Strategic fit and the societal effect: Interpreting cross-national comparisons of technology, organization and human resources', *Organization Studies* 12(2): 161–90.

Sorge, A. and Warner, M. (1986) *Comparative Factory Management: An Anglo-German Comparison of Manufacturing Management and Manpower*, Aldershot: Gower.

Thurley, K. (1988) 'The triangulation approach in international cross-cultural research', *STICERD Discussion Paper CIR/88/180*, London School of Economics.

Wakasugi, R. (1989) 'Kenkyu kaihatsu no soshiki to kodo' (Organisation and policy practices in Research and Development), in K. Imai and R. Komiya (eds) *Nihon No Kigyo* (The Japanese Enterprise), Tokyo: University of Tokyo.

Werskey, G. (1987) *Training for Innovation: How Japanese Companies Develop their Elite Engineers*, London: General Electric Company.

Westney, E. (1993) 'Country patterns in R&D organization: the United States and Japan', in B. Kogut (ed.) *Country Competitiveness: Technology and the Organizing of Work*, Oxford: Oxford University Press.

Part III

CHANGE IN
GENDER RELATIONS

10

CHECKING OUT
AND CASHING UP

The prospects and paradoxes of
regulating part-time work in Europe

Abigail Gregory
and Jacqueline O'Reilly

Since the early 1990s, interest in the issue of part-time work has emerged with attempts to develop a more integrated single European market. The White Paper on *Growth, Competitiveness, Employment* (Commission of the European Communities 1993) has sought to encourage a more extensive use of flexible working time (*Labour Research* 1994: 11), as one means of reducing unemployment in the community. However, concern has also arisen over the haphazard growth in part-time work which may encourage social dumping and/or a distortion of competition at the Community level. A major criticism of the development of part-time work has emphasised the disadvantageous conditions associated with this form of 'atypical' employment. In Britain criticism has focused on the way that hours thresholds affect the application of basic employment rights and social security entitlements: in 1988 over 2.1 million men and women were excluded from employment protection (Maier 1991), although a House of Lords' ruling (3 March 1994) should help reduce the levels of discrimination somewhat in Britain. In France, where labour law and social security provisions offer protection to a larger number of part-timers (approximately 400,000 men and women were without protection in 1988 according to Maier 1991), greater emphasis is placed on other forms of discrimination: fewer promotion prospects, less convenient working hours, less functional flexibility and more repetitive tasks (Marimbert 1992).

The disparity in working conditions for part-timers propelled the European Commission to develop common minimum standards of regulation throughout the European Union (EU). The draft directive on atypical work (COM (90) 228/I and II final of 29.6.90), although not yet adopted by the Council of Ministers, seeks to improve the conditions of employment for those not working on a full-time or permanent basis. This directive would give 'atypical' workers the same rights, such as training and holidays, as permanent full-time staff. Those working more than eight hours a week would also gain the right to social security benefits: both part-time employees and their employer would be obliged to pay social security contributions. A major concern arising from these developments revolves around the question of the role and impact of supra-national regulation in attempting to generate convergent employment practices and further integration within the EU.

These developments at the economic and political level have been discussed theoretically in relation to debates on globalisation, convergence, economic integration and political harmonisation. These debates have emerged from the growing literature and research comparing working practices in different countries (for example: Gallie 1978; Maurice *et al.* 1982; Sorge and Warner 1986). As Redding (1994) points out, such research has a long and varied tradition (see also O'Reilly 1994a: ch. 1).

Initially, comparative research suggested that industrial and technological imperatives would lead to a convergence in industrial organisation on several levels: economically, politically and socially. This idea, first popularised in the work of Kerr *et al.* (1960), received considerable criticism from later empirical work. Nevertheless, 'new' or revised versions of this idea have emerged in the growing literature on 'globalisation' (Ohmae 1990) or 'Europeanisation' (Mueller and Purcell 1992). The causes of globalisation, or pressures encouraging a convergence in management practices arise from the growing importance of multinational companies (MNCs), the free movement of capital and investments, as well as the desire to build on 'best practice' and the transfer of knowledge and technology. Even if there is considerable debate as to what constitutes a global firm (Hirst and Thompson 1992) there is, nevertheless, a conception that advanced industrialised countries have been exposed to similar pressures and changes. In the European context these economic pressures, as well as the exchange rate mechanism (ERM) and moves to develop European monetary union (EMU), have been coupled with a – sometimes ambivalent – desire to forge a political and social union within the continent. In sum, there have been encouragements for European economies to integrate and harmonise at all three levels. However, this process of integration has met with severe resistance from some quarters which has raised questions concerning the nature of convergence in Europe.

An opposing perspective to the globalisation school of thought has argued that despite universal pressures to conform to a single model, in practice what we find is a growing level of diversity. Gallie (1978) points out that in Britain and France, despite similar technology, working practices and social integration within firms varied between countries. Maurice *et al.* (1982) have argued that the social institutions in a given society have a significant impact on shaping the nature of working relations within firms in Germany and France. In South East Asia, Whitley

(1992) has shown that there are a variety of ways in which Japanese, Taiwanese and Hong Kong firms are structured. Further, Schmid *et al.* (1992) have argued that even within the European Union the development of social welfare schemes, such as unemployment insurance, have increasingly diverged, as opposed to a desired convergence. Much of this empirical work has focused on how institutional arrangements of a particular society affects work organisation at the firm level. In a similar vein, the work of Granovetter (1985) shows that the characteristics of economic relations are greatly influenced by on-going social relations and networks. Such a perspective is critical of a macro-economic perspective which ignores the specificity of such factors. Although the emphasis in these studies varies between those who give greater weight to the structural role of social institutions and those who emphasise the importance of actors in creating and re-creating specific social relations, the general conclusion to be taken from them is that the relations of economic life have shown a greater propensity towards particularity than similarity and convergence.

To some extent Mueller (1994) has attempted to assess the theoretical debates and empirical research concerned with arguments around convergence and divergence. He points out that there is often contradictory evidence for both perspectives, but despite this he argues for a more global approach. The aim of this chapter is to examine these debates by focusing on the way firms use part-time employment, and on attempts to regulate this activity at both the national and European level. We are interested in examining the tensions and developments which have occurred in relation to the growth and regulation of this form of employment. Employment regulation is taken here to mean not only national employment law and European directives but, also, collective bargaining and law court rulings. It is argued in this chapter that the extent of convergence in relation to the use of part-time work will depend on the outcome of conflicts and compromises arrived at by various actors at the firm, national and supranational level.

In this chapter we examine aggregate data for a range of European countries as well as focusing on case study data for the use of part-time work in Britain and France, both at the national and sectoral level. These data allow us to examine the general and specific trends in the use of part-time employment. Our case studies focus on the use of part-time work in the retail banking and the large-scale grocery retailing sectors in both countries. This is because there has been a relative neglect of service sector industries in employment research, in particular from a cross-national cross-sector perspective. The service sector in general has undergone considerable employment growth in both countries since the 1960s, growth which is attributable to a large extent to part-time work, particularly in Britain. The choice of Britain and France for comparison provides us with two countries where there are significant differences in the levels of part-time work. For example, as a percentage of the total labour force the rate of part-time work rose between 1973 and 1991 from 16 per cent to 24.5 per cent in Britain and from 7.2 per cent to 13.4 per cent in France (Maier 1991; Eurostat 1993). Further, a comparison of banking and grocery retailing also allows us to examine sectors where we might expect relatively low and high levels of part-time work respectively. In retail banking considerable product knowledge and personalised customer relationships are required. This is not the case in large-scale grocery retailing where self-service methods have facilitated the division of labour and the removal of functions from the retail outlet, resulting in the disappearance of the traditional skills of the shop worker (Fulop 1964).

Retail banking and large-scale retailing are particularly suitable sectors for examining the issues raised by the globalisation–national specificity debate. In terms of factors encouraging convergence, both sectors in each country have been subject to similar commercial pressures and technological changes. For example, in both sectors product markets have become increasingly saturated, which has led to a greater segmentation of services and products: in retail banking a broader range of accounts and financial services are now offered by most banks; in large-scale retailing there has been an increase in product differentiation and the introduction of high value-added goods. Automation has also had a profound impact on both sectors: in banking extensive use is being made of cash dispensers, computer networks and telephone banking; in retailing just-in-time delivery, scanning and Direct Product Profitability (DPP) have all been developed since the early 1980s. The site of service delivery has also changed: telephone banking has lead to a revised conception of the role of branch networks; in large-scale retailing there has been a growth in out-of-town shopping centres and mail order. Further, in both sectors there has been pressure to compete in terms of longer opening hours (Dawson 1982; Burt 1989, 1991; O'Reilly 1994a). Given such conditions these sectors provide an apposite, yet neglected, site of interest in which to examine the impact of political developments in the European context as well as theoretical debates on developments in industrial organisation.

The chapter begins by giving a brief overview of changes in the use of part-time work at national level in various European countries on the basis of Labour Force Survey data. It identifies trends in the use of part-time work since the mid-1970s. Second, drawing on comparative case-study research conducted in Britain and France in retailing and banking, common national and sectoral differences in the use of part-time work are examined. Third, explanations for the differences are found in the relationship between the nature of labour market regulation, the salient characteristics of business concerns and demand for labour, as well as the characteristics of the available sources of labour. Finally, the implications of these findings are examined in relation to developments within the

European Union. The main argument, developed on the basis of this research, is that the prospects and paradoxes of regulating and harmonising part-time work will depend on the interaction of actors at the local, national and European level. The conflicts and compromises that this will entail suggest that wholescale convergence is unlikely to occur and that the parameters of employment standards will continue to be a source of conflict, at several levels.

TRENDS IN THE USE OF PART-TIME WORK

Since the mid-1970s there has been a tendency for the use of part-time work to increase in several European countries. However, the rate of growth varies significantly between countries. High levels of use are found in the Netherlands, Denmark and Britain, whereas Germany, France and Belgium are examples of countries with relatively moderate rates of part-time work; Ireland, Italy, Spain, Luxembourg, Greece and Portugal have very low levels of part-time work (Maier 1991; Eurostat 1993; Fagan et al. 1994). Table 10.1 illustrates the rate of growth of part-time work in high to moderate use countries since 1973.

The Netherlands, which during the 1970s had a low use of part-time work, experienced a rapid acceleration after 1979 (de Neubourg 1985; de Olde 1994). In Denmark the use of part-time work has remained high and relatively stable. In Britain there has been a notable increase during the 1980s. Germany, France and Belgium have all experienced an increase in part-time work, although from different base rates (Maier 1991; Rubery et al. 1994).

If we break down these aggregate national trends we can identify distinct sectors where the use of part-time work has increased in each of these countries. An analysis of European Labour Force data presented by Rubery et al. (1994) shows that in all countries by far the greatest rates of female part-time work has been in 'other services' (Table 10.2). However, the rate of use varies: in the Netherlands 55 per cent of all employees in this sector were working part-time in 1991 compared to only 9 per cent in Portugal. Amongst high and moderate use countries the distribution sector also accounts for a significant share of part-time employment, although rates of part-time working also vary considerably from one country to another. In the banking and finance industry part-time work has increased very rapidly, particularly in Germany and Denmark. In the Netherlands, Germany and Denmark there has also been an increase in the use of part-time work in manufacturing and in transport and communications. These differences indicate the difficulty of identifying a common European model of part-time work and suggest that individual countries are following different working time patterns, rather than converging around a common single pattern. These findings give little

211

Table 10.1 Trends in the growth of part-time work in high to moderate use
countries in Europe[a]
(as a percentage of the total labour force)

	Netherlands	Denmark	Britain	Germany	France	Belgium
1973	8.7	na	16.0	10.1	7.2	3.8
1975	9.5	21.2	17.1	11.2	6.4	4.9
1977	9.7	22.0	17.2	11.7	7.8	6.1
1979	11.2	22.7	16.4	11.4	8.2	6.0
1981	21.8	23.7	17.9	12.0	8.3	6.4
1983	28.1	26.7	22.4	15.3	10.3	11.3
1985	29.3	26.5	24.2	15.2	11.9	12.5
1987	34.6	26.3	24.7	15.1	12.9	14.3
1989	36.6	25.2	26.3	16.0	13.4	14.9
1991	37.0	24.6	24.5	18.1	13.4	16.3

Sources: Maier 1991; Eurostat 1993: Table 28, p. 77)

Note: [a] Figures for 1973–81 are based on unpublished Labour Force Survey data presented in Maier (1991). Figures for 1983–91 are based on published Eurostat (1993) data. Figures for 1983–7 available from Eurostat (1993) appear to be higher than those presented by Maier (1991) although they also come from Labour Force Survey. This indicates one of the problems of the reliability of comparisons drawn from such data. Nevertheless, whether the later figures are an overestimate, or the earlier figures an underestimate, they still reinforce the pattern of differentiated uses of part-time work in Europe.

Table 10.2 Incidence of part-time employment by sector for a selection of
European countries 1991
(share of all employees who are part-time)

	Countries grouped by incidence of part-time work									
Sector	High			Moderate			Low			
	NL	UK	DK	D	B	F	IRL	I	E	P
Other services	55	41	38	29	25	22	17	8	13	9
Distribution	39	41	32	25	25	15	15	7	4	3
Agriculture	31	20	22	14	0	13	0	19	2	8
Finance and insurance	24	16	18	18	11	10	6	5	4	7
Public administration	19	13	17	13	11	16	7	2	2	1
Other manufacturing	23	13	18	12	6	6	4	4	2	2
Transport and communications	21	9	14	11	5	9	0	2	1	0

Source: Rubery *et al.* 1994: Appendix table 3.2

support to the arguments put forward by the convergence/globalisation/ Europeanisation school. They force us to ask why such divergence exists, and appears to persist.

Although labour force data can allow us to measure the rate of growth and the age and sex ratios of those who are employed part-time within a specific country, difficulties arise when we want to make direct comparisons between countries. This is because in each society employment status and occupational categories may be defined in a somewhat different way, as a result of a different evolution over time (these problems are discussed more fully in Beechey 1989; Dale and Glover 1989, 1990; Gregory 1989; O'Reilly 1994a). A further problem with survey data of this kind is that they cannot tell us in detail what types of work organisation employers adopt and the rationale for these patterns. While national studies can give some insights into these questions they rarely enable cross-national comparison at a sectoral level. Such information can be provided only by more qualitative case-study data, which also permits us to take account of differences in the meaning and reasons for using full- or part-time work in different countries.

COMPARING CASE STUDY EVIDENCE OF THE USE OF PART-TIMERS IN RETAIL BANKING AND LARGE-SCALE GROCERY RETAILING IN BRITAIN AND FRANCE[1]

In general, part-timers in France work longer hours than British part-timers (Barrère-Maurisson *et al.* 1989). This was supported by data from the case study banks and supermarkets. In France, part-timers were more likely to work between nineteen and thirty hours a week in both sectors. In Britain, there was a trend to shorten the length of shifts in both sectors: in the banks 'week on week off' contracts were being replaced by two and three days a week contracts, and in retailing shifts of less than four hours a day were being introduced.[2]

Length of shifts and the variety of tasks performed appear to be linked. Part-timers in the French supermarkets were more multi-skilled than those in Britain; this strategy was used by employers to compensate for the fact that they worked longer hours. A similar pattern was also found in the banking sector where French part-timers were better qualified and more likely to say they were expected to do a wider variety of tasks than part-timers interviewed in Britain (O'Reilly 1992b). Part-timers working longer hours are more likely to receive training, however minimal, than those on very short hours.

In Britain, employers in both sectors were able to offer a diverse range of part-time contracts and to change these as and when they needed (O'Reilly 1994b). In France, the use of part-time work is more formalised than in the UK, according to regulations in the *Code du Travail* and in collective agreements (notably in retailing where a minimum contract length is established). Also, in France employees often had more formal opportunity to select the types of shifts they wanted (within a specific set of formulae) than in the UK. For example, in a number of French super-markets semi-autonomous groups allocated shifts amongst themselves; in the banks individuals, as was typical among public sector employees, negotiated their preferred type of part-time work.[3] This element of choice in the French supermarkets was introduced to reduce labour turnover on unpopular shifts. In Britain part-time hours and shifts were stipulated by the employers. In Britain an on-call system was used in both sectors. An on-call system means that the company can call up former employees at very short notice and ask them to come in to work for a specific time period. According to Wood and Smith (1992) this is a common procedure in British firms. This practice, which contravenes French labour law legislation which requires working hours to be fixed, did not exist in the French banks and was used illegally in only very few French supermarkets. In the banks in Britain, part-timers were used to meet daily workload fluctuations, which was not the case in the French banks.

Attitudes towards the use of part-time work also seemed to vary con-siderably in the two countries and to some extent between sectors. In the banks in France, employers rarely perceived any strategic advantage for the company in the use of part-time work. Managers in the banking sector in France were more hostile to the use of part-time work, in a society where full-time employment was seen to be the norm. Part-timers in the banks were segregated to an area where their absence would not be too disruptive to an organisation centred on full-time employment.[4] Managers and supervisors interviewed often said that the advantages of part-time work accrued primarily to the employees rather than to the company. In France, employees in the banks could request to work on a part-time basis because of government legislation and negotiations accepting this with the unions (O'Reilly 1994a). In the supermarkets, employers were more willing to use part-timers to meet peaks in workload associated with customer activity, although this was associated with higher rates of labour turnover.

This case study evidence indicates that the use of part-timers in Britain and France varies between the two countries.[5] We have seen differences, not only in the length of their contracts, and their levels of skill, but also in employers' attitudes to these types of employees. Further research also indicates that there are significant differences in the attitude of part-time employees in each country, which are discussed in more detail later (Gregory 1989; Dex *et al.* 1993; O'Reilly 1994b).

HOW MUCH OF THE DIFFERENCES FOUND ARE EXPLAINED BY EMPLOYMENT REGULATION?

Three major factors can be identified which account for the differences in the use of part-time work in Britain and France. The model illustrated in Figure 10.1 outlines the approach developed here. First, the nature of employment regulation in each country shapes the way that employers construct their labour demand. However, this also has to be seen in the context of how business concerns account for the way firms identify their labour needs. The main elements of business concerns are the forms of competition, the way service policy has developed, and the key issues in personnel management for these companies. Also, we need to identify the characteristics and preferences of the available labour supply in each country. This includes taking account, not only of their levels of training and qualifications, but also of how the provision of child care, tax and benefit systems affect available workers' ability and desire to participate in paid employment.

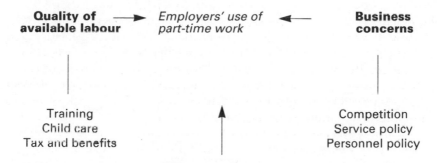

Figure 10.1 A model of labour market practices

REGULATION

The role of national legislation

A partial explanation for the lower levels of part-time work in French banking and retailing can be found in the greater employer reluctance to use part-time work compared with British employers. This reluctance stems from the differing costs and levels of protection associated with part-time work. In Britain, the trend of national policy has been to facilitate competition on the basis of low wages and limited employment protection. Until the House of Lords' ruling (March 1994), part-timers working less than sixteen hours required five years' continuous service with the same employer before they were entitled to employment protection; the legal ruling has equalised entitlement, for those working more than eight hours per week, to two years' continuous service. However, those working less than eight hours will still receive no protection. The national insurance system in Britain also encourages employers to use short weekly hours, especially for low skilled, low paid jobs like those found in grocery retailing. This is because national insurance contributions are paid only for workers earning over £56 a week (as at April 1994). The operation of the national insurance system has not been the only feature of the legislative framework to be conducive to the use of part-time work in retailing. The Selective Employment Tax (1966–73) caused retailers to look more critically at the composition and deployment of the workforce. This had an immediate impact on employment profiles (see Gregory 1989: 202). Also, it has been asserted that the Employment Protection Act 1975 and the Equal Pay Act 1970 provided a further economic incentive for the use of part-time work (see in particular Robinson and Wallace 1974; Hurstfield 1978). In sum, it has been easy and attractive for British employers to use part-time contracts which are cheaper and involve lower levels of protection. Common law traditions in British labour law also give British employers greater freedom to reorganise work contracts than countries like France with a Roman law tradition.

In France, by contrast, employers have traditionally shown greater reluctance to create part-time jobs, a characteristic which stems partly from its location in a more rigid framework for working time. Although Britain, owing to its earlier stage of industrialisation, was early to legislate for working time in the nineteenth century (Blyton 1985), working time in the twentieth century became the object of collective bargaining and minimal state intervention. In France, however, working time became the focus of much greater legislative intervention after 1936 when the French state introduced very progressive legislation – notably the introduction of the forty hour week and statutory paid leave – and a very strict framework controlling working time,[6] which effectively prohibited the use of part-time work. Other aspects of the French legislative framework also discouraged the use of part-time work: in particular the disproportionate cost of employers' national insurance contributions for part-timers until 1973 and other employment costs which were based on the number of employees and were not proportional to pay (Droulers 1972).[7]

After 1973, under the pressure of tight labour market conditions and employers' appeals for greater flexibility, the legislative framework was modified in order to make it easier to employ part-timers,[8] but the conditions of use remained so complicated that few employers had recourse to this form of work. Part-time work began to develop significantly only from the beginning of the 1980s when, under the dual pressure of growing unemployment and employers' demands for greater flexibility in the face of international industrial competition, left and right wing French governments took action to encourage the use of part-time work as part of a wider programme to increase flexibility in working time. In particular, the Socialist government (1981–6) sought to stimulate the supply of part-timers by ensuring that they were not discriminated against as far as their working conditions were concerned and by giving part-timers *pro rata* rights to full-timers. Indeed, in contrast with the situation in the UK, legislation in France has prevented all part-timers except those on very short weekly hours (whose numbers are usually limited by collective agreements) from being disadvantaged in terms of the payment of social security contributions (see Maier 1991). This has removed one incentive for employers to create part-time jobs comparable with those in the UK and it has inhibited the development of short weekly contracts (Fagan et al. 1994).

The development of flexibility in working time in the early 1980s was part of a wider debate in society on time, which has had no real equivalent in the UK, in which a greater flexibility in work and non-work time for men and women was favoured. This notion of flexibility was called *temps choisi* (Echanges et Projets 1980).[9] The Mitterrand government sought to develop its policy to increase flexibility in working time through the public sector where it introduced very favourable conditions for the use of part-time work in its 1982 legislation (*Ordonnance* of 31 March 1982), allowing part-time work to be available in *tranches* of 10 per cent, ranging from 50 to 90 per cent of a full-time job. This meant that in the extensive public sector in France part-time work took a more structured form than in Britain.[10]

The response to these government initiatives was relatively restrained (see Table 10.1), except for the public sector where the government has been able to exercise a more direct influence. Subsequent efforts by right wing governments to encourage the growth of part-time work have borne little fruit, a situation which may be explained in part by the characteristics and preferences of the labour supply as we shall suggest. In 1986 reductions in social security costs for part-timers were introduced. Under the Balladur government, all employers' contributions to employees' social security costs were removed, and other measures were taken to encourage the development of part-time work (see *Lettre de Matignon* 1993: 2–3). Nevertheless, the core aspects of employment protection for part-timers in France have been maintained.

Sector specific regulation is also more significant and restrictive in France than in the UK. For example, in the banking sector a working time decree from 1937 prohibits the use of overlapping shift work, and allows bank employees the right to two consecutive days' holiday, one of which must be a Sunday (O'Reilly 1994a: 229–30). Employers have been unsuccessful in attempts to have this decree derogated; such regulation prevents French employers developing part-time work in ways comparable to the British banks. In French food retailing it is illegal to use zero hours and on-call flexibility systems as these contravene labour law; in Britain no such restrictions apply. Also, in France the use of overtime, while permitted, is strictly controlled by this same legislation.[11] Added to these restraints the higher profile of working time in France and the widespread acceptance of the concept of *temps choisi* may contribute to an explanation for the more widespread use of employee-controlled flexibility in France.

The role of collective bargaining

The issue of working time has been dealt with differently by unions in the two countries (for a detailed analysis see Gregory 1989 and O'Reilly 1994a) and, in general, working time has been a higher profile issue for French trade unions than for their British counterparts. However, in France discussion of the issues of working time in the union movement has been characterised by disunity and in particular has been affected by the union leaderships' different visions of the levels at which bargaining over working time should take place. On the issue of flexible working time, for example, the CGT (Confédération Général du Travail) has opposed negotiations on flexible working time, including part-time work, whereas the CFDT (Confédération Française Democratique du Travail) have been more open and sought to maximise employees' choice in working patterns (Gregory 1989). Reactions to local initiatives have depended to a large extent on the degree of employer cohesiveness within a particular industry, as our examples in retailing and banking show. In Britain whilst the unions have generally adopted a more pragmatic stance towards negotiations on working time and have often been more willing to discuss the development of extended hours and shift work, they have not always been invited to participate in such negotiations.[12] Part-time work has not been opposed by British unions, which have sought instead to improve the conditions associated with this form of work.

In grocery retailing, in both countries, the unions have been hampered by recruitment difficulties and in Britain, food retailing trade unions have also found that the anti-union environment of the Thatcher years has weakened their negotiating position. Since the national collective agreement for food retailing – the Multiple Food Trade Joint Committee Agreement – became defunct in 1988, the main union in food retailing, the Union of Shop, Distributive and Allied Workers (USDAW), has been forced to adopt a very flexible position in relation to employers' demands in order to prevent negotiations from being completely severed (Gregory

1993). Its position with regard to the use of part-time work is also flexible: it accepts the fact that employees seek this form of work, but wishes to see part-timers' employment conditions improved. However, attempts to bring part-timers' conditions in line with those of full-timers have been thwarted. This is partly due to the fact that in the early 1990s many British large-scale retailers introduced job evaluation programmes to bring about equal pay for work of equal value. Although these have benefited part-timers at the bottom of the hierarchy because they have tended to raise pay, employers have been reluctant to improve part-timers' general conditions as well (Gregory 1993). In the area of pensions for part-timers, for example, they have had less success. Nevertheless, the unions have played a role in improving part-timers' conditions of work in as much as the continued pressure on employers to address equality issues has kept this on the agenda. They are also seeking to prevent the development of flexible contracts for part-timers such as zero hour contracts, although to date they have met with limited success (Gregory 1993). In terms of the day-to-day organisation of working time in retailing, the role of trade unions in Britain is, on the whole, limited and depends on the strength of local support. USDAW's main (indirect) influence on the daily organisation of work is the continuing application of the four hour threshold for rest breaks in firms belonging to the industry's collective agreement, which in turn has encouraged retailers to use daily shifts for part-timers of three and a half or three and three-quarter hours' duration.

In French food retailing, a formal machinery for sectoral level collective agreements exists and the agreement (*Convention Collective Nationale des Magasins de Vente d'Alimentation et d'Approvisionnement Général*) applies, in theory at least, to all employers in the sector. This is supplemented by narrower agreements such as the sector's agreement on part-time working (European Industrial Relations Review 1993, 231: 7), which dates from March 1993, and an increasing number of company agreements. Many of these provisions are inspired by existing legislation and practices currently prevalent in the sector. The main problem with the operation of the collective bargaining system in France is that members of the growing independent sector of food retailers are often not signatories to sectoral agreements and therefore employees in these outlets are not covered by their provisions until they are officially extended.[13] These retailers, like Leclerc and Intermarché, now account for 40 per cent of retail sales in supermarkets and in hypermarkets. Employment conditions in these non-signatory outlets seem to be deteriorating since they rely heavily on part-time work, temporary contracts and maximum use of overtime (Lallement 1993). Also, it now seems that in the context of weak sectoral-level bargaining and, given the growing importance of the unallied independent retailers, a relatively disunited employers' body,[14] company agreements on working time in food retailing are becoming widespread and increasingly threatening the basic conditions established in the Convention Collective (Lallement 1993).[15] However, in relation to working time, company agreements had allowed the introduction of semi-autonomous teams and new systems of breaks, both of which had a significant impact on work organisation. Finally, because of the weakness of the unions, industrial relations are often tilted in the favour of employers and employment regulation is not always observed. Despite this, our case study material suggested that in companies which applied the sectoral collective agreement legal provisions often had a considerable impact on working hours. For example, the minimum contract length allowed for part-time work in France was sixteen hours (now increased to twenty-two hours: *European Industrial Relations Review* 1993, 231: 7) and part-timers were required to work a minimum of three hours in one stretch, hence contributing to an explanation for the longer part-time contracts and longer part-time shifts, found in French large-scale grocery retailing.

In British banking, trade union weakness has been attributable to union divisions and inter-union hostility has made it increasingly difficult for the unions to co-operate or intervene effectively in workplace re-organisation. Also, the banking unions have traditionally never exercised job-property rights and, therefore, have been unable to intervene in job restructuring; as a result management have retained their prerogative to manage. With regard to the use of part-time work, the unions have sought to improve their rights and conditions. Successful gains include the right for part-timers to cheap loans and pensions. However, the banks' decision to improve conditions was largely a pre-emptive reaction to the European ruling on direct discrimination.

In France, the conditions of part-timers in the banking sector have benefited more from the protection provided to public sector workers, so that precarious forms of part-time work are prohibited from trade union gains obtained through collective bargaining. Most unions adopt an anti-part-time stance, seeing this form of employment as an attack on standard working conditions. The CFDT, however, has been prepared to compromise as long as such an approach can be collectively agreed.

In contrast to the British banks who have argued for shift work to meet employers' demands for flexible working hours, in France the unions have staunchly opposed this practice. The French unions have been opposed to any move which will undermine the 1937 decree on working time. Attempts to negotiate this issue have highlighted the tension between the unions over this, between the different levels of negotiations, as well as within the employers' association, the AFB. A good illustration of these tensions is the famous Credit Lyonnaise case in 1987 where the local Valence and Beziers branch of the CFDT made an agreement with an association of management workers, the SNB–CGC (Société Nationale Bancaire–Confédération Générale des Cadres).[16] The agreement conceded to union demands for shorter working hours in exchange for longer bank opening hours. This radical agreement was ratified by the National Confederation of the CFDT and received government support. However, the other unions were opposed to the local agreement, including the banking wing of the CFDT and the national SNB–CGC organisation. Moreover, such was the strength and unity of the banking employers' over-arching body – the AFB – which was in the process of negotiating the subject at branch level that the local agreement did not come into effect.

Clearly the nature of employment regulation at the national level has had an important impact in shaping the conditions under which employers have been able to develop forms of part-time work. Material drawn from these case studies indicate the complex and diverse conditions associated with part-time regulation at both the sectoral and the national level. It also shows that the way actors react to the issue of part-time work is closely related to these particular conditions. Such evidence further highlights the obstacles to developing harmonised working conditions in the European context. Nevertheless, we also wish to argue that it is not employment regulation on its own that needs to be taken into account in understanding the nature of these differences. In the following sections we propose to show how business concerns and the characteristics of labour supply also have a significant impact.

Business concerns

The convergence literature suggests that market factors, such as competition, technology and capital investments, will encourage firms to compete in similar ways, and therefore develop similar working practices. However, many of these generalisations have been based on studies of somewhat exceptional sectors, such as the car industry (Mueller and Purcell 1992). Generalisations derived from these studies have tended to overlook the fact that very few firms compete in similar global markets. Sorge and Maurice (1990) have pointed out how the machine tools industry in France has produced for a more customised market, compared to more standardised product development in Germany.[17] One of the key issues in these debates requires a more sophisticated analysis of the precise nature of the type of markets in which firms compete, and in what ways competition affects their organisational design.[18]

The use and demand for part-time work can be examined in relation to the way in which firms compete. Competition can take place on several levels, for example firms can compete in terms of access to services, opening hours, and the quality of service and goods provided. Firms can opt to offer a high quality service where staff are expected to have a broad product knowledge provided by the same employees; in other circumstances firms can fragment the services they provide, so that a number of different staff provide specialised services requiring a more limited or specialised product knowledge. Where a more integrated, high quality service with detailed product knowledge is the major element of competition, as in the French banks, less use is made of part-timers; where services are more fragmented and product knowledge is limited, a more extensive use of part-timers is found, as in the retail sector (O'Reilly 1992b).

Despite common pressures in both sectors in each country, significant differences in the competitive strategies and organisation of work were identified in Britain and France. In general, French companies had adopted a more extensive policy of task enlargement, whereas in Britain companies have been segmenting services; even British retailing companies seeking to offer a high quality service had adopted this approach. However, the motivation for enlarging task performance varied between sectors in France. In retailing, it was a response to a decision to limit the use of part-time work in order to avoid labour turnover problems, and was combined with a policy of offering longer part-time contracts. In banking in France, greater emphasis was given to offering a high quality service and detailed product knowledge, albeit with less complex products compared to the British banks. In French banking the application of till technology and work design (decentralised clearing) coincided with the approach taken to make limited use of part-time work, and give more emphasis to polyvalence. In Britain, the centralisation of clearing and till technology allowed companies to make greater use of part-time work (O'Reilly 1994a).

The basis on which firms compete in banking would seem to have affected the organisation of work and hence the use of part-time work in Britain and France. In food retailing, by contrast, the basis on which firms compete has not played a significant role. Rather companies' responses to the operation of different types of markets would seem to have generated different organisational structures: although since the 1980s discount food retailing has been more prevalent in France and competing on quality more common in Britain, policies on the use of part-time work have not matched competitive strategy; higher levels of part-time work are found in Britain where the policy of large-scale grocery retailers has been more quality-orientated.

In retailing and banking differences in the use of part-time work would also seem to have stemmed from dissimilar competitive pressures in the two countries and in particular from their impact on labour costs. In Britain food retailing suffered particularly from the economic recession in the 1970s: consumer expenditure on food showed no real growth between 1972 and 1982. Moreover, this situation was compounded by very high inflation rates which severely affected retailers' margins and growing price competition between retailers imposed by the new price consciousness of consumers during the 1970s (Gregory 1989). Under these conditions retailers 'set out to look for ways to improve the *status quo* in terms of their existing markets, and to reduce costs' (Reynolds 1985: para 2.03). In France, although sales growth in food retailing started to slow down from 1974, inflation was much lower over the same period. French food retailers did not experience comparable pressure to reduce labour costs until the beginning of the 1980s. This delayed pressure came about because of a substantial fall in household consumption due to recessionary conditions. Profit margins fell and, because of a relatively faster increase in employment in retailing than turnover, labour costs rose as a proportion of value added. It was from this point onwards that the use of part-time work became more widespread (Gregory 1989: 205).

In British banking there was less pressure to reduce labour costs during periods of limited competition between the banks. The cartel agreement on wages and grading between the major clearers and the potential for market expansion meant that labour costs were not a key issue. However, this situation changed after the breakup of the wage cartel in 1986, together with increased competition from building societies and a sudden fall in the market at the end of the 1980s. Profit instability created enormous pressures to reduce operating costs in general. In French banking competition has been a perennial characteristic, regardless of state control of the banks. Despite lower capital/assets ratios than British banks, French banks have had greater profit stability. Added to this has been government reluctance to encourage a mass displacement of jobs. So although the French banks have been concerned about overstaffing for longer than the British banks, changes in the size and shape of their personnel have been introduced in a more incremental and socially managed fashion. British banks, especially since 1986, have been under greater pressures to look for short-term measures to manage changing markets and organisational design.

Differences in staff allocation systems can also contribute to an explanation for the different uses of part-time work in each country. Part-timers can be most effectively used when they can be fitted precisely into a total hours schedule. In Britain, in both sectors a more detailed, Taylorist labour measurement system allowed the British companies to employ more part-timers than in France. For example, in the banks, time and motion studies were commonly used and staff numbers were allocated to within a decimal point; in France, the number of accounts determined the number of staff in a given branch. Similarly in British large-scale grocery retailing, a more sophisticated labour allocation system allowed a more extensive use of part-timers than in France, where these systems were less developed and staff numbers were mostly related to the turnover of a store (for a detailed explanation of the systems in retailing see Gregory 1989).

Finally, personnel policy, which in itself is affected by labour market conditions, also explained cross-national and cross-sectoral similarities and differences in the use of part-time work. In terms of personnel policy, part-time work has often been seen as an alternative source of labour in times of labour shortages; it has also been used to reduce full-time staff and cut labour costs by employing staff for peak periods. In the banks in France and Britain, part-time work was used to some extent to reduce staff numbers and cost. In the banks in France, as a result of recruiting thousands of low qualified staff during the period of branch expansion in the 1970s, the banks are now faced with a disproportionate number of relatively low-skilled, middle-aged staff in the middle to low grades of their organisation (Bertrand and Noyelle 1988; Cossalter 1990; Conseil National du Crédit 1989). Part-time work has been one 'legitimate' way for the banks to tackle the 'problem' of the age pyramid and reduce the number of full-time staff, in particular amongst older women employees. In British banking the situation was somewhat different to the extent that during the boom period at the end of the 1980s, companies were more concerned with the predicted decline in the number of school leavers entering the labour market. Several case study companies tried to adapt their traditional recruitment practices to encourage more women to work part-time to make up for this shortfall. However, at the beginning of the 1990s with the effects of recession, the pressure to reduce staff numbers and costs became a greater concern and part-time was used as a method to achieve these cost reductions. In retailing in both Britain and France, part-time work was used to reduce labour costs and meet constraints in terms of working hours, although the importance of reducing labour costs (notably through the avoidance of national insurance contributions) was a greater preoccupation in Britain. Arguably, the greater focus on labour costs in Britain may be a reflection of higher levels of competition in British retailing where large-scale grocery retailing accounts for a larger proportion of retail sales and is more highly concentrated than in France (Gregory 1991b). In British retailing, as in British banking, a policy of recruiting more women returners and retired people on a part-time basis was adopted during the boom period in the 1980s (Lennon 1990). This policy is now of less significance (see for example, Milne and Donovan 1992).

Clearly both sectors in both countries have been subject since the late 1980s to severe and more intense competitive pressures which have forced them to re-assess how they deploy their labour and what use they make of part-time work. However, the nature of these competitive pressures has been variegated and firms have responded with different organisational strategies. The reason why firms do not develop convergent working practices needs to be seen in the light of the detailed nature of competitive pressures and the labour demands they generate.

Labour supply

The demand for labour is highly contingent on the characteristics and preferences of the available labour supply. A number of comparative studies have shown how firms organise jobs according to the level of skills they can attract (Prais and Wagner 1983; Steedman and Hawkins 1993). This argument can be developed in relation to the demand and availability of part-time workers. In global terms there has been an increase in the number of women taking up paid employment in the post-war period. However, the extent of this varies between countries. In terms of previous debates concerning globalisation or divergence, the key issue is whether these differences actually matter. It will be argued here that the differences in the quality and quantity of female employment affect the way employers organise work, both in terms of shaping and accommodating preferences for different forms of working time. In the case of Britain and France the differences in the use of part-time work are closely tied to the fact that the characteristics, preferences and availability of female labour in each country differs significantly.

The age distribution of part-time workers tends to be concentrated in the prime 25–49 age group in both countries. In 1993, 53 per cent of part-timers in Britain came from this age group compared with 58 per cent in France (Eurostat 1995: 109). This reflects the tendency to see part-time work as a suitable form of employment for mothers in both countries. However, this similarity disguises the differences in the extent of part-time work amongst specific age groups. In Table 10.3 we can see that in 1987 the proportion of part-timers in the 25–64 age groups is twice as high in the UK as in France. Further, a much larger proportion of women over 65 work part-time in the UK than in France (83.1 per cent in the UK compared with 45.3 per cent in France). For British employers there clearly seems to be a larger pool of available labour amongst married and older women willing to work part-time than is the case in France. In the UK a much larger proportion of women working part-time are married: 83.2 per cent in the UK compared with 69.4 per cent in France. In France a much higher proportion of part-timers are single: 21.6 per cent in France compared with 9.8 per cent in the UK (Maier 1991: Table 8). This shows how the characteristics of part-timers in each country varies.

These patterns in the use of part-time work reflect well-documented differences in patterns of women's activity across their working lives in the two countries, despite very similar activity rates (see for example, Hantrais 1990; Dex *et al.* 1993). In the UK part-time work is used extensively by married women as a way of returning to the labour force and of combining paid work with family responsibilities after children are born. For an older generation of women it has become an important way of returning to the labour force after a long period out of paid employment. In France, where

Table 10.3 Proportion of female part-timers of all employees in
each age group, 1987

Age group	France	UK
14–24	24.4	20.5
25–49	21.3	50.2
50–64	27.3	54.9
65+	45.3	83.1

Source: Maier 1991: Table 4

combining full-time work with family responsibilities has become the norm for working mothers since the late 1960s, these figures reveal the continuing importance of full-time working in the child-rearing years and the particularly important role of part-time work as a means of integrating younger women into the labour force (see also Bouffartigue *et al.* 1992). Explanations for the differing patterns of labour force participation of women in Britain and France have been made in terms of a wide range of factors which include: the availability of child-care provision, the operation of tax and social security payments, the level of education and the availability of part-time work (see Barrère-Maurisson 1989; Hantrais 1990; Dex *et al.* 1993; O'Reilly 1994b).

The differing place of part-time work in women's activity patterns is also related to their level of satisfaction with this form of work. The evidence suggests that in France a large proportion of women working part time would prefer full-time work if it were available. In a European survey (Taddei 1991), it was found that although 77 per cent of full-timers claimed that they wanted to work part time, 89 per cent of French part-timers, most of whom are women, would prefer to work full time. The same survey showed that in the UK the figures are reversed: 89 per cent of part-timers would not want full-time work, while similar proportions (75 per cent) of full-timers were attracted by the idea of part-time work. British and French women have different reasons for working part time, and in Britain women give greater emphasis to hours which suit their domestic responsibilities (see also O'Reilly 1994b).

There would also seem to be a distinction in France between those who choose to work part-time and those who do it because they cannot find full-time employment (see Gregory 1989; Dex *et al.* 1993). Indeed, in France satisfaction with part-time work would seem to be strongly related to the sector of the economy: in the private sector, for example, where part-time work is concentrated (representing approximately 75 per cent of part-time jobs) and has developed rapidly in shops and cleaning, it would appear that part-time work is often the only form of work available (Nicole-Drancourt 1989) and women often work part-time because it is 'better than nothing' (Maruani and Nicole 1989). Among a number of French retailers the large numbers of women taking part-time work only because full-time work was not available deterred them from developing this form of work. High levels of dissatisfaction with part-time work also caused employers to introduce measures to reduce labour turnover: various forms of employee-controlled flexibility, and the adoption of differing shift systems (rotating shifts). By contrast, in jobs where part-time work is 'chosen', it is often made available to all men and women in a collective agreement and provides for very good conditions of employment, such as the freedom to move freely from part-time to full-time work and to negotiate the number of part-time hours worked. It would seem that these jobs are relatively small in number and are found mainly in the public sector, banking and in insurance, a finding which our case study material supports.

As a result of this distinction between chosen and imposed part-time work in France, there would seem to be greater dissatisfaction with part-time work in France than in the UK, especially in low-skilled jobs, with consequences for employers' policies. Overall, it would seem that British employers benefit from and construct part-time jobs in the knowledge that women in Britain need to work part-time if they are going to work at all during the period when they are raising a family. French employers find less demand for part-time work and a greater dissatisfaction among those who do work part-time.

CONCLUSIONS: REGULATION AND THE SINGLE EUROPEAN MARKET

This chapter set out to examine the prospects and paradoxes associated with the regulation of part-time employment in the process of European integration. We have seen that no one European model for part-time work exists and that the development of part-time work in Britain and France has been very different. We have seen that despite differences between the two sectors in their use of part-time work, firms tend to be influenced by regulatory, commercial and social conditions created within a particular country. Nevertheless, attempts at the European level have aimed to integrate and standardise employment regulation in the Union. Harmonisation, however, has met several obstacles. These include the existing differences in the basis of employment law and social security systems, as well as resistance from those national governments which see such regulation as potentially undermining the basis of their competitive advantage.

The Commission's attempts to improve the conditions for part-timers is still in the process of negotiation: this negotiation reflects the current power struggle between the Commission and the Council of Ministers and remains to be resolved. The goals of the Commission in encouraging a protected form of part-time work were to balance efficient labour market management and the protection of social rights at the European level. However, although for example the French government was prepared to accept these changes, there was much greater resistance from Germany and the UK. This was because such a change would entail greater reforms of their national laws on taxation thresholds and employment protection, than was the case for France.

Improvements in the employment status of part-timers since the 1980s have largely resulted from individual legal cases of sexual discrimination. This development has arisen from the fact that the overwhelming majority of part-timers are women. Key cases taken to the European Court of Justice have argued that unequal treatment between part-timers and full-timers amounts to a contravention of article 119 of the Treaty of Rome. For example, the case of Bilka-Kaufhaus vs. Weber von Hartz (*Industrial Relations Legal Information Bulletin* 1989) was significant in extending an interpretation of discrimination to include indirect sexual discrimination. This had important consequences for part-timers in Britain. One repercussion of this decision was to make some firms improve the conditions for part-timers in their organisations. This was in anticipation of potential disputes which might result from this legal decision (O'Reilly 1994a: ch. 9). The House of Lords' ruling of 3 March 1994 harmonised the distinction between part-timers working below or above sixteen hours a week in Britain. Whilst this can be seen as a gradual improvement towards some degree of harmonisation, it is still a long way off from the entitlements of French part-timers (Grahl and Teague 1992).

These cases illustrate how change has come about not only through the ground rules laid down by European directives, but also by local actors in the form of individuals and trade unions appealing to supra-national jurisdiction. In this way we need to recognise that regulation is not only a matter of senior heads of government attempting to find some form of consensus, but also includes the role for the courts and trade unions to be actively involved. The level at which effective regulation and harmonisation in employment practices and attendant conditions will take place is still to be negotiated. Rubery (1992) suggests that attempts at harmonisation will occur at several levels, subject to various political and economic influences.

> The enthusiasm with which the European idea is embraced will depend on how it complements or contradicts agendas at a local level. The actual implementation of European policies is thus likely still to reflect specific cultures and political agenda, with countries implementing policies selectively to suit their internal requirements. Such a scenario does not suggest, however, stagnation in social and cultural systems, but evolution, through the interplay of trans-national, pan-European and domestic influences.
>
> (Rubery 1992: 257)

Convergence at the economic level requires convergence in the system of social reproduction, at the level of 'family systems', income maintenance as well as education and training (Rubery 1992). The case of part-time work highlights the differences in the forms of social reproduction systems in Europe and the characteristics and preferences of the women available to work on a full- or part-time basis in different countries. In some countries part-time work is used by women to manage the period of child rearing, in other countries this is not the case. These differences imply that a more differentiated form of integration is likely to take place. This perspective suggests that centralised top-down change on its own will have only limited success. Instead, a conception of change and integration needs to give greater recognition to the role of business needs, supply side characteristics and the role of trade unions in shaping the nature of employment relations in Europe. The interaction of these factors, together with national and supra-national forms of regulation will mean that the road to integration may take many twists and turns. It is argued here that a more fruitful way of understanding the nature of regulation within Europe on issues related to employment relations is to think of regulation in terms of co-habiting tensions between different actors at the local, national and supra-national levels. While harmonisation will prove difficult, it should not be assumed that attempting such change is futile, and that existing relations are static.

NOTES

1 The case study research presented here is based on empirical research conducted in both countries over the period 1985–91. In-depth interviews were
held with the head of personnel in the banks and large-scale grocery retailers.
Survey, interview and observational data were collected from branch banks,
administrative clearing departments and large-scale grocery outlets under
study. This involved detailed discussions with shopfloor staff and supervisors.
The case study research was supplemented with interviews in both sectors and
in both countries with employers and trades union bodies. Additional work on
British retailing has been carried out by Gregory (Gregory 1991; 1993).

2 This evaded the now defunct Multiple Food Trade Joint Committee agreement
which covered a number of the major food retailers – Argyll, Tesco, Morrison,
and the former W.M. Low in Scotland. The agreement stipulated that part-
timers had to receive a paid break of fifteen minutes after working four hours
continuously. In France employees are often entitled to breaks on the basis of
a set number of minutes for each hour they work. These can be accumulated
but must be given during the working period. Also, according to the sector's
collective agreement, part-timers in France are not permitted to work for less
than three hours on one day.

3 However, in retailing there was strong evidence that arrangements over
working hours arrived at informally often lead to greater satisfaction among
part-timers in Britain than in France.

4 See also the example of the use of part-timers at Régis Renault cited in
Thurman and Trah (1989: 206).

5 More details about these case studies can be obtained from Gregory (1989) and
O'Reilly (1994a).

6 The law stated that working hours should be the same for all employees working in an establishment or in any section of one. Together with the prohibition of rolling and overlapping shifts, this severely limited the use of part-time work.

7 For a detailed explanation for the growth of part-time work and the development of working time in France, see respectively Droulers (1972) and Marimbert (1992), and Gregory (1989).

8 In particular the national insurance payment system was altered so that employers could be reimbursed for overpayment made when part-timers were employed.

9 Indeed, the debate over working time resurfaced in France in the early 1990s under conditions of rising unemployment. Notions of *temps choisi* were evoked in the debate over the four-day working week. This resulted in an experimental agreement to encourage substantial reductions in working time and annualised working hours (Gregory 1995).

10 The public sector accounted for 25 per cent of all employment in France in 1992 (Szarka 1992: 60).

11 An employee can work overtime up to 130 hours per year provided the overtime does not take weekly working hours above 48 hours per week and 46 hours averaged over twelve weeks. Overtime hours above the 130 hours quota have to be agreed with the *Inspecteur du Travail* and the *Comité d'Entreprise*. All hours over 39 per week have to be paid at overtime rates (+25 per cent for the first 8 hours and +50 per cent for subsequent hours).

12 In Britain there is no legal obligation for unions to be drawn into negotiations on working time. In France, by contrast, employers are under an obligation to negotiate plans for more flexible working hours with the unions represented at company or outlet level, or in their absence with worker representatives. Furthermore, in France there is a tradition of inter-professional negotiations on working time, which began in 1978 when the first attempts to make working time more flexible were made (Boulin 1992).

13 This is the procedure by which when collective agreements, and the unions negotiating them, satisfy a number of conditions established in the *Code du Travail*, the agreement can be applied beyond the signatory companies.

14 Although diversity is the rule on the French employers' side, the merger of three of the employers' organisations in 1988 has produced slightly more cohesiveness. There are now two main employers' organisations in food retailing: the merger of the wholesalers' organisation, the FE DI PAC, the MAS (*Syndicat des maisons à succursales multiples* – the multiple chain stores' organisation) and some members of the GNH (*Groupement National des Hypermarchés*) produced the FE DI MAS and the Association pour le Commerce Moderne, an organisation which centralises and rationalises the administrative, financial and commercial resources of the FE DI MAS. The hypermarkets outside the FE DI MAS still belong to the GNH. It is the FE DI MAS which is the major player in regulating working conditions in the industry (Lallement 1993).

15 These were encouraged by the 1982 Auroux reforms with the aim of better matching employers' and employees' working time requirements.

16 The Auroux laws allowed company agreements on working time to derogate from higher level agreements under certain circumstances.

17 It is quite plausible and important to consider that machine-tool making firms can thus almost be the inverse of the norm structures applying in their clientele. A manufacturing industry dominated by large batch or mass production firms and large concerns will be congenial to manufacturers of customized machine-tools which have a market strategy and personnel

structure that is opposed to that of their clients. A manufacturing industry in which small-batch production of investment goods for more differentiated markets is more typical, will go together with a machine-tool industry that makes more flexible standard machines, and hence has a market orientation, production systems and personnel structure of a more industrial kind, i.e. closer to that of its clients.

(Sorge and Maurice 1990: 149–50)

18 An interesting example from Germany is that of a former East German Kombinat, now run as a management buy-out competing with a formidable West German multinational cosmetics company. Both companies compete in the same market with a very similar product (face cream), but their size and organisation are very different.

REFERENCES

Atkinson, J. and Meager, N. (1986) *Changing Working Patterns: How Companies Achieve Flexibility to Meet New Needs*, London: National Economic Development Office.

Barrère-Maurisson, A-M., Daune-Richard, A-M., and Letablier, M-T. (1989) 'Le travail à temps partiel plus développé au Royaume-Uni qu'en France', *Economie et Statistique* 220: 47–56.

Beechey, V. (1989) 'Women's employment in France and Britain: some problems of comparison', *Work, Employment and Society* 3(3): 369–78.

Bertrand, O. and Noyelle, T. (1988) *Ressources humaines et stratégies des entreprises: Changement technologique dans les banques et assurances: Allemagne, Etats-Unis, France, Japon et Suède*, Centre pour la recherche et l'innovation dans l'enseignement, Paris: Organisation for Economic Co-operation and Development (OECD).

Blyton, P. (1985) *Changes in Working Time*, London: Croom Helm.

Bouffartigue, P., de Coninck, F. and Pendariès, J-R. (1992) 'Le nouvel âge de l'emploi à temps partiel', *Sociologie du travail* 4: 403–28.

Boulin, J-Y. (1992) 'Les politiques du temps de travail en France: la perte du sens', *Futuribles* 165–6: 41–62.

Burt, S. (1989) 'Trends and management issues in European retailing', *International Journal of Retailing* 4(4): 1–97.

—— (1991) 'Trends in the internationalisation of grocery retailing: the European experience', *Distribution and Consumer Research* 5(1): 487–515.

Commission of the European Community (1993) *Growth, Competitiveness, Employment: The Challenges and Ways Forward into the 21st Century*, White Paper, Luxembourg: Office for Official Publications of the European Communities.

Conseil National du Crédit (CNC) (1989) *Modernisation et gestion sociale des établissements de crédit: rapport de mission*, Paris: CNC.

Cossalter, C. (1990) *Renouvellement des qualifications et de la gestion des ressources humaines dans les banques et les assurances*, Collection des Etudes no. 53, Paris: CEREQ (Centre d'études et de recherches sur les qualifications).

Cox, A. (1994) 'Derogation, subsidiarity and the Single Market', *Journal of Common Market Studies* 32(2): 127–48.

Dale, A. and Glover, J. (1989) 'Women at work in Europe: the potential and pitfalls of using published statistics', *Employment Gazette* June: 299–308.

—— (1990) *An Analysis of Women's Employment Patterns in the UK, France and the USA: The Value of Survey Based Comparisons*, Department of Employment Research Paper 75, London: HMSO.

Dawson, J. (1982) *Commercial Distribution in Europe*, London: Croom Helm.

DeLange, W. (1986) 'Control of working time: attuning working time to organisational or individual needs', *Labour and Society* 11(1): 97–106.

de Neubourg, C. (1985) 'Part-time work: an international quantitative comparison', *International Labour Review* 124(5): 559–76.

de Olde, C. (1994) 'Teilzeitarbeit in den Niederlanden und in Deutschland: Modelle für Praxis'. Paper presented to the Deutsche Gesellschaft für Personafuhrung e.V. 28 June, Düsseldorf.

Dex, S., Walters, P. and Alden, D. (1993) *French and British Mothers at Work*, London: Macmillan.

Droulers, M-F. (1972) *Le Travail à temps partiel*, Valenciennes: M-F. Droulers.

Echange et Projets (1980) *La Révolution du temps choisi*, Paris: Albin Michel.

EIRR (European Industrial Relations Review) (1991) *Working Time in Europe: The Duration and Flexibility of Working Time in 17 European Countries*, Report no. 5, London: EIRR and Industrial Relations Services.

—— (1994a) 'France: new rights for working parents', *European Industrial Relations Review* 248: 19.

—— (1994b) 'Germany: government launches part-time work initiative', *European Industrial Relations Review* 247: 21–2.

European Commission (1994) *Leave Arrangements for Workers with Children: A Review of Leave Arrangements in the Member States of the European Union and Austria, Finland, Norway and Sweden* (European Commission Network on Childcare and other measures to reconcile Employment and Family responsibilities), V/773/94-EN, Luxembourg: European Commission.

Eurostat (1993) *Labour Force Survey Results*, Luxembourg: 3C Statistical Office of the European Community.

—— (1995) 'Erhobung über Arbeitskräfte Ergebnisse 1993', Luxembourg: Statistical Office of the European Communities.

Fagan, C., Plantenga, J. and Rubery, J. (1994) 'Does part-time employment reduce or reinforce sex inequality? Lessons from the Netherlands and the UK'. Discussion paper FS I, Berlin: Wissenschaftszentrum Berlin für Sozialforschung.

Fulop, C. (1964) *Competition for Consumers: A Study of the Changing Channels of Distribution*, Institute of Economic Affairs, London: André Deutsch.

Gallie, D. (1978) *In Search of the New Working Class: Automation and Social Integration within the Capitalist Enterprise*, Cambridge: Cambridge University Press.

Gospel, H. (1992) 'The Single European Market and industrial relations: an introduction', *British Journal of Industrial Relations* 30(4): 483–94.

Grahl, J. and Teague, P. (1992) 'Integration theory and European labour markets', *British Journal of Industrial Relations* 30(4): 515–28.

Granovetter, M. (1985) 'Economic action and social structure: the problem of embeddedness', *American Journal of Sociology* 91: 481–510.

Gregory, A. (1987) 'Le travail à temps partiel en France et en Grande-Bretagne: temps imposé ou temps choisi?', *Revue Française des Affaires Sociales* 3: 53–60.

—— (1989) 'A Franco-British comparison of the patterns of working hours in large-scale grocery retailing, with specific reference to part-time work', unpublished PhD thesis, Aston University.

—— (1991a) *Les Processus d'introduction des nouvelles technologies et leur négociation en Grande Bretagne, enquête monograpique, le cas de la grande distribution alimentaire*, Paris: Association de Recherche et d'Information Sociales.

—— (1991b) 'La grande distribution alimentaire en Grande-Bretagne: le rôle du travail à temps partiel', *Formation Emploi* 36: 36–46.

—— (1992) 'Recent developments in part-time work in France: what implications for women's employment?', paper presented to the Gender Research Workshop, UMIST, 23 September.

—— (1993) *Working Time in British Retailing*, a working document, April.

—— (1995) 'Patterns of working hours in large-scale grocery retailing in Britain and France: convergence after European Union?', in P. Cressey and B. Jones (eds) *Work and Employment in European Society: Integration and Convergence*, London: Routledge.

Hakim, C. (1987) 'Trends in the flexible workforce', *Employment Gazette* 95(11): 549–60.

Hantrais, L. (1990) *Managing Professional and Family Life: A Comparative Study of British and French Women*, Aldershot: Dartmouth.

Hantrais, L., Clark, P.A. and Samuel, N. (1984) 'Time–space dimensions of work, family and leisure in France and Great Britain', *Leisure Studies* 3: 303–17.

Harrop, A. and Moss, P. (1994) 'Working parents: trends in the 1980s', *Employment Gazette* October: 343–52.

Hirst, P. and Thompson, G. (1992) 'The problem of "globalisation": international economic relations, national economic management and the formation of trading blocs', *Economy and Society* 21(4): 357–96.

Hurstfield, J. (1978) *The Part-Time Trap*, Low Pay Unit Pamphlet 9, London: Low Pay Unit.

Industrial Relations Legal Information Bulletin (1989) 388, 7 November: 9.

Kerr, C., Dunlop, J.T., Harbison, H.H. and Myers, C.A. (1960) *Industrialism and Industrial Man*, Cambridge, MA: Harvard University Press.

Labour Research (1994) 'Europe's "Flexi-mania"', *Labour Research*, July: 11–12.

Lallement, M. (1993) 'France: the case of retail trade', paper given at the meeting on flexible working time arrangements, the roles of bargaining and government intervention, Paris: OECD, 3–4 May.

Lennon, P. (1990) 'Facing the demographic challenge', *Employment Gazette* January: 41–4.

Lettre de Matignon (1993) 'Pour une dynamique durable de l'emploi', *Lettre de Matignon* 420, 20 septembre: 2–3.

Maier, F. (1991) 'The regulation of part-time work: a comparative study of six EC-Countries', Discussion paper FS I 01–9, Berlin: Wissenschaftszentrum Berlin für Sozialforschung.

Marimbert, J. (1992) *Situation et perspectives du travail à temps partiel*, Rapport au Ministre du Travail, de l'Emploi et de la Formation Professionnelle. Rapport présenté le 18 mars.

Maruani, M. and Nicole, C. (1989) *Au Labeur des dames*, Paris: Syros.

Maurice, M., Sellier, F. and Silvestre, J-J. (1982) *Politique d'éducation et organisation industrielle en France et en Allemagne*, Paris: Presse Universitaire de France.

Milne, S. and Donovan, P. (1992) 'Gateway faces heavy job cuts', *Guardian* 11 February: 10.

Mueller, F. (1994) 'Societal effect, organisational effect and globalisation', *Organization Studies* 15(3): 407–28.

Mueller, F. and Purcell, J. (1992) 'The Europeanisation of manufacturing and decentralisation of bargaining: multinational management strategies in the European automobile industry', *International Journal of Human Resource Management* 3(1): 15–34.

Nicole-Drancourt, C. (1989) 'Organisation du travail des femmes et flexibilité de l'emploi', *Sociologie du Travail* 2: 173–93.

Ohmae, K. (1990) *The Borderless World: Power and Strategy in the Interlinked Economy*, London: Collins.

O'Reilly, J. (1992a) 'Banking on flexibility: a comparison of the use of flexible employment strategies in the retail banking sector in Britain and France', *International Journal of Human Resource Management* 3(1): 35–58.

—— (1992b) 'Where do you draw the line? Functional flexibility, training and skill in Britain and France', *Work, Employment and Society* 6(3): 369–96.

—— (1994a) *Banking on Flexibility*, Aldershot: Avebury.

—— (1994b) 'What flexibility do women offer? Comparing the use of and attitudes to part-time work in Britain and France in retail banking', *Gender, Work and Organisations* 1(3): 138–50.

Prais, S.J. and Wagner, K. (1983) 'Some practical aspects of human capital investment: training standards in five occupations in Britain and Germany', *National Institute Economic Review* 105 (August): 46–65.

Redding, G. (1994) 'Comparative management theory: jungle, zoo or fossil bed?', *Organization Studies* 15(3): 323–60.

Reynolds, J. (1985) *Innovation and Structural Change in UK Grocery Retailing*, University of Edinburgh: Coca Cola Retail Research Foundation.

Robinson, O. and Wallace, J. (1974) 'Wage payment systems in retailing', *Retail and Distribution Management* 1(6) November/December: 28–31.

Rubery, J. (1989) 'Precarious forms of work in the UK', in G. Rogers and J. Rogers (eds) *Precarious Jobs in Labour Market Regulation: The Growth of Atypical Employment in Western Europe*, Geneva: International Institute for Labour Studies.

—— (1992) 'Productive systems, international integration and the single European market', in A. Castro, P. Méhaut and J. Rubery (eds) *International Integration and Labour Market Organisation*, London: Academic.

Rubery, J., Fagan, C. and Smith, M. (1994) *Changing Patterns of Work and Working Time in the European Union and the Impact on Gender Relations*, Report to the European Commission (DGV Equal Opportunities Unit), Manchester: Manchester School of Management, University of Manchester Institute of Science and Technology (UMIST).

Schmid, G., Reissert, B. and Bruche, G. (1992) *Unemployment Insurance and Active Labour Market Policy: An International Comparison of Financing Systems*, Detroit, IL: Wayne State University Press.

Sorge, A. and Maurice, M. (1990) 'The societal effect in strategies and competitiveness of machine-tool manufacturers in France and West Germany', *International Journal of Human Resource Management* 1(2): 141–72.

Sorge, A. and Warner, M. (1986) *Comparative Factory Organisation: An Anglo-German Comparison of Manufacturing Management and Manpower*, Aldershot: Gower.

Steedman, H. and Hawkins, J. (1993) *Mathematics in Vocational Youth Training for the Building Trades in Britain and Germany*, mimeo, London: National Institute of Economic and Social Research.

Szarka, J. (1992) *Business in France: An Introduction to the Economic and Social Context*, London: Pitman.

Taddei, D. (1991) *Temps de travail, emploi et capacités de production: la réorganisation-réduction du temps de travail*, rapport final de la mission auprès de la Commission des Communautés Européennes, Brussels.

Thurman, J. and Trah, G. (1989) *Conditions of Work Digest: Part-Time Work* 8(1), Geneva: International Labour Organisation.

van Kersbergen, K. and Verbeek, B. (1994) 'The politics of subsidiarity in the European Union', *Journal of Common Market Studies* 32(2): 215–36.

Watson, G. (1993) 'Working time and holidays in the EC: how the UK compares', *Employment Gazette* September: 395–403.

Whitley, R. (1992) *Business Systems in East Asia: Firms, Markets and Societies*, London: Sage.

Wood, D. and Smith, P. (1992) *Employers' Labour Use Strategies: First Report on the 1987 Survey 'Social and Community Planning Research'*, Department of Employment Research Paper 63, London: HMSO.

11

THE TRAILING WIFE: A DECLINING BREED?

Careers, geographical mobility and household conflict in Britain 1970–89

Irene Bruegel

The argument explored in this chapter is that decisions about household migration and location implicitly involve conflict between the interests of the different household members. Commonplace though this observation may be, it has largely escaped social science concerns with labour market change, migration behaviour and household relations in Britain.

The 'trailing' wife has been taken by some writers to be a declining breed. Her partner is seen to be largely a creature of Fordist industrial organisation (Scase and Goffee 1989); pressures on employees to accept transfer between regions are argued to have abated with a structural shift away from internal labour markets (Savage *et al.* 1992). Others find 'trailing' status unproblematic. Bonney and Love (1991) see any locational conflict associated with migration as limited to the very small number of dual career households. On the whole dual earner households can absorb any transfer requirements of the main breadwinner, since women's jobs are fairly ubiquitous. Indeed some women may do better as a result of a move to a new labour market.

This chapter takes a contrary standpoint. Rather than dismissing the problem of trailing wives, it explores how far the ability or inability of 'working wives' to constrain household migration might be indicative of wider social changes in the way households and careers are constructed. Far from being overtaken by events, mobility requirements associated with career development are a continuing element in the differentiation of 'men's' work from 'women's'. The theoretical basis for this view is discussed in the first section, followed by a discussion of the evidence for the alternative stances cited above. This is followed by an analysis of the migration behaviour of men and women living 'as a couple' since the mid-1970s in Britain, using data from the Labour Force Survey and the OPCS Longitudinal Sample.

MIGRATION AND THE HOUSEHOLD

Migration behaviour is taken to reflect power relations within the household and the degree of mutuality in decision-making processes, much as Rose and Fielder (1988) use a hypothetical question about tied migration to develop a measure of traditional and egalitarian gender relations within households. Though labour market migration is a relatively rare event – with less than 3 per cent of couples making such moves in any one year – decision making around it is likely to be more explicit and hence more amenable to analysis than the more day-to-day accommodations that feature in most sociological analysis of household relationships (Anderson *et al.* 1994). As Odland and Ellis (1988) have suggested, the less autocratic the decision making, the more unanimity required, the lower the chances of migration. Migration behaviour also helps to clarify the layering of household membership. The weaker the economic and emotional ties between members of a household, the more likely that migration possibilities will lead to household fragmentation (Schaeffer 1987). In the case of young people leaving home, this is hardly problematic. In the case of couples, as micro-economic household models would predict, marital breakdown may be the way conflicting interests are eventually resolved.

Though migration may well involve explicit decision-making, actual outcomes reflect compromise, and conflict may never become manifest. Scase and Goffee (1989) imply that the path of transition from the work-centred to the home-centred manager has been relatively smooth. In reality, overt conflict may be contained by wives suppressing any individual aspirations. Finch discusses how women may subsume their individual desires to the priority of male career building and, where necessary, select types of employment consistent with frequent changes of location (Finch 1983). In this way the issue of tied migration raises a rarely considered differentiation between male and female jobs, that is differentiation along a dimension of ubiquity or 'portability' (Mincer 1978). This form of differentiation may link to primary/secondary segmentation in labour markets (Gordon 1993), skill differentials (Bonney and Love 1991) or involvement in occupational rather than organisational labour markets (Crompton and Sanderson 1990).

Alternatively the 'costs' to trailing wives may be contained and conflict minimised in other ways. If moves are made to large rather than small labour markets, the effects on wives' ability to find work will be lower and resistance is likely to be more muted. The relative youth of labour migrants and the coincidence of male career-based migration with early parenthood and a mother's temporary exit from the labour market, may also contain overt conflict and reduce any 'drag' factor.

There are, at the same time, a number of longer term trends which might be thought to aggravate potential stresses of household location decisions, including the tendency towards employment dispersal into more rural areas, the rise of male unemployment and the rising qualifications and labour market aspirations of married women.

HOUSEHOLD CONFLICT AND LABOUR MOBILITY

Underlying all this is the question of the relation between individual choices, household choices and structural constraints and, indeed, the meaningfulness of concepts of choice and strategy in such circumstances (Anderson *et al.* 1994). Though household migration has been described as 'a battlefield of personal utility maximisation' (Shihadeh 1991), economic and geographical analyses of migration have treated potential conflict within the household inconsistently.

Four different theorisations of intra-household relationships can be discerned in the literature on migration: the unified household; households as coalitions; households as gendered but unified collectives; households as arenas of potential conflict.

The unified household

This, the most common type of migration analysis, treats the household as a single unit with a common preference function. The analogy is made with a *team*, in which all individual preference functions are identical to the family preference function (Schaeffer 1987). As Anderson *et al.* (1994) put it, the household is reified. Such theorisations write out of account potential conflicts of interests between household members. It has frequently been criticised, not just for its sexism, but also as breaking with the tenets of methodological individualism that otherwise underlie neo-classical micro-economics.

Households as coalitions

This orientation conceptualises households as voluntary coalitions, entered into by individuals only where their expected benefits exceed the expected costs. Schaeffer (1987), in discussing the modelling of migration in Third World countries, distinguishes families that operate as a foundation or a coalition from the 'family as *team*' model: a family is a foundation where individual preferences differ yet the ranking of choices is still consistent. Families are *coalitions* when there is no necessary consistent ranking of alternatives. Responses of such families to migration possibilities will vary, with coalitions likely to break up when the benefits of joint migration vary greatly between members.

Schaeffer's model gives equal weight to the preferences of each member of a household. Thus tied migration will take place only where the 'trailing' partner values staying in the partnership and is relatively indifferent about where they live. His analysis acknowledges differentiation between family types and allows for separable interests, but does not reflect differential power between members, nor the interactive nature of preference formation.

Households as gendered but unified collectivities

Mincer's analysis of 'family' migration decisions recognises gender differences and unequal returns from migration. He observes that women are more likely to be 'tied movers', because of the greater economic importance of men's jobs within most households and that women may lose out in employment status as a result. He also observes that men, especially those with working wives, may be 'tied stayers'.

In essence this type of analysis sees decisions to migrate as 'family decisions'. They are decisions to maximise total utility irrespective of its distribution, with gains to husbands assumed to compensate for losses to wives. Otherwise, as in a co-operative game (coalition) model, the collectivity would dissolve through divorce or separation. The superior rewards to the husband arise from his higher investment in human capital and higher earnings, not directly from his gender. A corollary of such an analysis is that household migration would be expected to decline, other things being equal, with a rise in married women's economic activity.

Holmlund's (1984) study of inter-labour market (inter-county) migration in Sweden adopts a household utility maximisation approach. He found that the propensity of couples to migrate was related to the degree of *income dispersion* across the couple; the closer the income grouping, the lower the propensity to migrate. Thus 'tied' labour migration is still more a feature of 'traditional' couples than 'non-traditional', but this is because of differences in the relative net costs in the two cases, not because of independent differences in sex role orientations and aspirations.

Households as arenas of potential conflict

Game theoretical models in the early 1990s break in one way or other from the simple picture of 'income and consumption sharing' of the New Household Economics (Carling 1992; Seiz 1991). Game theory allows for the way each person may need to consider the impact of their decision on others, but it still rests on individualistic foundations. The concept is one of outwitting an opponent with whom negotiation is restricted. This may not be entirely relevant to households either, given the interdependency of preferences and elements of reciprocity within families (Sen 1990; Jordan *et al.* 1994). What is required is a model which understands the way accommodations are eventually arrived at through iterative household interactions in a framework of social rules and norms, where some groups have power over others (Folbre 1994; Anderson *et al.* 1994).

Shihadeh (1991) begins to use such an approach in his analysis of Canadian migration. His is a simpler alternative to Mincer's 'family migration decision model', based around the concept of gender role socialisation. Here the pattern of social expectations is critical to the eventual response to career based migration opportunities, but his model lacks any dynamic quality. There is little sense that such expectations can change or any concern with how they might.

These models have been laid out here to clarify the various ways that gender relations within the household have been treated, ignored or skated over in the migration literature, as the background to our hypothesis that the shift to a more external, career-centred femininity has increased the *potential* conflict over household migration, without reducing the male centredness of most resolution of such conflict. This male centredness is taken to be reflected in the degree to which 'working wives' inhibit household migration or operate as a 'drag' on it, when compared to single (sole-male) earner households. While cross-sectional analyses of migration have sometimes included such a drag effect, evidence on its scale is not consistent (Yu *et al.* 1993), nor has there been any previous attempt to measure changes in such an effect over time in Britain, or to understand its dynamics.

In this chapter we present some results of an on-going analysis of secondary data on migration from the OPCS Longitudinal Sample (LS) and the Labour Force Survey (LFS). No attempt is made to test the models discussed above against the empirical evidence but we are particularly interested in attempting to distinguish between income maximising and behavioural change approaches. Mincer's model implies that changes in patterns of household migration in Britain in the years since 1971 can be explained purely as income maximising behaviour. Shihadeh's approach, in contrast, would suggest that the decline of the single earner household will have changed behaviour over and above the direct effect of any increases in the share of household income coming from women. A full analysis of any such changes in values or relations of power would, of course, require a much more qualitative approach than is available here. This work can be viewed as a preliminary to more qualitative research on the issue.

Before looking at the results of our analysis of 'drag' effects, it is necessary to clarify which types of migration are being considered, particularly because Mincer (1978) found that the scale of any drag effect depended on how 'voluntary' the move was. Where the man had been made redundant or where he was being transferred within the company, the employment status of wives at the time had little effect.

DISTINGUISHING TYPES OF MIGRATION

While there are undoubtedly conflicts between household members over *residential* migration, this chapter sets out to consider only migration between labour market areas.[1] This reflects a concern with a potential conflict between the logic of fostering a spatially mobile labour force and that of calling on the supply of two or more workers from stable households. For this reason the analysis discussed here is restricted to migration that is tied in two distinct senses. First, it is concerned with migration (or staying) that is tied because the potential migrants are members of a household containing a couple.[2] (In principle the analysis should apply equally to homosexual as heterosexual couples, but data deficiencies make a comparative historical analysis of homosexual couples difficult.) Second, migration is tied by the need for at least one member of the household to seek employment/earn a living. Thus retirement migration and student migration are largely ignored.

The employment–migration tie can take different forms, which relate intimately to the type of labour market occupied by household members. Using Brown's (1982) typology of 'middle class' (male) careers which makes a three-fold distinction between self-employed entrepreneurs with capital resources; those with educational capital associated with occupational skills; and those who pursue organisational careers, it is possible to identify 'typical' migration patterns. Small entrepreneurs are rarely regionally mobile, since local links to suppliers, markets, etc., are likely to be particularly important for them. *Occupational* careers are likely to be associated with voluntary migration, with moves between areas being associated with changes of employer, but not of broad occupation. Those who pursue *organisational* careers are more likely to move between locations at the instigation of their employer and hence remain with their employer on moving location.

We can also identify a stream of migration associated with entry and re-entry into the labour market. Some is at the beginning of a career, after further or higher education. A small but highly variable element is re-entry into jobs after a period of unemployment (Jackman and Savouri 1992). Such entry and re-entry migration is for the most part excluded in what follows.

TIED MIGRATION AND TRANSFER MIGRATION

The concept of tied migration harks back in some ways to sociological discussions of dual career households and spiralist careers and 'organisation men' of the 1960s and early 1970s (Pahl and Pahl 1971; Fogarty *et al.* 1971). It is therefore worth considering whether organisational exigencies, which produce the spiralist manager moving from location to location with family in tow, still hold, before attempting to interpret changes in labour market migration as a whole. Certainly management literature, particularly that associated with *transfers* across national borders, suggests that the problems of the 'trailing' wife are still rife. Cooper (1988) speaks for a wider group when maintaining that frequent relocation is 'one of the chief sources of pressure for the executive family' (Munton 1993; British Institute of Management 1991; Incomes Data Services 1991; Institute of Manpower Studies 1987).

Savage (1988) argues, however, that there has been a decline in employer induced 'transfer' migration in line with a decline in the salience of the internal labour market and a decline in average job tenure by managers. This theme is developed further in his joint research where such a decline is seen to stem from the restructuring and fragmentation of Fordist organisations, the rise of the small firm and the shift towards professionalisation in employment in large public and private bureaucracies (Savage *et al.* 1992). The view that there has been such a structural change also suggests that women will not be hampered in managerial careers by any lack of independent mobility.[3] The evidence Savage gives for a decline in transfer migration is of two kinds. First, he points to a fall in overall inter-regional migration levels between 1979 and 1983/4 (from 1.5 per cent p.a. to 1 per cent p.a.) and second, he shows that for the period 1966–81 *relative* migration rates for professionals and managers (Socio-Economic Group SEG 1–4) fell. He does not attempt to distinguish transfer migration from all inter-regional migration by these socio-economic groups.

Other empirical evidence suggests no sustained decline in the rate at which professional and managerial labour is subject to transfer migration, despite the dramatic fall in the average number of years spent by managers with a single employer (Nicholson and West 1988). This is because transfer migration is largely concentrated on younger employees, in the early years of their jobs (Nakosteen and Zimmer 1992; Salt 1990). Moreover, much of the decline cited by Savage can now be seen to be cyclical, not structural. This is particularly evident when looking at migration of employed people as a whole (Rosenbaum and Bailey 1991; Jackman and Savouri 1992), but can also be seen to apply to managerial migration. Though research on migration trends in the 1970s and early 1980s appears to confirm a relative decline in inter-regional migration for managerial staff (Hughes and McCormick 1984; Pissarides and Wadsworth 1989), Gordon (1993) found that transfer migration 'grew markedly in importance' (relative to other types of migration) from 1974 up to about 1983. For the later period Owen (1992) records a rise in job related mobility of managers from 2.6 per cent in 1980/1 to 4.8 per cent in 1986/7. While this was followed by a decline associated initially with the widening regional house price differentials, and later, with rising unemployment, transfer migration is not shown to be in structural decline.

241

Estimates of the number of transferees vary. Salt (1990) puts the annual figure for the UK at 150,000–180,000 people, accounting for about one-third of moves over 20 km. On the basis of a survey of employees of six organisations Atkinson (1987) put it at 250,000 a year in 1986/7. Defining transfer migration as permanent moves of residence made for job-related reasons while remaining with the same employer, analysis of the 1989 Labour Force Survey suggests that about 170,000 transfers are made a year. Some 125,000 of these involved married or cohabiting men. Defining transfers in this way leaves open the possibility that some of these moves were sought by the employees themselves. Over-estimation may also arise where respondents worked for large multi-site employers like the NHS. Although they may have had to go through much the same job recruitment process as everybody else, technically, they remained with the same employer and hence may therefore have been classed here as having been transferred. On this definition, it is also clear that transfer migration is not confined to managerial grades in organisational labour markets(Gordon 1993).

THE IMPACT OF MOVES ON PARTNERS

The second argument for dismissing any 'drag' effect is to argue with Bonney and Love (1991) that tied moves generally have negligible effects on partners. Partners are unlikely to resist moving if they do not perceive migration as a problem, and in such circumstance employers would be unlikely to experience problems in implementing mobility policies.

Bonney and Love argue that male career mobility is an issue only for the small minority of career women and that women geographers and sociologists who have raised the problem are effectively generalising from their own perspective. The majority of the women in their sample of households moving to Aberdeen in the 1980s who gave up jobs with their husband's career move did not view their own employment prospects as damaged by the move. There are three problems with such an analysis: the empirical question of how general Bonney and Love's findings actually are; the issue of selectivity in studies which cover migrants only; and the longer term implications for women's employment prospects of gender-biased adaptation to tied migration.

Empirical evidence on the effects of tied migration

Not surprisingly the evidence of the effects of a partner's labour market migration will vary with the circumstances. At the time of Bonney and Love's research Aberdeen was still an expanding labour market. Even if net migration veers towards more buoyant local economies, it is not helpful to generalise from Aberdeen in the 1980s. Individual men moving for work-related reasons often move to areas that are relatively depressed (Greenwood 1985). The higher the level of the man's job, the more likely this is to be the case, but many of their wives may still find themselves with limited job choices.

Writing of the USA (where mobility is generally much higher), Mincer (1978) observes that 'tied migration ranks next to child-rearing as an important dampening influence on women's life cycle wages'. He found that even after five years the wives of migrants had higher unemployment rates than those of stayers, with the husbands displaying the contrary pattern. Sandell (1977) in a similar type of analysis attempted to measure the long- and short-term effects of tied migration on women's income in the USA. While men who moved between labour market areas increased their earnings on average by nearly $1,000 relative to non-migrants, their wives' incomes fell by $950 on average, compared to non-migrant wives. Contrary to Mincer, Sandell argues that most of the fall came from a temporary reduction in hours worked over the year as moving house and locality absorbed large amounts of women's time and energy. Similar results have been obtained elsewhere. In a longitudinal analysis of three West German cohorts (born between 1929 and 1951), Wagner (1989) found that the job careers of women were negatively affected by migration, in strong contrast to those of men.

There is no comparable British study of the income effects of migration on partners in a couple. Existing studies tend to consider single groups of women (Snaith 1990), specific places (Bonney and Love 1991; Johnson et al. 1974) or regions (Congdon 1989; Fielding 1989). Snaith's (1990) studies of childless married graduates of 1965 and 1972 found that almost 40 per cent felt that migration in pursuit of the husband's career had damaged their own. Johnson et al. (1974) looking at migrants to four towns in the 1960s found that 40 per cent of the wives of migrants had given up their job following the move. Neither Congdon nor Fielding look explicitly at women in heterosexual couples, but their results also suggest that women may well be disadvantaged where they lack independent mobility. Congdon's analysis of mobility in London covers all people (irrespective of marital/couple status) who were in employment in both 1980 and 1981. He shows that, keeping age and income level constant, women were far less likely to have experienced upward occupational mobility than men even though they had much the same rate of inter-borough mobility (Congdon 1989).

Fielding's study of migration in and out of the South East of England suggests differential effects too. He found that routine white collar workers (mainly women) moving from the South East to other regions experienced increased unemployment (Fielding 1989). This he attributes to reduced opportunities associated with tied migration. In his more recent analysis with Halford, however, he found that flows to the South East Region are relatively to the advantage of women's careers compared to those of men (Fielding and Halford 1993). However, this may be because Fielding and Halford's data included a high proportion of moves by single men and women.

Selectivity

Studies which restrict themselves to migrants, such as Bonney and Love's, may well select out those households and partners who anticipate problems on moving, correctly or otherwise. This means that they ignore the issue of 'tied stayers'. Their findings therefore leave open the question of partner-related constraints on geographical mobility. This can be addressed only by using longitudinal data sets which allow for comparison between households that migrate and those that remain. Both the Labour Force Survey and the OPCS Longitudinal Study used in this analysis include information on the respondent's residential location one year before the date of interview. However, neither provides information about explicit offers to migrate during the year in question. Hence some of the observed differences between movers and non-movers may arise from unobserved differences between those who were offered such an opportunity and those who were not.

Analysis of the 1989 LFS sample of 40,000 households containing a married or cohabiting couple shows that there are both losers and gainers amongst the wives of men making 'job moves' (Table 11.1). The movers in this table are all households who moved house between 1988 and 1989 and in which the male head of household said that the move was job related. By and large such moves will be to a new local labour market area, new, at least for women, who operate in fairly limited spatial labour markets (Green *et al.* 1986).

The unemployment rate amongst women in such migrating households rose sharply between 1988 and 1989, as compared to that for women in

Table 11.1 Economic activity of women in 1988 and 1989, by whether the household moved between 1988 and 1989 for reasons of a male partner's job

	In employment (%)		Unemployed (%)	
	1988	1989	1988	1989
No move made related to man's job	63.5	64.0	2.7	3.9
Moved for man's job	55.2	50.5	3.5	11.3
N = 30,953				

Source: Labour Force Survey 1989 (unpublished)

households that either stayed put or moved for a reason not associated with the man's job. At the same time as many as 4.6 per cent of women in 'mover' households entered paid employment following a move to a new area, that is around 40 per cent of those who were not employed in 1988 (Table 11.2). This compares to the rate of labour market entry of 32 per cent for the non-mover group. This may well be a reflection of the relative youth of the job migrants. It may also reflect a tendency of women to anticipate tied moves by postponing labour market re-entry until after an expected move.

Table 11.2 Contrasts in employment of women, by whether household moved between 1988 and 1989 for reasons of a male partner's job

	Movers (%)	Non-movers (%)	All (%)
Employed 1988 and 1989	36.0	56.0	56.0
Employed 1988 only	43.0	27.0	27.0
Not employed 1988 or 1989	5.4	7.6	7.5
Employed 1989 only	4.6	3.6	3.7
	N = 630	N = 29,686	N = 30,316

Source: Labour Force Survey 1989 (unpublished)

Gender bias in tied migration and its longer term implications

As one would expect, very few wives in the LFS sample were instigators of household migration between labour markets. Such events are still sufficiently rare to invite media attention. In the LFS 1989 it was possible to identify 42 women (out of 40,000) who said they had made a job-related move, where their partners did not.[4] There were a number of instances of both partners in the LFS sample saying that a change of residence had been 'job-related'. In some cases this was where both partners were self-employed, probably working together, but in most such cases, it would seem that the woman in the couple classed a move made for her partner's job as 'job related' herself. Research by Rose and Fielder (1988) on attitudes to male and female career-induced migration shows that such traditional views of the primacy of male careers remain common amongst women.[5] Faced with a possibility of household migration to improve their partner's job, a fair majority of women (63 per cent) thought that a woman should 'encourage the partner to take the job and look for any job she could do there', with only 12 per cent thinking she should 'ask the partner not to accept before she could be sure of finding as good a job there as she has now'. There were differences between women related to their education, but there was no evidence of any strong 'perception that a partner's migration ought to be resisted.

Gender bias in tied migration is not then in dispute. Bonney and Love (1991) would not deny that women experience periods of unemployment or non-employment associated with a 'tied move', but argue that few women regard this as a problem. They are probably right to see this subjective response to tied migration as linked to the relative ubiquity of 'female' jobs. This ubiquity of 'women's work' may explain Gordon's (1993) apparently perverse finding that men and women doing such jobs were *more* likely to have been 'voluntary' (as against transfer) migrants than those in 'male' jobs. The implication is that women's work is easier to enter from a distance than are such 'male' jobs.

The long-term consequences of this split in the geographies of 'male' and 'female' jobs is not, however, unproblematic. Mobility requirements attached to jobs have been identified as potentially discriminatory (Equal Opportunities Commission (EOC)1985). Gordon (1993) found that women were significantly less likely to be transferees in 1988/9 *after* allowing for differences in qualification levels, job types and in economic activity rates. Thus geographical mobility that is generally associated with career progression (i.e. transfers) remains slanted towards men, even after characteristics of the job and the worker (other than their gender) are accounted for. In the formal investigation of the Leeds Permanent Building Society, the EOC provided some evidence that female applicants for managerial posts were less mobile than male, and recommended that any mobility *requirement* be restricted to intra-regional mobility between branches (though it also suggested that a firm might indicate to its staff 'that faster progression might be achieved by staff who were prepared to be more widely mobile' (EOC 1985: 2.47[5]; Crompton and Sanderson 1990: 118–21). Thus the value of mobility to employers was accepted together with the implicit linkage of spatial and career mobility. Such a linkage will continue to impede women seeking organisational careers, so long as their mobility remains more 'tied' than that of men by domestic obligations. To explore this issue further we turn to look at trends in tied mobility to see how the rising employment aspirations of women have affected the scale of job-related mobility for married men.

ANALYSING MIGRATION CHANGE

The discussion so far has shown that male job-related mobility, while subject to a number of socio-economic trends, does not appear to have been affected by any changes in the regime of accumulation, as posited by Savage *et al.* (1992). In effect, there has been no sustained decline from the demand side. We now turn to the so-called supply side to see whether we can identify any increasing reluctance of managers and others to move as a result of the increasing contribution of women's earnings to household incomes. This may show how resilient the male breadwinner model has been when it comes to decisions about long-distance migration. We assume it holds where men are unemployed (Morris 1990) and concentrate on looking at changes in migration behaviour for sole-male and dual earner households, making some allowances for changes in tenure, demographic structure and male occupational profile in the period.

Analytically changes in migration behaviour of such households over time can be separated into those that are due to the shift towards dual earner households and those due to changes in the behaviour of dual and sole-male earner households, treated as independent groups, which may in turn reflect changes in tenure, occupation and age characteristics of the groups. A household income maximisation model, like Mincer's, would suggest that rising economic activity rates would of themselves herald a decline in husband-centred migration, as the proportion of household income attributable to women's earnings rises. If there had been no change in the propensity of either sole-male or dual earner households to migrate, the rise in the proportion of married women in employment (from 55 per cent to 68 per cent) would, of itself, have reduced migration between regions from 4.1 per cent in 1971 to 3.8 per cent in 1991, on the basis of migration rates of both types of household in 1970/1. Such a model would not, however, anticipate any knock-on effect of rising economic activity rates on the acceptability of different types of behaviour. If women had succeeded in shifting accepted norms, the propensity of dual earner households to migrate could be expected to have declined, reducing total expected migration below 3.8 per cent. In the event regional migration by couple households reached 7.7 per cent in 1991, as a result of a number of other social changes in the period, illustrating the difficulty of isolating any one component of change.

To evaluate whether there has been any change in the willingness of women to be moved about 'like a piece of furniture' (Snaith 1990: 170), we analyse what has happened to the *difference* in the probability of migration of dual and single earner households over the period 1970/1 to 1988/9. The results of a logistic regression of LFS 'couples' for 1988/9 are given in Tables 11.A1 and 11.A2 in the Appendix. These show that after allowing for tenure, life cycle status and male occupation, dual earner households were less likely to have undertaken a male job-related move of residence than sole-male earner households. There was then a statistically significant drag effect in 1988/9.

Unfortunately there is no consistent measure of labour market migration yet available for Great Britain (or England and Wales) for the whole period (see note 1) to enable direct comparison with years before 1980. In Table 11.3 we present a series of comparative estimates of the drag effect, using the OPCS LS for 1970/1 and 1980/1 and the LFS for 1988/9. Migration is defined differently in the two sources; as moves between travel to work areas for 1970/1 and 1980/81 and as 'job-related' permanent moves for 1988/9.

Table 11.3 Propensity to move between labour markets/for job-related reason: single and dual earner households 1970/1,[a] 1980/1[a] and 1988/9[b]

| | | % all | Proportion of households migrating | | |
			% single earner (A)	% dual earner (B)	ratio (B/A)
All couple households					
1971	N = 131,368	9	10.5	7.5	0.71
1981	N = 198,333	2.3	2.5	2.00	0.80
1989	N = 30,206	2.8	3.3	2.4	0.73
Owner occupiers					
1971	N = 36,353	6.9	7.5	6.2	0.83
1981	N = 14,229	5.3	5.3	5.3	1.00
1989	N = 23,123	2	2.7	2	0.74
Owner occupiers male professional					
1971	N = 11,727	8.8	10.3	7.4	0.72
1981	N = 11,909	4.3	4.8	4	0.83
1989	N = 2,060	4.3	5.8	3.1	0.53
Owner occupiers male manager					
1971	N = 19,641	10	11.1	9.2	0.83
1981	N = 33,817	3.4	4.1	2.9	0.71
1989	N = 5,169	3.9	4.8	3.4	0.71
Owner occupiers households with dependent children					
1971	N = 38,170	6.03	7.04	4.40	0.62
1981	N = 106,231	2.1	2.9	1.3	0.45
1989	N = 16,196	2.7	4	2.10	0.53
Logit model odds					
1971	N = 127,219				0.89
1981	N = 181,704				0.801
1989	N = 40,166				0.82

Sources: Labour Force Survey 1989 (unpublished); OPCS Longitudinal Survey Crown Copyright

Notes: [a] Movement between travel to work areas
[b] Movement for reasons 'related to man's job'

For technical reasons a logit analysis was undertaken, rather than a logistic regression, to establish the relative odds of such migration between the years. While the rates of migration from the two sources are not strictly comparable, the relative odds ratios (i.e. the differential effect of women's economic status on the probability of undertaking a given form of migration) are more validly compared. These odds are based on the coefficient for women's economic activity in a loglinear model which included tenure (three categories); male occupation (four categories) and life cycle stage (three categories). These categories are described in the Appendix, Table 11.A3. This gives the relative odds as identified in a saturated model as well as the 'best fit' model for each data set. The coefficient for women's economic activity status was statistically significant for each of the logit analyses of migration. Table 11.3 shows the relative odds derived for the best fit model as well as the ratios for some specific categories of household.

The results presented in Table 11.3 (last column) suggest that there has been no consistent or marked change in the 'drag effect', the degree to which employed women (i.e. dual earner households) are willing and/or able to forestall inter-regional migration, as compared to full-time housewives (sole-male earner households), despite the potentially negative effects of such moves on their own earnings. These results are in line with the data provided by Pissarides and Wadsworth (1989) from the 1977 and 1984 Labour Force Surveys. Their data suggest that, over the period in question, the odds of that households with women in paid work would have been involved in an inter-regional move, relative to a single earner household, only changed for households headed by men working in non- manual jobs.

At first sight this result might appear to justify Mincer's approach. There is no evidence of a sustained shift in attitudes. It is also possible that the apparent stability in relative migration propensities of the two types of household stems from shifts in the characteristics of working wives, such as a shift towards part-time work and towards earlier labour market re-entry. To evaluate this the 1088/9 migration behaviour of different types of dual earner households was analysed in more detail. When dual earner households are disaggregated, between those where the wife worked full time before the move and those where she was employed on a part-time basis, Mincer's income maximisation model appears equally problematic.

TRAILING WIVES IN THE LATE 1980s

The degree to which a woman's employment acts as a 'drag' on such migration is not, as one might have expected, generally greater for women who work full time than those who work part time. Table 11.4 shows that other things being equal part-time women workers are less likely to be trailing wives than are full-time women workers, across different groups in the population. Moreover the nature of a woman's job does not appear to have the 'expected' effect on migration rates (Table 11.5).

Table 11.5, which covers only the subset of the 1989 sample for whom information on the occupations of both partners was available, suggests that migration for job reasons was particularly high for households in which both partners were working as managers. This would appear to negate the view that male job migration is facilitated by women operating in occupational and ubiquitous labour markets, rather than in organisational markets. Before drawing such a conclusion, it is worth noting that

Table 11.4 Proportion of households moving for reasons of a male
partner's job 1988/9

| | All (%) | Wife's employment status 1988 | | |
		Full-time employment (%)	Part-time employment (%)	Full-time housework (%)
Tenure group				
owner occupier	2.0	2.1	1.3	2.4
other tenure	5.3	6.1	4.2	5.4
Husband's occupation				
managerial	5.4	5.3	3.4	6.8
professional	4.3	3.2	2.0	5.8
other	1. 5	1. 9	1.1	2.3
Youngest child				
below school age	3.5	3.1	3.0	3.9
school age	1.7	1.7	1.3	1.9
no child below 18	2.7	3.0	1.6	2.7
All households	2.7	1.7	1.8	3.5
	N = 40,163	N = 8,964	N = 9,444	N = 21,755

Source: Labour Force Survey 1989 (unpublished)

Table 11.5 Proportion of dual earner households moving for reasons of the
man's job 1988/9, by type of occupation of both partners
(N = 10,994)

| Wife's occupation | All husbands | Husband's occupation 1989 | | | |
		Managers	Professionals	Other	
Manager	4.2	5.9	2.0	3.3	N = 1,724
Professional	2.1	3.8	2.2	0.5	N = 1,257
Clerical/ associate prof	4.3	3.0	2.0	1.6	N = 2,173
Other	1.9	3.4	2.5	1.4	N = 5,840

Source: Labour Force Survey 1989 (unpublished)

many of the women concerned appeared to operate in 'entrepreneurial'
labour markets. Managerial wives of managers were twice as likely to be
self-employed, as all working wives of managerial husbands. Though our
predictions were that self-employed people would be less likely to move, in
the case of married women, self-employment may provide the required
flexibility. Or it may be that the couples work for the same organisation,
and that their employers facilitated their combined moves. Overall, however, neither the income maximisation nor the ubiquitous women's
employment model appears to fit migration behaviour in Great Britain in

1988/9: the occupational level of the wife does not appear to alter her desire or ability to limit job migration for her husband's career.

There are four possible explanations for our finding that neither full-time employment nor managerial status appear to have limited the level of a male partner's job-related migration, relative to part-time or more traditional 'women's' work.

A neglected resource effect

Male centred migration may be higher for wives who work full time in higher grade jobs because higher overall incomes facilitate migration. This may be important when house price differentials and difficulties of selling raise the costs of migration, as was the case in the period in question. It may be that, just as high incomes may enable women to buy-in household service and child care, they may enable managerial/professional women to overcome more usual constraints of tied migration, specifically by financing a second car. With independent local mobility, allowing women to retain their jobs by commuting, dependent geographical migration may be less of a problem. Certainly there is evidence that women's journeys to work have lengthened over the twenty years to 1991 (Department of Transport 1993; Bruegel and Pearson 1996).

There may be a selectivity effect

Those who migrate are an unknown proportion of those offered the opportunity to migrate. It is possible that men with full-time working wives are more likely to be offered such an opportunity. This may be because they are younger, or more forward looking. Table 11.5 shows some such selectivity operating. The higher rate of male job-centred migration amongst managerial women may be partly attributed to their choice of partner. They are more likely to be married to managers and professionals, occupations where migration opportunities are more often available. Having a managerial husband is not the complete explanation for the higher migration rates of managerial wives. Amongst the group of women with managerial husbands, women with managerial jobs are still more likely to be 'trailing wives', than those in apparently more ubiquitous jobs.

The measure for change in attitudes is mis-specified

Choosing to look at the differential odds of male job-centred migration between working and non-working (and full-time and part-time working) women makes the assumption that effects of changes in expectations relate to the current employment status of the wife. They may equally have had effects on what non-working wives are prepared to accept. Indeed, it has been argued (Seidenburg 1973) that having a job reduces the problems of

251

being moved about 'like furniture', since it aids integration into a new area. There may also be another selectivity effect; other things being equal, women who work full time are more able and willing to contemplate the upheaval of migration.

Changes in geographical accessibility are more complex

Although the initial suggestion was that geographical change, specifically the urban–rural shift, may have attenuated the conflict within dual career households, changes in patterns of geographical accessibility to higher level jobs are becoming more complex. The rise in dual car households is one issue that can be investigated using the new data for 1991 of the OPCS LS. A second is the geographical pattern of migration by dual career households. It may be that such migration is more focused on London and other large labour markets at the top of the urban hierarchy than labour market migration by other groups.

CONCLUSION

Our results suggest that the trailing wife has neither been killed off by organisational changes nor by rising career aspirations amongst women. At most the breadwinner model may have been modified, rather than transcended. As Jordan and his collaborators note, 'to read accounts of women facing . . . changes . . . brought about by their partner's pursuit of career advantage . . . is to become aware of their relative powelessness in the face of . . . men's control over the household's destiny' (Jordan *et al.* 1994: 162), though some of the men they interviewed had sought to soften the blow of a 'forced' move in various ways.

This chapter shows some of the strengths and weaknesses of the analysis of large data sets for understanding processes of change. In quantitative terms, organisational labour markets involving the transfer of staff between regions can be seen to remain important. It was also possible to show that working wives continue to inhibit male career migration when migration rates are set against those for comparable households where wives are not in work. It is not, however, entirely clear what the direction of causation is, because the anticipation of a career move may itself be inhibiting woman's labour market participation. We found indeed (Table 11.2) that the economic activity rates of women in mover households were lower before the move than those of 'non-movers'.

The findings on the relatively high rate of 'trailing' by full-time women workers and women in higher occupational groups, while confounding the initial assumptions of the study, also throw into question a household income maximisation model of migration choices. Given the evidence of women's unemployment levels following a male-centred move, the opportunity costs of such migration are likely to be higher for full-time working women and for higher status jobs and yet they are *more* likely to be involved in such migration, *ceteris paribus*, on our evidence.

As with the much discussed issue of female economic activity in households with an unemployed male head (Morris 1990), when the issue comes to a head, male breadwinner status may take precedence. As McLaughlin's research suggests, economic rationality and household income maximisation are circumscribed by the 'unthinkable' in these circumstances with wives 'trying to avoid having too much power'(McLaughlin *et al.* 1989: 67), a response which is almost impossible to explain in a thoroughgoing household income maximisation perspective.

Our results suggest, too, that Bonney and Love's (1991) findings for Aberdeen need to be put into context: it is not just women in low level jobs who appear unwilling or unable to stake a claim to remaining in their existing neighbourhoods. (Whether they would subsequently feel satisfied, or at least say they felt satisfied, is a different question.) It might be interesting to see how far any such apparent acquiescence to male-centred moves is affected by experience or risk of unemployment in different local labour markets.

If this apparent acquiescence to tied migration is in fact sustained by increased independent mobility, with as many as 30 per cent of adults now living in households with two or more cars, it suggests that a process of polarisation of women with respect to tied migration may be developing. For the majority of women in 'women's work', the problem posed in this chapter will be met by an extra twist to a segmentation cycle, as is indeed implicit in Bonney and Love's (1991) research and Gordon's results (1993). 'Tied migration' is facilitated by women restricting themselves to ubiquitous jobs and opting out of jobs which require transfer flexibility but provide some chance of occupational mobility. Other women who have managed to acquire a foothold further up the ladder – probably as a result of higher education – face fewer personal constraints from 'tied migration' and can take full advantage (or fuller advantage) of their headstart as a result. Peter Hall (1971) once suggested, when discussing dual career households, that motorways liberate women. Our results suggest that – in a strictly limited sense – he may have a case. However, such a solution to the coupling constraints of tied migration may be prove to be ecologically unsound as well as socially divisive.

ACKNOWLEDGEMENTS

Thanks to Simon Gleave of the Social Science Research Unit, City University, and John Shanks of South Bank University Computer Centre for their help; Ian Gordon for comments and Peter Hall for tracking down his 1971 article.

APPENDIX A

Table 11.A1 Analysis of the probability of male job-related migration 1988/9 (relative to private tenants with no children; men over 30 years, in manual job; woman not employed)

Variable	Definition	Regression Coefficient	(st. error)	(Waldinger)
Tenure	Owner occupier	−2.0397	0.0975	434.2
1989	Council tenant	−1.9226	0.1690	129.5
Life cycle	No child/			
1989	male under 30	1.1106	0.1413	61.8
	Child under 18 years	0.4703	0.0999	22.2
Male occupation	Managerial	0.7607	0.1012	56.5
1988	Professional	0.7372	0.1569	22
	Other non-manual	0.5088	0.1219	17.4
Wife's employment	Full time	−0.3959	0.1083	13.4
1988	Part time	−0.6588	0.1075	37.5
Constant		−2.349	0.1274	340
Number of cases	24,889			
−2 log likelihood	5,241			
Goodness of fit	25,109			

Source: Labour Force Survey 1989 (unpublished)

Table 11.A2 Predicted probabilities of single and dual earner households undertaking job-related migration 1988/9

	Single earner (A)	Dual earner (B)	Relative likelihood (B/A)
Private tenant, no child, man under 30 in managerial job	0.383	0.268	0.700
Owner occupier, child, man in managerial job	0.041	0.024	0.600
Owner occupier, child, man in professional job	0.040	0.036	0.898
Council tenant, child, man in non-manual job	0.036	0.021	0.599

Source: Labour Force Survey 1989 (unpublished)

Table 11.A3 Comparison of the relative odds of dual and single earner
households making a male job-related move 1970/1, 1980/1 and 1988/9
using logit models

Model 1 saturated model[a]	*1970/1* N = 127,219	*1980/1* N = 181,704	*1988/9* N = 40,166
Parameter estimate			
Dual earners	–0.07778	–0.0612	–0.0754
(z value)	(z = –7.18)	(z = –3.33)	(z = –4.5)
Relative odds			
Dual/single earner			
households	0.86	0.88	0.86
Model 2 best fit model[b]			
Parameter estimate			
Dual earners	–0.0599	–0.1278	–0.0527
(z value)	(z = –3.57)	(z = –14.56)	(z = –4.72)
Relative odds			
Dual/single earner			
households	0.89	0.80	0.82

Sources: Labour Force Survey 1989 (unpublished); OPCS Longitudinal Study Crown
Copyright

Notes:

[a] saturated model variables
tenure: owner occupiers; public renters; private renters
male occupation: managerial; professional; non manual; other (SEG based)
lifecycle: no child and male under 30; child under 18; no child and man over 30
wife's employment: employed; not in employment
[b] best fit model variables
as saturated plus: woman has a degree, does not have a degree

NOTES

1 The exact definition of 'migration between labour market areas' varies,
depending on which data set is used. In the LFS for 1989 which charts migration behaviour for 1988/9, each respondent was explicitly asked whether a
move of residence was 'made for job reasons'. A move between labour markets
in our analysis from the LS is defined somewhat differently. In the LS households were coded according to whether or not they had moved between Travel
To Work Areas (as defined by the 1981 census). Moves between Travel To
Work Areas may not in fact involve a change in the location of work . Therefore
cases in which households had moved to a local authority in which they were
employed in 1971 or 1981 were excluded from the category of job migrants.
Households with heads over the age of 65 were excluded. Moves associated with
early retirement and mature higher education entry are also excluded, as far
as possible.

The spatial area of the internal migration varies between the two data sets.
The LFS covers movements between parts of the UK, while the OPCS LS covers
only England and Wales. In both cases the analysis is restricted to internal

migration, though the theorisation may equally well apply to certain types of international migration.

2 Even by 1989 a very small proportion of women living with men were classed as cohabitees. It would seem that the majority of cohabitees were recorded as the wife of the head of household. For this reason all female partners are termed wives in this chapter, even if they are not actually married.

3 This is the gist of Savage's argument that women's exclusion from large sectors of the service class work relates to 'patriarchy' rather than spatial immobility (Savage 1986: 559).

4 These 42 women, unsurprisingly, had a much higher occupational profile than the sample as a whole (half were working in professional and managerial jobs), while the occupational profile of their husbands was weighted towards service and manual jobs.

5 They find men to be less 'traditional' , but that is likely to be an artifact of the hypothetical nature of their questions.

REFERENCES

Anderson, M., Bechhofer, F. and Gershuny, J. (eds) (1994) *The Social and Political Economy of the Household*, Oxford: Oxford University Press.

Atkinson, J. (1987) *Relocating Managers and Professionals*, Brighton: Institute of Manpower Studies.

Bonney, N. and Love, J. (1991) 'Gender and migration: geographical mobility and the wife's sacrifice', *Sociological Review* 39 (2): 335–48.

British Institute of Management (BIM) (1991) *On the Move: Manager Mobility in the 1990s*, London: BIM.

Brown, R. (1982) 'Work histories, career strategies and the class structure', in A. Giddens and G. Mackenzie (eds) *Social Class and the Division of Labour*, Cambridge: Cambridge University Press.

Bruegel, I. and Pearson, R. (1996) *Putting Women in Place*, Cambridge: Polity.

Carling, A. (1992) 'Rational choice and household divisions of labour', in S. Arber and C. Marsh (eds) *Families and Households*, Basingstoke: Macmillan.

Congdon, P. (1989) 'Population and social change in London wards', *Transactions Institute of British Geographers* 14 (4): 478–90.

Cooper, C. L. (1988) *Living with Stress*, Harmondsworth: Penguin.

Crompton, R. and Sanderson, K. (1990) *Gendered Jobs and Social Change*, London: Unwin Hyman.

Department of Transport (1993) *National Travel Survey, 1984–5 and 1989–91*, London: HMSO.

Equal Opportunities Commission (EOC) (1985) *Formal Investigation: Leeds Permanent Building Society*, Manchester: EOC.

Fielding, A. (1989) 'Inter-regional migration and social change: a study of South East England based upon data from the Longitudinal Study', *Transactions Institute of British Geographers* 14 (1): 24–36.

Fielding, A. (1992) 'Migration and social mobility: South East England as an escalator region', *Regional Studies* 26(1): 1–15.

Fielding, A. and Halford, S. (1993) 'Geographies of opportunity: a regional analysis of gender specific social and spatial mobilities in England and Wales 1971–81', *Environment and Planning* 25(1): 421–40.

Finch, J. (1983) *Married to the Job: Women's Incorporation in Men's Work*, London: Allen & Unwin.

Fogarty, M., Rapoport, R. and Rapoport, R.N. (1971) *Sex, Career and Family*, Beverly Hills, CA: Sage.

Folbre, N. (1994) *Who Pays for the Kids? Gender and the Structures of Constraint*, London: Routledge.

Gordon, I. (1988) 'Interdistrict migration in Great Britain', *Environment and Planning A1* 20 (7): 907–924.

Gordon, I. (1993) *Migration in a Segmented Labour Market*, paper to Institute of British Geographers Annual Conference, Egham, Surrey, 5–8 January.

Green, A., Coombes, M.G. and Owen, D. (1986) 'Gender-specific local labour markets', *Geoforum* 17(3): 339–51.

Greenwood, M. J. (1985) 'Human migration: theory, models, empirical studies', *Journal of Regional Science* 25(4): 521–44.

Hall, P. (1971) 'Motor lib', *New Society* 25 February.

Holmlund, B. (1984) *Labor Mobility: Labor Turnover and Migration in the Swedish Labor Market*, Stockholm: Industrial Institute for Economic and Social Research.

Hughes, G. and McCormick, B. (1984) 'Migration intentions in the UK: which households want to migrate and which succeed?' *Economic Journal* 95 (conf): 113–23.

Incomes Data Services (1991) *Relocation*, IDS Study 491, October, London: IDS.

Institute of Manpower Studies (1987) *Relocating Managers and Professional Staff*, Brighton: IMS.

Jackman, R. and Savouri, S. (1992) 'Regional migration in Britain: an analysis of gross flows using NHS central registry data', *Economic Journal* 102: 1432–51.

Johnson, J.H., Salt, J. and Wood, P.A. (1974) *Housing and the Migration of Labour in England and Wales*, London: Saxon House.

Jordan, B., Redley, M. and James, S. (1994) *Putting the Family First*, London: UCL Press.

McLaughlin, E., Millar, J. and Cooke, K. (1989) *Work and Welfare Benefits*, Aldershot: Avebury.

Mincer, J. (1978) 'Family migration decisions', *Journal of Political Economy* 86 (5): 741–73.

Morris, L. (1990) *The Workings of the Household*, Cambridge: Polity.

Munton, A . (1993) *Job Relocation*, London: John Wiley.

Nakosteen, R. A. and Zimmer, M. (1992) 'Migration, age and earnings: the case of employee transfers', *Applied Economics* 24 (7): 791–804.

Nicholson, N. and West, M. (1988) *Managerial Job Change*, Cambridge: Cambridge University Press.

Odland, J. and Ellis, M. (1988) 'Household migration', *Demography* 25(4): 565–79.

Owen, D. (1992) 'Migration and employment', in J. Stillwell, P. Rees and P. Boden (eds) *Migration Processes and Patterns Vol. 2*, London: Belhaven.

Pahl, J.M. and Pahl, R.E. (1971) *Managers and their Wives*, Harmondsworth: Penguin.

Pissarides, C. and Wadsworth, J. (1989) 'Unemployment and inter-regional mobility of labour', *Economic Journal* 99: 739–55.

Rose, M. and Fielder, S. (1988) *The Principle of Equity and the Labour Market Behaviour of Dual Earner Households*, ESRC Social Change and Economic Life Initiative paper (mimeo), Oxford.

Rosenbaum, M. and Bailey, J. (1991) 'Movement within England and Wales during the 1980s, as measured by the NHS Central Register', *Population Trends* 65 (autumn): 24–33.

Salt, J. (1990) 'Organisational labour migration: theory and practice in the United Kingdom', in J.H. Johnson and J. Salt (eds) *Labour Migration: The Internal Geographical Mobility of Labour*, London: Fulton.

257

Sandell, S. (1977) 'Women and the economics of family migration', *Review of Economics and Statistics* 59 (4): 406–14.

Savage, M. (1988) 'The missing link: the relationship between social and geographical mobility', *British Journal of Sociology* 39: 554–77.

Savage, M., Barlow, J., Dickens, P. and Fielding, A. (1992) *Property, Bureaucracy and Culture: Middle Class Formatiom in Contemporary Britain*, London: Routledge.

Scase, R. and Goffee, R. (1989) *Reluctant Managers*, London: Unwin.

Schaeffer, P. (1987) 'A family model of migration', *Socio-Economic Planning Science* 21 (4): 263–9.

Seidenberg, R. (1973) *Corporate Wives – Corporate Casualties*, New York: AMACOM.

Seiz, J.A. (1991) 'The bargaining approach and feminist methodology', *Review of Radical Political Economy* 23 (1): 22–9.

Sen, A. (1990) 'Gender and co-operative conflict', in I. Tinker (ed.) *Persistent Inequalities*, New York: Oxford University Press.

Shields, G. and Shields, M. (1989) 'Migration theory and a new direction', *Journal Economic Surveys* 3 (4): 277–303.

Shihadeh, E. (1991) 'The prevalence of husband centred migration; employment consequences for married mothers', *Journal of Marriage and the Family* 53 (2): 432–44.

Snaith, J. (1990) 'Migration and the dual career household', in J. H. Johnson and J. Salt (eds) *Labour Migration*, London: Fulton.

Wagner, M. (1989) 'The spatial determinants of social mobility', in J. van Dijk, H. Folmer, H.W. Herzog and A.M. Schottmann (eds) *Migration and Labour Market Adjustment*, Dordrecht: Kluwer.

Yu, L. C., Qi Wang, M., Kaltrieder, L. and Chien, Y.-Y. (1993) 'The impact of family migration on the employment status of married college educated women', *Work and Occupations* 20 (2): 233–46.

12

WOMEN AND MEN MANAGERS

Careers and equal opportunities

Judy Wajcman

Since the 1980s there has been much talk of a glass ceiling preventing women from 'getting to the top' in management careers. The barriers to women's advancement that have been identified include the lack of family-friendly employment policies, poor access to training and the pattern of career development. However, after some years of the implementation of equal opportunity policies, there is increasing recognition of the informal barriers that inadvertently maintain and reproduce a world in which there are so few senior women managers. This is the case even in the flagship Opportunity 2000 companies. As a result, there is now a concern with the ways in which organisational cultures are themselves gendered and whether gender stereotypes prevent women from being seen as having the appropriate leadership qualities for senior management.

The aim of this chapter is to investigate particular aspects of the gender relations of senior management in a post-equal-opportunities world. The research explores the interaction between formal equal opportunity in employment policies and the extent to which organisational processes, particularly in a context of corporate restructuring, continue to obstruct women's career advancement. The strength of this research is that it compares the attitudes and experiences of women and men managers, rather than the more usual study of equal opportunities issues which looks exclusively at women. It demonstrates that the women who have made it into senior positions are in most respects indistinguishable from men in equivalent positions. However, this is not enough to guarantee success. Despite their own efforts, their career progression is ultimately blocked. Women's experience of management suggests it is still men who have the power to define what constitutes occupational success, and men who dominate it.

BARRIER METHODS:
SEXUALITY AND ORGANISATIONS

There is now a growing interest in women at higher levels in organisations. Most of the writing on this theme has been within the mainstream management literature and in fact there has been a reluctance on the part of feminist sociologists studying women and work to delve into this area, the key exception being Marshall (1984). As privileged individuals who have competed successfully in a man's world, women managers have not been feminism's favourite daughters. The more pressing problem for feminists and sociologists has been to research the continued prevalence of low pay for women's work, the failure to break down the gender segregation of the labour market, and the concentration of women in under-valued part-time work. However, as Coyle (1989: 119) observed, 'whilst management is the site of decision-making and power, we [feminists] cannot afford to ignore it'. More recently, women managers have been seen as a symbol and measure of organisational change, an indicator of the success of equality policies. The presence of women in senior management positions is perceived to be a more direct challenge to male power within organisations, and to offer hope for all women of change from the top down. So how women managers are faring in this equal opportunities climate, and to what extent they are able to make a difference in their organisations, deserves careful investigation.

The under-representation of women in top management jobs is well documented. In an extensive study using data from 533 UK based companies over the years 1989 to 1992, Gregg and Machin (1993) found that only 8 per cent of top executives are female and their relative share falls dramatically as one moves towards the top of the corporate hierarchy. They earn significantly less for the same jobs as men, with the largest pay gap at the extreme top of the corporate structure. The report concludes that the glass ceiling blocking the promotion of women to the highest jobs does not appear to be cracking. A national survey of management salaries (Institute of Management 1994) actually recorded a fall in the number of women managers overall from 10.2 per cent in 1993 to 9.8 per cent in 1994. It shows a considerable variation in employment by function, with women concentrated in personnel and marketing and least represented in research and development, manufacturing and production. There is also a considerable variation by sector, with women managers more often found in banking, finance and insurance. The small numbers of women overall, particularly at the most senior levels, and the downward trend, are similarly recorded in the USA, Europe and Australia (Fagenson 1993).

Some of the reasons for such low numbers and little change in a whole range of occupations are well rehearsed. Perhaps the most common explanation is that women themselves lack the necessary attributes to succeed in management. Human capital theory stresses that because women's primary orientation is to their child-rearing role they voluntarily choose to invest less in education and training than do men. They therefore tend to lack the professional qualifications that have become increasingly necessary for promotion to senior positions. More recent developments in human capital theory suggest that workers' choices to engage in household labour are important determinants of their labour market outcomes (Becker 1985). Specifically, individuals who engage in a significant amount of household labour will choose less demanding positions that are also less rewarding in terms of earnings and other outcomes. Applying this logic to managers, the model suggests that women managers, who engage in considerably higher levels of household labour than men, will be employed in positions that are less demanding in that they require fewer hours of work per week, as well as less education, less training and less commitment.

Other more psychologically based theories focus on personality traits and an individual's attitude towards the job (Davidson and Cooper 1992). According to this perspective, women are socialised into feminine patterns of behaviour which are ill-suited to the managerial role. They lack the confidence, drive, and competitiveness which are seen as key to effective performance as a manager. As Purcell (1988) points out, even within mainstream sociology of work there is a long history of claims about gender differences in motivation, aspiration and commitment to work. Women are said to be less instrumentally motivated, less interested in career advancement, and less committed to work generally.

In all these different explanations, the focus is on the individual characteristics of women as the major determinants of career progression. These are seen as the result of processes that occur outside the workplace, before women even enter the world of paid employment. Dominant sociological approaches also focus on factors outside of work, but locate the explanation in family structures and the domestic division of labour. Women's life-cycle patterns of work and childbearing role have not fitted them for a career in management. Reflecting this, equal opportunity policies have been largely preoccupied with enabling women to combine family responsibilities with a career, as this is seen as the main block to their career advancement. Indeed, there is a widespread perception that it is now much easier to have both. The empirical evidence is equivocal to say the least, as I shall go on to discuss. The point here is that this approach tends to explain women's relation to employment as solely derived from their family experiences.

Much feminist research has now moved away from explanations in terms of the sphere of reproduction, to examining how the gender relations of employment are produced at work. There has been growing interest in the ways in which gender divisions are actively created and sustained in the processes of organisational life. In particular, researchers have asked how ideas of masculinity and femininity are constructed at work and how jobs themselves are sex-typed. Out of a dialogue between feminist theory and organisation theory, a concern with the way in which organisations are themselves gendered has emerged. This body of work, which is known as gender and organisational analysis, is concerned to explore the male culture of organisations and how this shapes gender relations at work (see Wajcman 1993). Several themes are developing in this literature, and I shall briefly outline those of most relevance to an understanding of the gender relations of management.

The central argument of this literature is that gender relations are constitutive of the structure and practices of organisations and that this is key to understanding how men define and dominate organisations (Acker 1990; Cockburn 1991; Hearn and Parkin 1987; Savage and Witz 1992). These gendered processes operate on many levels, from the explicit and institutional to the more subtle, cultural forms that are submerged in organisational decisions, even those that appear to have nothing to do with gender. They include the way men's influence is embedded in rules and procedures, formal job definitions and functional roles. For example, the structure of a management career, based on men's experiences, needs and life-cycle patterns, assumes a history of continuous, full-time employment. Or the way in which gender is mapped onto organisational authority resulting in a sexual division of labour whereby it is prescribed that women are better suited to personnel management than other management functions (Legge 1987).

The main strength of this literature lies in its analysis of gendered cultural processes, like the way people talk to each other, how they interact informally, and their taken-for-granted assumptions, values and ideas. It is largely through this set of cultural representations and meanings that people construct their understandings of the gendered structure of work and opportunity within their own organisations. It also provides the necessary scripts for gender-appropriate behaviours and attitudes. The dominant symbolism of organisations is suffused with images of masculinity such that a successful organisation is lean, mean, aggressive and competitive with a tough, forceful leader. Managerial work itself is conceptualised as involving constant action, the image is of a fire-fighter dealing with constant pressure, doing rather than thinking – 'action man'. Thus the social construction of management is one in which managerial competence is intrinsically linked to qualities attaching to men. These persistent male stereotypes of management serve to make 'natural', and thereby help to generate, the close identification between men and management. The resulting culture is one that marginalises women: women are out of place in a 'foreign territory'.

Sexuality, in its diverse forms and meanings, is implicated in each of these gendered cultural processes. Since the mid-1980s, literature from this perspective has been concerned with the relationship between gender, sexuality and organisational power, emphasising the significance of sexuality in workplace interaction (Adkins 1995; Burrell 1984; Hearn *et al.* 1989; Pringle 1988). Male socialisation leads men to sexualise and objectify women and this is crucial in perpetuating women's exclusion from spheres of power and influence within organisations. Male collective behaviour suggests that men prefer each other's company, as Kanter (1977) pointed out in her discussion of 'male homosociability'. Male managers share a common language and understanding with others of their own kind. They appear to feel most comfortable communicating with each other and promote 'clones' of themselves. For women, however, the demands of being a woman and being a manager are set up as contradictory ones for them to balance. Their success depends on how they negotiate their sexuality and manage their 'femaleness'. The central argument here is that theorising male power in organisations involves seeing organisations as arenas of men's sexual dominance.

Many of the theories canvassed above, particularly in relation to questions of organisational culture and management style, have been elaborated with very little empirical foundation. Furthermore, the existing research tends to treat women managers in isolation from men. Failure to examine the experience of men within the same organisation inevitably limits our understanding of how managers are made. This study aims to correct the imbalance by presenting comparative material on women and men managers. In bringing the results of my research to bear on the issues I have outlined, I hope to illuminate the strengths and weaknesses of the theoretical approaches developed to date, and point in some future directions.

RESEARCH METHODS

Given the paucity of empirical investigation of many of the claims made about women managers, particularly from the organisational perspective, it seemed appropriate to adopt a primarily quantitative methodology. There are few up-to-date, hard data available and, although this project does have a qualitative dimension, the purpose of this chapter is to report on the quantitative analysis. I shall be exploring the interview research in depth elsewhere.

I approached five multinational companies, all of whom agreed to participate. The companies operate in the technologically advanced sectors of oil, chemicals, and computing services. I selected the companies for the following reasons. First, they are companies which are widely acknowledged to be at the forefront of equal opportunity policies. The project thus set out to investigate best practice companies. Second, it seemed best to study the private sector as most current research in this area is on the public sector, for example, the NHS. Finally, it is often claimed that the new fast-growing high-tech industries might provide easier access to women managers because they have not inherited long-standing organisational structures. The case most often referred to is Apple Computer in the United States, where women represent 33 per cent of management and 40 per cent of professionals (Fagenson 1993: 61). In fact, no such sector effect was evident. An issue this chapter will not explore is differences between the companies. These appear to be a product of organisational politics within the companies rather than any evident sector, age, or country of ownership effect.

Although the companies in the study were selected from 'leading edge' cases, in fact women are still seriously under-represented at senior levels of management in all the companies. Thus the women managers in my sample are all working in very male-dominated workplaces. In order to get a reasonable sample size, given how few genuinely senior women there are, for the purposes of this study senior managers are defined as those earning over £40,000 p.a. in 1993. This level of managerial salary is consistent across the five companies involved and £40,000 is a recognised cut off between senior and middle management. It produced a remarkably similar number of women (on average 24) across all the companies.

The questionnaires were sent to 439 managers between October and December 1993. All of the senior women managers and a representative sample of men in equivalent grades have been surveyed. Of the 324 managers who completed the questionnaire, 108 are women and 216 are men. The response rate of 74 per cent (89 per cent for the women and 68 per cent for the men) is exceptional for a mailback questionnaire, indicating a high level of interest in the subject matter of the survey. Male managers have been included, both in their own right and as a control group in relation to the women. A simple random sample of the men would have been, on average, more senior than their female counterparts. It was thus crucial to the research design to match the sample of men with women so that they are similar to the women in all respects other than gender. The findings presented here are based on the aggregate data from the five companies and all the differences referred to in this paper reach the conventional level of statistical significance.

PROFILE OF THE SAMPLE

The profile of women who have achieved senior management positions in all the companies is similar to that of their male colleagues in many respects. Crucially, as stated above, the research design controlled for differences in managerial level. In terms of age, as Table 12.1 shows, the highest proportion of managers in the survey (56 per cent) is middle-aged, concentrated

Table 12.1 Percentage distribution of respondents in senior management
sample according to their age

Age categories	Men	Women
Under 25	0	0
25–34	9	23
35–44	56	56
45–54	33	21
55 and over	2	0

within the 35–44 age range. The majority of both men and women are in this age range or the 45–54 range, reflecting the age distri-bution for this occupational group in national labour force surveys. Women managers tend to be younger and have more recently joined the organisation. However, there is no sex difference in the age of first managerial appointment: 87 per cent of both men and women reach managerial level by the age of 35. Respondents move around within the company and this is reflected in the fact that over 80 per cent of both men and women were recruited to their present post through internal promotion. So men and women have had equal exposure to the promotion system in their company.

While human capital theory emphasises women's supposed lack of qualifications, recent studies have found that women are generally better qualified in formal terms for equivalent jobs. Interestingly, no gender differences in educational qualifications emerged in this study, with almost half the respondents having degrees and a further third with some sort of postgraduate qualification. With regard to the related issue of training, once again the same proportion (74 per cent) of both men and women have been on a training course financed by the company that they suggested for their own self-development.

Respondents were asked about their job title. A higher proportion of the men than women describe themselves as managers (85 per cent of men and 69 per cent of women) whereas 31 per cent of the women describe themselves as professionals. A substantial proportion of both men and women in the study describe themselves as 'general managers' – 26 per cent and 20 per cent respectively. When asked about their principal management function (see Table 12.2), the women are more likely to be in 'personnel/human resources/industrial relations' and 'service func-tions', whereas men are more likely to be in 'marketing and sales'. This broadly reflects the wider labour market patterns of the gender specialisation of management functions, although if anything there is less concentration of women in the human resources function than one might expect (see Legge 1987).

Table 12.2 Percentage distribution of respondents in terms of principal management function

Stated functional specialism	Men	Women
Administration/company secretary	1	2
Management services	1	0
Finance/accounting	9	12
Education/training	1	2
Personnel/human resources/industrial relations	5	14
Production/manufacturing	2	2
Computing/IT	10	7
Development/strategic affairs	8	7
Marketing/sales	31	21
Corporate affairs/public relations	2	4
Management consultancy	4	6
General management	24	18
Other	2	5

However, where there is a marked sex difference is in the numbers of people for whom the respondents are directly responsible. Whereas 64 per cent of the women manage fewer than 10 people, this is true for under half of the men. Over 20 per cent of the men manage more than 50 employees, whereas only 12 per cent of the women carry similar line-management responsibilities. Men are more than twice as likely as women to have responsibility for over 100 employees. It should be noted, however, that this is not independent of management function. As more of the women are professional specialists, they are less likely to have extensive responsibilities for subordinate employees.

HOURS OF WORK

Since the 1980s, there has been increasing discussion of the intensification of work pressures on managers which has resulted in a significant length-ening of the working week. For example, Scase and Goffee (1989) reported that most of the managers in their study worked an average week in excess of 50 hours (and were generally working harder than ever before). Similarly, a more recent survey of NHS top managers found that their average working hours is 56 per week (NHS Women's Unit 1994). The issue has been raised about whether these long hours act as a disincentive to middle management seeking promotion, in particular for women. Not only is this issue of hours key to human capital theorist's explanations of women's position, but also it is at the heart of the current conceptions of the 'macho' manager. The idea is that being a manager requires total commitment and sacrifice to the organisation and that the job comes first, above all else. Because it is actually very difficult to measure the quality or productivity of managerial work, commitment is often measured in terms of time spent at the workplace. If women's commitment to paid work is less than men's, it would thus be expected that they would work shorter hours than men.

This study did not find significant sex differences in the hours respondents worked. Over 60 per cent of women and men reported that they work an average week in excess of 50 hours, with over 16 per cent of both men and women working over 60 hours. When asked 'how many nights a month do you spend away from home on business?', the replies were as follows: 8 per cent of men and 18 per cent of women spend no nights away. Of those who spend some nights away, 74 per cent of men and 66 per cent of women spend between one and four nights; 12 per cent of men and 13 per cent women spend between five and eight nights; 6 per cent men and 4 per cent women spend nine or more. Even when asked about changing their hours of work, no differences emerged. Of those (64 per cent) who expressed a desire for change in their working hours, over two-thirds of both men and women said they would prefer to work shorter hours and a third said they would like different hours. The NHS survey referred to above also found no significant gender differences in the hours worked. The finding that there is no significant difference in the hours worked by men and women in senior management positions is contrary to the common perception that men work longer hours than women. The need to work long hours should not therefore act as a barrier to women's promotion. However, perceptions about women's ability and willingness to work long hours differs from the reality and continue to negatively influence women's promotion paths.

MOTIVATION

It is commonly assumed that there are major gender differences in motivation to work. Thus women are said to be less instrumental, less interested in career advancement, and generally less committed to work. For example, Davidson and Cooper (1992: 16) and Goffee and Scase (1992: 372) argue that women managers are more likely than men to be *job* rather than *career* oriented, concerned with the intrinsic rewards of the task at hand rather than with future career benefits. This is accounted for in terms of women's response to their more frequent experience of career disappointment than men. However, I found few sex differences in the overall responses to questions about motivation to work. Interestingly, the main sources of motivation for both men and women are intrinsic to the work itself, that is, a sense of achievement and enjoying the job (see Table 12.3).

After probing, two marginal differences between men and women did emerge. Women appear to enjoy power more than men and they are slightly less concerned about financial reward. The latter difference, that

Table 12.3 Percentage of respondents mentioning each source of motivation

	Very important		Fairly important		Not very important		Not at all important	
	Men	Women	Men	Women	Men	Women	Men	Women
Prospect of promotion	24	20	51	52	22	26	3	3
Financial reward	35	24	55	56	8	19	2	—
Status	6	16	59	44	32	34	3	6
Sense of achievement	85	88	15	10	—	—	1	2
Fear of failure	14	17	33	37	41	26	12	20
Contributing to company	44	45	48	47	7	9	1	—
Enjoying the job	75	86	25	14	4	—	—	1
Meeting targets	44	47	49	44	6	8	1	2
Respect from colleagues	48	55	44	42	8	3	—	—
Developing people	36	37	54	55	9	8	1	—
Enjoying power	13	21	40	48	40	22	7	10

women are less instrumentally motivated, is much less than the sociological literature would suggest. This may be explained by the high proportion of men (40 per cent) in the survey who are supporting full-time housewives, while only a tiny number of the women were financially supporting their partners. It might also be an adaptation by women to limited career opportunities. Similarly women may enjoy power more because they are generally less accustomed to it, or have had to succeed against greater odds to achieve it. Indeed women may attach more significance to the exercise of power precisely to compensate for reduced financial rewards. Overall, however, this research found little evidence for the traditional assumption that women's motivation to work is different from men's.

HOUSEHOLD TYPE

So far I have been examining the individual characteristics of managers in the survey and have found little difference between the women and the men. In relation to family structures and the domestic division of labour, however, the contrast between the situation of men and women could not be more stark. A brief overview of the data here is instructive.

The marital status of the men and women managers is very different: 93 per cent of male managers are married or living with a partner, compared to 73 per cent of their female colleagues. Women managers are much more

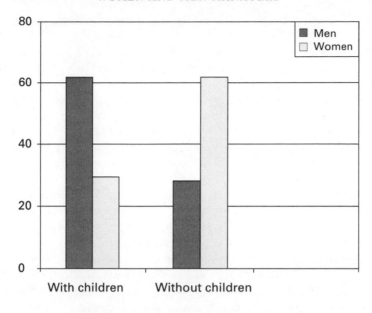

Figure 12.1 Managers living with and without children

likely to be single, divorced or separated: 27 per cent in comparison to 7 per cent of men. As Figure 12.1 shows, over two-thirds of the women managers surveyed do not have children, while over two-thirds of the men do have children living with them. However, the data show that, by and large, the men do not take primary responsibility for the care of their children. Of respondents with children, 94 per cent of women, compared to only 15 per cent of men, reported that they have primary responsibility for their children. The resulting average weekly hours of housework (defined as cooking, cleaning, laundry, shopping, and childcare) reported by the women in the survey is 19 hours, whereas the average weekly total for men is 10 hours, reinforcing previous findings that even in dual-career households, women are likely to shoulder more domestic work and child-care than their partners (see, for example, Hochschild 1990). The key factor in understanding the allocation of housework is the employment status of partners. In the male sample, the highest proportion (40 per cent) had non-employed partners, nearly a third (31 per cent) had partners who worked part-time and only 27 per cent had partners who were also full-time employees. Conversely, most of the women who had partners were in dual-career households: 88 per cent with full-time employed partners and the remaining minority had partners who were retired or worked part-time.

The point that needs to be stressed here is that these striking differences in household type and reported domestic responsibilities do not result in sharply sex-differentiated attitudes to and hours of work, as indicated above.

It should be noted in this context that the majority of managers were in fact reliant to a greater or lesser extent on paid domestic services to enable them to do their jobs. Most paid domestic help is used by women who live in dual-career couples (79 per cent), whereas the least is used by men with full-time housewives (28 per cent). The most common form of help is cleaning (80 per cent employ a cleaner), followed by ironing (53 per cent), gardening (35 per cent) and childcare (28 per cent). Although these women managers do less housework than women who work part-time or are housewives, they still do almost twice the amount of housework as the men in the sample. Even so, the women managers do the same number of hours of paid work as the men. This would appear to cast considerable doubt on Becker's (1985) theory that more domestic labour is traded off for fewer hours of paid employment. Given that women's lack of promotion into senior management cannot simply be derived from either their individual characteristics or their family situation, indeed that most women have forgone having children for a career, I shall now turn to factors within the workplace that may act as barriers to careers.

CAREER PROGRESSION AND BARRIERS

It is important to note the organisational context. As already indicated, the companies in the study were chosen because of their exemplary equal opportunities policies. The companies are all 'flagship' members of 'Opportunity 2000', a business-led campaign launched in 1991 to 'increase the quality and quantity of women's participation in the workforce'. They all have explicit and highly visible policies to increase the number of women at all levels of their organisations by the year 2000, although in fact the main focus has been on the progress of women in management. Common initiatives include flexible work arrangements, the provision of some kind of childcare or career break option, generous maternity leave provisions, and critical monitoring of recruitment and promotion practices. Some of the companies also have a women's network, provide women-only training courses, and have policies on sexual harassment. These policies fit within the broader framework of their human resource management policies and are regarded as just one facet of their systems for maximising human potential within the workforce. In general, these companies would see themselves as operating the textbook model of 'soft' human resource management (Sisson 1994). This approach is essentially people-centred – emphasising communication, motivation and leadership. The personnel managers responsible for the implementation of these equality policies all spoke about the need to promote profound cultural change through such initiatives as intensive workshops to raise consciousness about equality issues. In sum, these are companies who profess a serious commitment to equal opportunities at the very highest levels of decision making in the organisation.

A number of questions in the survey addressed the theme of career progression and at this point marked sex differences begin to emerge. Men and women express very different views of women's prospects within their organisation. Whereas 70 per cent of men think that men and women have equal chances of promotion in their company, fewer than 40 per cent of the women think so. In fact, nearly three-quarters (71 per cent) of women believe that a 'glass ceiling' exists limiting women's ability to move up the ladder, and almost a third of the men agree with them. Clearly this finding raises questions about the limited success of equal opportunity policies in these companies.

Nearly twice as many women as men say they have experienced barriers in their career. When asked about the three principal barriers in their careers, over a third (34 per cent) of the men but only 18 per cent of the women said they had not experienced any barriers. Of those who had experienced barriers, the four most commonly cited by both men and women are that senior management is perceived to be a 'club', the prejudice of colleagues, the lack of career guidance, and family commitments. Table 12.4 reveals the surprising finding that fathers and mothers are equally likely to have cited 'family commitments' as a barrier and the women are scarcely more likely than the men to have seen 'lack of adequate childcare' as a barrier. It is perhaps surprising that in companies with such developed human resource policies that the lack of career guidance is perceived to be such a major barrier for both sexes.

However, there are substantial differences in the kinds of barriers that women and men experience. Significantly more women than men perceive the prejudice of colleagues and the 'cliquiness' of senior management as an obstacle to their progress. It is striking that as many as 76 per cent of women as against 43 per cent of men mention senior management seen as a 'club'/ prejudice of colleagues as a barrier. Coe (1992) also reports that the greatest barrier encountered by senior women managers in their career is the 'men's club/old boy network'. Furthermore, there is a marked difference between men and women in their reporting of sexual discrimination/ harassment as a barrier to their career development with 17 per cent of women saying they had experience of this compared to only 1 per cent of men. In a separate question which asked respondents if they had ever experienced any form of discrimination at work, just over half of the women said they had experienced sexual discrimination. A slightly higher proportion of women with children (59 per cent) have experienced sexual discrimination. Finally, it is worth noting that when listing sources of positive support in their careers, three times as many women (22 per cent) as men mentioned the importance of a female boss or female role model.

Table 12.4 Percentage of respondents mentioning principal barriers in their career

	Men	Women
Inflexible working patterns	6	14
Family commitments[a]	44	43
Lack of adequate childcare	3	8
Lack of career guidance	45	50
Lack of training provision	9	5
Prejudice of colleagues	11	23
Lack of personal motivation/confidence	19	21
Senior management seen as a 'club'	32	54
Social pressures	1	10
Sexual discrimination/harassment	1	17
Insufficient education	11	13

Note: [a] Here the data refer only to respondents with children.

ATTITUDES TOWARDS WOMEN MANAGERS

That these processes of prejudice and discrimination are hidden is evidenced by the lack of major differences between women and men in their views about the role of women in management. Asking people to respond to a set of attitude statements on a scale tends to promote conventional answers, but I was curious to compare my respondents with a similar survey. The following set of statements mirror those asked by Coe (1992) in a report on members of the Institute of Management. The statements are: 'women managers have positive skills to bring to the workplace'; 'male managers are more committed to the organisation than women managers'; 'there should be positive discrimination for women managers; 'women should not combine a management career and motherhood'; 'all managers should be treated the same, regardless of family responsibilities'; 'I do find it/would find it difficult to work for a woman manager'. The results are set out in Table 12.5.

Overall there is not much difference between the views of women and men in relation to these statements, both being overwhelmingly positive about women managers' skills, commitment, and ability to combine a career and motherhood. However, as in Coe's survey, some differences emerged in the strongly held views. Twice as many women as men 'strongly agree' that women managers have positive skills to bring to the workplace; well over twice as many women as men 'strongly disagree' that male managers are more committed to the organisation than women; a higher proportion of women 'strongly disagree' with the statement that women should not combine a management career and motherhood; and men are more likely than women to 'strongly disagree' with the statement that

Table 12.5 Percentage distribution of respondents' attitudes towards
women managers

	Strongly agree		Agree		Disagree		Strongly disagree	
	Men	Women	Men	Women	Men	Women	Men	Women
Women managers have positive skills	41	80	56	19	3	1	—	—
Male managers are more committed	1	2	13	7	65	39	21	52
There should be positive discrimination	1	2	10	10	45	56	44	32
Women should not combine career and motherhood	1	—	10	3	51	35	37	62
All managers should be treated the same	38	42	47	39	12	17	2	2
Difficult to work for a woman manager	1	1	9	3	49	42	41	54

there should be positive discrimination for women managers. In fact, there was very little support for positive discrimination among men or women.

In answer to a separate set of questions about preferences for male or female managers they work *with* or *for*, most men and women expressed no preference. In addition, most respondents (86 per cent) said that neither men nor women make better managers. In this context it is worth noting that 45 per cent of the managers report that they have actually worked for a woman manager, with a slight tendency for women to be more likely to have done so.

However, in sharp contrast to these views, when respondents were asked whether they would prefer to work for a manager of their own sex, a size-able proportion (21 per cent) of men say that they would prefer to work for male managers. Interestingly, 10 per cent of women also said that they pre-fer to work for male managers. However, neither men nor women expressed a preference for a woman manager. This would indicate that women are still far from being fully accepted in senior management positions.

GENDERED CULTURAL PRACTICES

How is it that systematic barriers to women's advancement into senior positions still operate in companies with such model equal opportunity policies? While it has been relatively easy for women to gain employment at the lower levels of these organisations, it is much more difficult for them to reach middle and senior executive positions. In all the companies there is a clearly identifiable level past which even the few senior women do not advance – a classic 'glass ceiling'. There is a considerable divergence between espoused company policy, which is to eliminate discrimination on the grounds of sex, and organisational reality. The lack of significant sex differences in respondents' overall attitudes is striking when compared to the very marked sex differences in perceptions of career barriers. It suggests that equal opportunities policies have been more successful in modifying managers' general views, especially men's, than they have been in transforming deeply held beliefs and behaviours.

In order to explore these processes I shall refer briefly to some of the detailed interviews with managers I conducted in the case study company. What emerges is the salience of informal gendered cultural practices which continue to operate despite considerable changes in the formal norms of these companies. This gender stereotyping is especially strong at the most senior levels. Studies show that adopting procedures that are apparently fair does not guarantee fair outcomes. Strict adherence to suitability criteria can still lead to the continued appointment of white men (Webb and Liff 1988). These criteria are themselves tainted by gender bias.

Discrimination operates not necessarily as a conscious process but as normal, taken-for-granted, practice. While men may express support for equal opportunities their influence is embedded in organisational rules and procedures and in the very character of the job. If jobs themselves are gendered, as the literature discussed earlier demonstrates, masculinity still constitutes an essential qualification for most managerial positions. The effect for women, as reflected in my interviews with managers, is that they never seem quite right for the job, or not quite ready, they are too narrow in experience and they can't take the pressure. In describing the fate of two senior women managers, a male respondent told me that: 'some women were given opportunities but it was tokenism. . . . They weren't competent to do the jobs they were invited to do . . . one of them had a nervous breakdown and the other just realised she was climbing the walls and got out before the same thing happened'. Most importantly, however, women are usually not even thought of when senior jobs are filled. Women do not fit the highly visible stereotype of management that prevails in these companies.

This point about visibility is directly connected to one of the main findings of the survey, the existence of the 'senior management club'. Although the survey found that some men also feel excluded by this club, this is a much greater barrier for women. As one woman expressed it: 'It's always been men at the top of this company and the top of the company I was in before. They all know each other. They've all come up the same route together. . . . Now the only way to get into senior management is to

Force nothing; be unforced

Accept no giant miracles

to prove by counterfeit your.

know people in the senior management clique, but how can you know them when you are invisible?' Many of the managers spoke about the pervasive power of this male network and its subtle operation. At its core is a group of men with a shared background, who have worked with each other over many years, and met socially at conferences and in local pubs. Since the recession has hit hard there are far fewer opportunities to meet outside the workplace but it appears that this has in no way weakened their influence.

Finally, it is clear from my research that a key factor in the durability of career ceilings for women is the business context. The current climate of almost continuous corporate restructuring and job losses has greatly intensified work for senior managers and means that opportunities for promotion for both sexes have severely contracted. In fact, the major topic of conversation amongst managers at one of the fast contracting companies is the size of the redundancy package. Insecurity about the future is pervasive but these trends are having a differential impact on the careers of male and female managers. As the Head of Human Resources explained to me: 'With huge job retrenchment and managers spread so thin, I need a known quality, and often the known quality to a man is another man.' Viewing the appointment of women as a bit of a gamble, she said that at this point she could not subject the business to that kind of risk: an ironic view for a successful woman who clearly saw herself (rightly) as atypical.

Gendered custom and practice reassert themselves in this environment. Many of my interviewees commented that with the 'downsizing', management was returning to a more traditional hierarchical structure, and macho management was again in the ascendancy. One, the most senior woman manager in her company, explained: 'The culture of the organisation is becoming much more directive, much more controlled from head office The word that is being used is discipline . . . and these changes in management style favour a male style . . . management say the right things on diversity issues, but the actual tangible results are getting worse'. Male managers also expressed concern about the changes that were taking place, for example:'We have returned to the 1960s military style of management by brutality, shouting louder, hit them harder and threaten them to death until they're frightened and they do what they're told'. In other words, while the management 'rhetoric may be the people-centred approach of the "soft" version: the reality is the cost reduction approach of the "hard" version' (Sisson 1994: 15). Indeed, men's resistance to equal opportunities, as constituting a threat to their own career prospects as well as to their identities (well-documented by Cockburn 1991), is likely to intensify in this climate. The picture for women managers looks particularly bleak.

CONCLUSION: WHY CAN'T A WOMAN BE MORE LIKE A MAN?

The data from the survey show that the few women who have succeeded in these companies are the ones who have very similar backgrounds and attitudes to the men. They work the same long hours as men. Therefore we cannot explain women's career barriers in terms of individual characteristics, such as their motivation or commitment to work. Neither can women's lack of progress at senior levels be explained by their greater involvement in housework and childcare. Many of the women up against the infamous glass ceiling have already found it necessary to forgo having children. Although the structure of the family is key to the careers of both men and women, men do not have to make the same kind of choice between family and work.

We must therefore look elsewhere for a satisfactory explanation of the glass ceiling. The results suggest that organisational structures and practices are central to an understanding of the ways women are marginalised and ultimately excluded. Clearly a fuller exploration of these cultural processes requires a qualitative study of women's and men's experience as managers. I will be developing this theme in the next phase of my research.

At this stage what has emerged most strongly is that women have had to become more like men to pursue successful management careers. This is a severely restricted model of equality in which it is women who do the accommodating to pre-existing norms. Relatively few women can benefit from this model. To achieve genuine sex equality in organisations will require more fundamental changes in the gender relations of management.

ACKNOWLEDGEMENTS

This research was carried out at the Industrial Relations Research Unit, University of Warwick, which is a Research Centre of the Economic and Social Research Council. Thanks to Val Jephcott, who provided invaluable assistance in the preparation of the data used in this analysis. Thanks also to Paul Edwards, Sonia Liff, Paul Marginson, Helen Newell, Jeremy Waddington and Colin Whitston.

REFERENCES

Acker, J. (1990) 'Hierarchies, jobs, bodies: a theory of gendered organizations', *Gender and Society* 4: 139–58.

Adkins, L. (1995) *Gendered Work: Sexuality, Family and the Labour Market,* Buckingham: Open University Press.

Becker, G. (1985) 'Human capital, effort, and the sexual division of labor', *Journal of Labor Economics* 3 (2): 33–58.

Burrell, G. (1984) 'Sex and organizational analysis', *Organization Studies* 5 (2): 97–118.

Cockburn, C. (1991) *In the Way of Women: Men's Resistance to Sex Equality in Organizations*, London: Macmillan.

Coe, T. (1992) 'The key to the men's club', *Institute of Management Report*, London: Institute of Management.

Coyle, A. (1989) 'Women in management: a suitable case for treatment?', *Feminist Review* 31 (spring): 117–25.

Davidson, M. and Cooper, G. (1992) *Shattering the Glass Ceiling: The Woman Manager*, London: Paul Chapman.

Fagenson, E. (ed.) (1993) *Women in Management*, Newbury Park, CA: Sage.

Goffee, R. and Scase, R. (1992) 'Organizational change and the corporate career: the restructuring of managers' job aspirations', *Human Relations* 45 (4): 363–84.

Gregg, P. and Machin, S. (1993) 'Is the glass ceiling cracking? Gender compensation differentials and access to promotion among UK executives', *National Institute of Economic and Social Research* Discussion Paper 50, London: NIESR.

Hearn, J. and Parkin, W. (1987) *Sex at Work: The Power and Paradox of Organization Sexuality*, Brighton: Wheatsheaf Books.

Hearn, J., Sheppard, D., Tancred-Sheriff, P. and Burrell, G. (eds) (1989) *The Sexuality of Organization*, London: Sage.

Hochschild, A. (1990) *The Second Shift: Working Parents and the Revolution at Home*, London: Piatkus.

Institute of Management (1994) *The 1994 National Management Salary Survey*, London: Institute of Managment.

Kanter, R.M. (1977) *Men and Women of the Corporation*, New York: Basic Books.

Legge, K. (1987) 'Women in personnel management', in A. Spencer and D. Podmore (eds) *In a Man's World*, London: Tavistock.

Marshall, J. (1984) *Women Managers: Travellers in a Male World*, Chichester: John Wiley.

NHS Women's Unit (1994) *Creative Career Paths in the NHS*, Report no. 1. Top Managers, London.

Pringle, R. (1988) *Secretaries Talk*, Sydney: Allen & Unwin.

Purcell, K. (1988) 'Gender and the experience of employment', in D. Gallie (ed.) *Employment in Britain*, Oxford: Blackwell.

Savage, M. and Witz, A. (1992) *Gender and Bureaucracy*, Oxford: Blackwell.

Scase, R. and Goffee, R. (1989) *Reluctant Managers*, London: Routledge.

Sisson, K. (ed.) (1994) *Personnel Management*, Oxford: Blackwell.

Wajcman, J. (1993) 'Organisations, gender and power', *Warwick Papers in Industrial Relations* 48, December, Coventry: Industrial Relations Research Unit.

Webb, J. and Liff, S. (1988) 'Play the white man: the social construction of fairness and competition in equal opportunities policies', *Sociological Review* 36 (3): 532–51.

INDEX